The Anthropology of Friendship

The Anthropology of Friendship

Edited by
Sandra Bell and Simon Coleman

Oxford • New York

First published in 1999 by
Berg
Editorial offices:
150 Cowley Road, Oxford, OX4 1JJ, UK
838 Broadway, Third Floor, New York, NY 10003-4812, USA

Berg is the imprint of Oxford International Publishers Ltd.

Library of Congress Cataloging-in-Publication Data

A catalogue record for this book is available from the Library of Congress.

British Library Cataloguing-in-Publication Data

A catalogue record for this book is available from the British Library.

ISBN 1 85973 310 7 (Cloth)
1 85973 315 8 (Paper)

Typeset by JS Typesetting, Wellingborough, Northants.
Printed in the United Kingdom by Biddles Ltd, King's Lynn.

**To Sir Raymond Firth
for his contribution to the study of
friendship and his support of this volume.**

Contents

Contents

Notes on Contributors

Dr Ray Abrahams has carried out a wide range of research in East Africa (Tanzania and Uganda) and north-eastern Europe (Finland and Estonia). He has published several books and many papers on this work. In 1991 he became the first Western scholar to carry out field research in modern rural Estonia, and he was awarded the Rivers Medal of the Royal Anthropological Institute in 1996 for his work on socialism and its aftermath in that country and elsewhere. His most recent book, *Vigilant Citizens* (1998) is a comparative study of vigilantism and the state in a variety of historical and contemporary contexts. Dr Abrahams is a Fellow of Churchill College, Cambridge.

Mario I. Aguilar is Chair of Ritual Studies, School of Divinity at the University of St. Andrews, Scotland. His latest books include *Being Oromo in Kenya* (1998), *The Rwanda Genocide* (1998), and an edited collection *The Politics of Age and Gerontocracy in Africa* (1998).

Sandra Bell teaches anthropology at the University of Durham. She has carried out fieldwork among Buddhists in Britain and with an international theatre company, leading to publications in several academic journals including the *Journal of Contemporary Religion*, *Novo Religio* and *The Contemporary Theatre Review*. With Elisa Sobo she is co-editor of *Celibacy, Culture and Society: The Anthropology of Sexual Abstinence*, University of Wisconsin Press (in press).

James G. Carrier teaches anthropology at the University of Durham. He has done fieldwork in Papua New Guinea and historical research on exchange and circulation in Western societies. His most recent books are *Gifts and Commodities: Exchange and Western Capitalism since 1700* (Routledge, 1994) and *Occidentalism: Images of the West* (Oxford, 1995), *Meanings of the Market* (Berg, 1997, editor) and *Virtualism: A New Political Economy* (Berg, 1998, co-edited with Daniel Miller).

Simon Coleman teaches at the Department of Anthropology, University of Durham. His other research interests include the globalization of conservative Protestantism, and pilgrimage. He has carried out fieldwork in Sweden, England and the United States. Recent works include *Pilgrimage: Sacred Travel and Sacred Space in the*

World Religions (1995, with J. Elsner) and *Anthropology: A Resource Guide* (1998, editor, with R. Simpson).

E. Paul Durrenberger is professor of anthropology at Penn State University. He received a Ph.D. in Anthropology from the University of Illinois at Urbana-Champaign in 1971. He was on the faculty of the University of Iowa for twenty-five years and was chair of the Anthropology Department when he left for Penn State in 1997. He has done ethnographic fieldwork in highland South-East Asia, lowland South-East Asia, Iceland, Mississippi, Alabama, Iowa, and Chicago. Recent books include *Gulf Coast Soundings* (University Press of Kansas, 1996), *Dynamics of Medieval Iceland* (University of Iowa Press, 1992), *It's All Politics* (University of Illinois Press, 1992), *Icelandic Essays: Explorations in the Anthropology of Modern Life* (Rudi Publishing, 1995), with Gísli Pálsson, *Images of Modern Iceland* (University of Iowa Press, 1996), and with Kendall Thu, *Pigs, Profits and Rural Communities* (State University of New York Press, 1998). With Suzan Erem he has recently published ethnographic work on a union in Chicago in various anthropological journals, including AA.

Robert Paine is Professor Emeritus at the Memorial University of Newfoundland. He has published widely from his fieldwork in Newfoundland, Norway and Israel. His publications on the subject of friendship include 'In Search of Friendship: An Exploratory Analysis in "Middle-Class" Culture' in *Man* (N.S.) Vol.5:1, 1969 and 'Anthropological Approaches to Friendship' in *Humanitas* Vol.VI:2, 1970.

Gísli Pálsson is Professor of Anthropology at the University of Iceland and, formerly, Research Fellow at the Swedish Collegium for Advanced Study in the Social Sciences in Uppsala, Sweden. He has done fieldwork in Iceland and the Cape Verde Islands. His writings include several books and a number of articles on ecological anthropology, fishing and language. His latest book is *The Textual Life of Savants: Ethnography, Iceland and the Linguistic Turn* (Harewood Academic Publishers, 1995).

Nigel Rapport is Professor of Anthropology in the School of Philosophical and Anthropological Studies at the University of St Andrews. He has conducted participant-observation research in England (1980–81), Newfoundland (1984–85; 1986) and Israel (1988–89). He is author of *Talking Violence: An Anthropological Conversation in the City* (ISER Press, 1987); *Diverse World-Views in an English Village* (Edinburgh University Press, 1993); '*The Prose and the Passion' Anthropology, Literature and the Writings of E.M. Forster* (Manchester University Press, 1994) and is co-editor of *Questions of Consciousness* (Routledge, 1995). He is also editor of the World Heritage Press book series 'European Studies in Social and Cultural Anthropology.'

Deborah Reed-Danahay is Associate Professor of Anthropology at the University of Texas at Arlington. She is author of *Education and Identity in Rural France* (Cambridge, 1996) and editor of *Auto/Ethnography: Rewriting the Self and the Social* (Berg, 1997). She has conducted extensive fieldwork in the Auvergne region of France, and is currently undertaking a study of published memoirs written by people who grew up in French villages.

Claudia Barcellos Rezende received her Ph.D. from the London School of Economics. She is Assistant Professor of Anthropology at the Universidade Estadual do Rio de Janeiro, Brazil. She has conducted fieldwork in London and in Rio de Janeiro. Her publications include the entry on friendship for the *Encyclopedia of Social and Cultural Anthropology*, edited by Jonathan Spencer and Alan Barnard (Routledge, 1996), and the articles 'A Amiga Brasileira: Amizade e Trabalho de Campo em Londres' (*Comunicações do* PPGAS, June 1995) and 'A Empregada na Televisão' (*Cadernos de Antropologia e Imagem*, 5 (2), 1997).

Alan Smart is an Associate Professor at the Department of Anthropology at the University of Calgary. He has conducted research on squatters, housing and development in Hong Kong (1982–87), on cross-border investment from Hong Kong in China (1987), and on social restructuring in Canadian cities (1995–). He is the author of *Making Room: Squatters Clearance in Hong Kong* and of articles in *The International Journal of Urban and Regional Research, Cultural Anthropology, Critique of Anthropology, City and Society, Society and Space* and a number of edited volumes.

Preface

I congratulate the editors on their perception and enterprise in organizing this set of essays on friendship, and I am complimented in having been asked to write a preface to the volume.

Friendship is an important social phenomenon. Among the many issues it raises I consider briefly only its ubiquity, its diversity (even ambiguity) and its practicality.

Indication of the ubiquity of the concept and practice of friendship is given by the range of essays in this volume. My own personal experience would support this. Over a long life I have had friends – many now dead – from numerous countries and spheres of interest. These have included kin-friends, a real category to be distinguished from simple kin. My friends have given me their trust, support, understanding and affection in a variety of circumstances. Some friendships have arisen from my professional career, special anthropological colleagues in China, Malaysia, Japan, Hawaii, Australia, South Africa, New Zealand, Scandinavia, as well as in Britain and North America. Other of my friendships, stemming in part from common interest in art and music, have been with an Austrian family, a Swiss wool buyer, a Russian teacher of languages. With two school-friends in New Zealand, one in later life a journalist and the other a zoologist and the director of the national museum, I maintained contact until they died, more than sixty years after our first acquaintance. I have reason to think that in all these cases enough threads of intellectual exchange and reciprocated sentiment were present to entitle the relationship to be termed friendship, despite cultural differences.

A special kind of anthropological friendship may come from the circumstances of fieldwork. At work in the field anthropologists rely very greatly on help from particular men and women. As their intimacy grows with what has been called their chief or key informants, in day by day talk and sharing of experiences, a sympathy and understanding can develop with a certain individual as mentor and confidant, so that a definite personal relationship is formed and acknowledged by both. Often such relationship has a special vernacular name, equivalent to friendship. Sometimes the ties created are of such ritual kind that they may be described, as I have termed them, 'bond-friendship'. Nearly forty years ago Joseph B. Casagrande edited a set of essays in which a score of anthropologists wrote of their relationship with friends among the people whom they studied (Casagrande 1960). Because the relation usually bridged two cultures, showed great reciprocity and differed from friendship between people of a similar background, Casagrande described it as unique among the forms of human association. Without entirely agreeing with this uniqueness, I would affirm its striking character. I also note, as Cassagrande has pointed out, its analogy to the relation between psychiatrist or psychoanalyst and patient, where a considerable degree of intimacy is established. But the differences bring out the essential quality of friendship. A patient is dependent upon the analyst, whose skill gives him or her a permanent superiority, whereas initially it is the anthropologist who is dependent on the informant, whose local skills, especially in the vernacular language, he/she tries to learn and match. The anthropologist's command of material resources is usually the greater, but as time goes on and equality of personality is reached, this aspect of their relationship tends to be built into their mutual exchanges or be relatively ignored. As respect and trust develops, so does emotional attachment and interplay of ideas, in which the anthropologist reveals her/himself in a way which a psychiatrist or psycho-analyst never does. In my own case, the bond-friendship which I formed in 1929 with Pa Fenuatara, son of the leading chief in Tikopia (Solomon Islands) and a man of great dignity and intelligence, was such that when I visited the island community after more than twenty years without communication we greeted each other with great warmth and affection.

Friendship in one form or another has a long literary history. The real or legendary names and exploits of friends such as Achilles and Patroclus, Damon and Phintias (Pythias), Orestes and Pylades are well known to classical scholars. Of more popular appeal as a model has been the friendship of David and Jonathan in which 'the soul of Jonathan was knit with the soul of David'. The medieval Japanese tale of Genji has many references to the hero's 'particular friends'. And literary explorations of friendship have ranged from analysis by Cicero of the concept of *amicitia* through study by the early Christian fathers of friendship and neighbourly love (White 1992) to scrutiny of female friendship in Victorian fiction (Coslett 1988). Psychologists too have been interested in friendship, as part of their focus on personal relationships in general.

All such studies show that friendship is of a very diverse and complex, even ambiguous, nature. In early literature as in rather formal modern English, 'friend' is often only a neutral term, a general salutation, a recognition that a person has entered into a relationship with oneself. It may indicate a simple common member-ship of a corporate body such as the Religious Society of Friends (Quakers) or Friends of the Western Buddhist Order. It may show interest – backed by donation – in some special idea or project, as Friends of Covent Garden (opera) or of Sadler's Wells (theatre). It may be of even vaguer import, such as the oddly named Friends of Friendless Churches. The concept of friendship can vary greatly in intensity, from simple well-wishers to familiar, close, dear, intimate, bosom, boon-companion friend, each with its own subtle quality, though each of a positive order. But the more colloquial 'crony', originally a university term for fellow student, and 'chum', originally used (according to the dictionary) by 'schoolboys, students, criminals etc.' have a somewhat disparaging air.

Definition of the concept of friendship is not easy, because of its diversity. Historically, benevolence and loyalty between friends seem to have been assumed. But about the degree of loyalty demanded there was question. Friends could strive in rivalry to give each more than each received, but how far does self-sacrifice go? A friend is a second self, but what does the 'sharing of the soul' mean? Is it limited to an emotional or spiritual exchange or is there a physical, perhaps sexual element as well? The relation of *agape* to *eros* in some such meaning has even occupied the attention of modern theologians. For early Christians the secular idea of personal friendship was in possible conflict with the religious injunction to love thy neighbour as thyself. Then, granted that friendship often involves gifts or exchanges of material or immaterial benefit, is a putative friendship to be seen as based on unworthy motive?

Given all this questioning, there is a practical side to all such study of friendship. It is clear that friendship in any developed sense can be of genuine support to individuals. Apart from any material benefit obtained from a friend, the tolerance, trust, sharing of private thoughts offered by a friend can be of great value in helping to strengthen a person's sense of identity. So it is that psychologists have examined the significance of friendship for social living. Some clinical psychologists have given detailed analysis of the nature of friendship, how it may arise and be maintained, for individuals with emotional difficulties or learning disabilities (Firth and Rapley 1990). They have also indicated some of the difficulties and pitfalls that may occur in friendship formation, especially in 'befriending' schemes by well-wishers, which may interfere with the development of personal identity by those being helped.

In this volume many of these general issues, together with others I have not mentioned, are treated by the editors and contributors in a variety of contexts, historically and over a range of cultures. The essays are informative and thought-provoking in themselves, and will stimulate further studies in this subject of universal interest.

Sir Raymond Firth

References

Bloom, A. (1993), *Love and Friendship*, New York: Simon and Schuster.

Casagrande, J.B. (1960), *In the Company of Man: Twenty Portraits by Anthropologists*, New York: Harper and Brothers.

Coslett, T. (1998), *Woman to Woman: Female friendship in Victorian Fiction*, Brighton: Harvester Press.

Firth, H., and Rapley, M. (1990), *From Acquaintance to Friendship: Issues for People with Learning Disabilities*, Kidderminster: BIMH Publications.

White, Caroline (1992), Christian Friendship in the Fourth Century, Cambridge: Cambridge University Press.

The Anthropology of Friendship:
Enduring Themes and Future Possibilities
Sandra Bell and *Simon Coleman*

In his 1999 Reith Lectures, entitled 'Runaway World', the sociologist Anthony Giddens makes the following claim: 'There is a global revolution going on in how we think of ourselves and how we form ties and connections with others.'[1] According to Giddens, new forms of intimacy are replacing older connections in three key areas of our lives: sex and love; parent-child relations; and friendship. He argues that these transformations are occurring 'almost everywhere', differing only in degree and the cultural context in which they take place.

This is a book about one of the areas highlighted by Giddens: friendship. We hope to demonstrate that some fundamental and important transformations are indeed taking place in this aspect of human life. We agree with the argument of 'Runaway World' that social and economic forces affecting sex, love and the family can also have an impact on the creation and maintenance of relations between friends. However, while the world evoked by Giddens is one that appears to be tightly linked by common assumptions – 'We find the same issues almost every-where', he says – our approach is comparative and frankly sceptical of generic claims to characterize 'global' realities. Our conclusion is that friendship is much more complex than Giddens implies. It is also much more interesting.

For Westerners in general, friendship is a topic with much moral weight. From our friends, we hope to derive emotional support, advice and material help in times of need. Through the ambiguities and ambivalences involved in establishing and keeping friendships alive, we learn about how others see us and therefore, in some sense, how to view ourselves. Can Western notions of friendship and intimacy be seen as evident in other societies, however? Our book juxtaposes case-studies drawn from contemporary Europe with others focusing on China, East Africa, Brazil[2] and ancient Iceland in order to provide some answers to this question.

For anthropologists, the study of friendship is particularly pertinent at the moment. Some thirty years ago, Robert Paine noted that ethnographers conducted lives in which friendship was probably just as important as kinship; yet their academic preoccupations tended to dwell far more on the significance of blood ties for the construction and maintenance of social relations (1969:505). Currently, anthropology is attempting to reappraise traditional ethnographic topics and methods, impelled partly by observing numerous challenges to older social bonds based on kinship or proximity. A consideration of the role of friendship in social life, not least as a means of producing an anthropology that understands kinship more explicitly in the context of other forms of social ties, is – we argue – long overdue.

The task is of course a challenging one, posing fundamental questions about our understandings of agency, emotion, creativity and the self; but it is a challenge we cannot afford to ignore. After all, the development of some form of friendship is inherent within anthropological practice. Fieldworkers usually have to establish cordial and even close relations with informants if they are not to become like ethologists, observing interactions while remaining aloof from close social contact. The ambiguity and complexity of the fieldwork relationship offer us, however, some initial clues to the questions to be posed by any comparative study of friendship: Do both sides of the cultural 'divide' understand the relationship in compatible ways?; How does friendship differ from, say, 'comradeship' or extended collaboration?; Can we describe as friendship something that has a necessarily highly pragmatic, as well as a possibly affective, dimension? Reflecting on field-work in Morocco, Paul Rabinow concludes with a description of his friend and informant, ben Mohammad (1977:162):

> Through mutual confrontation of our own situations we did establish contact. But this also highlighted our fundamental Otherness [. . .] I could understand ben Mohammad only to the extent that he could understand me – that is to say, partially. He did not live in a crystalline world of Otherness any more than I did [. . .] Different webs of significa-tion separated us, but these webs were now at least partially intertwined. But a dialogue was only possible when we recognized our differences [. . .]

We perhaps understand why, towards the end of the book (Rabinow 1977:160), a picture of ben Mohammad is included with the poignant caption: 'A wish for friendship may arise quickly but friendship does not.' Rabinow's broad comments, influenced by a phenomenological approach to ethnographic analysis, illustrate some of the questions of interpretation involved in establishing and understanding social relationships in the field. Implicit within them is not merely the issue of how two individuals are to regard each other, but also the question of whether it makes sense to think of friendship as existing in mutually comprehensible ways across cultures. It is this second issue that lies at the heart of our book. Paine (1969:506) warns us that it is important to be aware of whether one is talking about friendship as 'a cultural artefact and a social arrangement, or as a set of universal needs'. We leave aside, for the most part, the question of whether friendship expresses and meets trans-cultural requirements for human well-being and emotional satisfaction. Such issues have been more directly addressed by social psychologists although their data have largely been drawn from studies of interpersonal relations in contemporary, Western societies (Duck 1983; Bliezner and Adams 1992). We are more concerned with the cultural and social aspects of friendship as they are explored in the varying case-studies that make up the chapters of this volume. Generally, we focus less on relationships between fieldworkers and informants than on local understandings of friendship, mediated through the interpretation of the ethnographer.

In the process, we must be prepared to acknowledge the particularities and ambiguities inherent within our own perceptions of intimacy. Pitt-Rivers (1973:90; see also Carrier's paper in this volume pp.21–38) points to the difficulties of transferring certain notions of motive and selfhood to cultures that do not share the individualism of European and North American societies. Paine notes (1969:513) that the Western, middle-class idea of friendship as involving a personal, spontaneous, private relationship between particular individuals implies a degree of autonomy that is a 'sociological luxury', unaffordable in many other societies. Here, he is writing in a Simmelian tradition according to which the personal and the collective exclude each other.

Voluntarism as a defining quality of friendship is also challenged in a cross-cultural survey presented by Cohen (1961). He shows that relationships are frequently prearranged in many contexts and, even where an element of choice exists, friends often cannot terminate their relationship without pain of serious social sanctions. Neither are all friendships accurately described as informal in as much as they may be ritually sanctioned and formally regulated to the point of invoking incest taboos. For example, Cohen discusses the Kwoma of New Guinea where friendship between men who are not 'true kin' is instituted through blood bonds, while incest taboos apply to the friend's close female relatives (356). Such observations cannot be taken to deny the importance of the voluntary principle in many examples of what ethnographers call friendship: they can however be used to deny the principle's universality in the sense understood by most people in the West.

Even while advocating the possibilities of comparison across cultures, Brain feels it necessary to characterize forms of friendship in terms of Western/non-Western distinctions that would be familiar to Cohen. Brain argues (1976:105–6) that friendship has lost emotional expression and ceremonial patterning in Western cultures: it seems to provide a means of escaping from rigid role structures so that formalization is seen as the antithesis of a genuinely friendly relationship. In societies where friendship plays a more specific role, according to this view, the rights and duties between partners are often more overtly and formally expressed.

Nonetheless, the study of friendship can involve the fieldworker in observing a phenomenon that does not necessarily contribute to community ideologies and institutional stability in obvious or easily recordable ways. Relevant relations between persons may in some societies (despite Brain's and Cohen's points about formality) have inchoate, irregular and sometimes even secret dimensions. Much work in anthropology has instead reflected attempts to discern regular, long-term patterns of social organization, particularly in societies where centralized political control has been absent or distant. Brain (1976:13; cf. Fortes and Evans-Pritchard 1940) emphasizes, for instance, the importance attributed to kinship by many anthropologists in search of overtly expressed principles of arranging social groupings:

> Text-books decry the lack of any detailed treatment of 'bonding' and 'amity' as elements in social organization, but most anthropologists, having made a ritual obeisance to the importance of emotional ties outside structured kin groups, have apparently despaired of describing them in detail – most probably due to their delicate and non-articulate nature.

Aside from kinship and affinal relations, corporate associations linked with principles of territorial, political or ethnic affiliation have tended to provide the organizational means through which anthropologists have identified order in human relationships (Jacobsen 1973:5). Analyses of the processual, the idiosyncratic, the affective and the non-public aspects of social relations – all elements of at least some models of friendship – have often been far less evident. Admittedly, notions of the appropriateness of affect as well as Western privacy and idiosyncrasy in relations of friendship cannot be assumed to be universal. However, we argue that it is important to examine long- or medium-term social relations that, even if influenced by social rules and conventions, may involve relatively 'unofficial' bonds constructed between persons. More broadly, we contend that relationships such as those of friendship that often do not depend solely or predominantly on ties of kinship, fixed positions of roles and statuses, permanent geographical proximity, ethnicity or even common cultural background, are becoming more evident in everyday experience, both in the West and elsewhere. They are therefore emerging – or should be emerging – as an increasingly important aspect of ethnographic analysis and representation.

A non-Western case that illustrates the shifting yet socially highly significant creation of networks of amity is provided by Jacobsen (1973). He describes the personal bonds developed between itinerant urban élites in Mbale, Uganda, as emerging in contexts of geographic mobility, where tribalism and kinship ties are seen as a liability (12). While 'lower-class' Ugandans are perceived by élites as being concerned only with parochial issues, Jacobsen's informants seek ties of sociability and companionship with perceived equals – those people unlikely to make economic demands on them or burden them with social obligations. Networks of connections are thus constructed which reduce the anonymity of urban society without involving participants in taking the responsibility for constituting a fixed corporate group, and which are sufficiently flexible to accommodate the likelihood that individuals will move to other towns in response to the demands of work. Aguilar's paper in this volume (pp.169–184) similarly shows how East African pastoralists transcend or at least bypass localized kin by developing 'globalized friends', in other words contacts required to secure people's inclusion in regional and even national networks of association.

Aguilar's chapter also reflects a shift in the perspective of anthropology that has great relevance to an understanding of models of friendship. Many scholars have concluded that the literary device of describing societies or cultures as isolated social and cultural units fixed in islands of time and space is both methodologically and ideologically dubious (Fabian 1983; Wolf 1982). Furthermore, the scale of trans-national, or at least supra-local, interactions between individuals and groups is on the increase (though this is not to say that such interactions are understood in similar ways by all participants). These processes can hardly be said to be new in themselves, of course, as for instance non-industrial forms of trade have indicated. The likelihood is nevertheless growing that the people who are important to one's social relations will not live locally (Allan 1996:20). In many shifting social contexts, ties of kinship tend to be transformed and often weakened by complex and often contradictory processes of globalization. At the same time new forms of friendship are emerging. Such processes incidentally transform the relationship between informant and anthropologist. We live in a shrinking world, where friends and collaborators, including those from 'the field', read our products (Grindal and Salamone 1995:2). Our relationships with those we describe must be accountable in new ways if we are not to destroy relations of amity established with those whom we study.

Thus the development of an anthropology of friendship is overdue on a number of counts. Anthropologists are focusing the ethnographic gaze on Western societies more than ever before and are forced to confront contexts where unstable networks of intimacy, frequently unrelated to kinship ties, constitute key arenas of social interaction and identity formation. In addition, the oft-quoted division between Western and other societies, even if a useful shorthand descriptive strategy, is becoming an increasingly crude way of delineating supra-local processes that are breaking down old cultural divides and erecting new ones in unpredictable places. Both physical and mediated contacts between representatives from all parts of the globe have increased, with the result that new etiquettes for mutual interaction are being devised all the time. More generally, the study of friendship may force us to pose key questions of all of the taken-for-granted social and cultural fields in which we live and work. It may for instance require us to reconsider the role of affect in the lives of the people we study as well as in our own fieldwork experiences.[3] We must also ask whether our disciplinary expertise in the study of kinship has encouraged us not only to neglect other forms of human association but also to privilege its distinctiveness as a means of organizing social relations.

Friendship and Kinship

Many anthropological and sociological works contrast friendship with kinship along lines of achievement/voluntarism versus ascription/constraint in the establishment and maintenance of social relations (see also the brief discussion in Abrahams, this volume, pp.155–156). For Allan (1996:84), the fact of being aware of a formal, ascribed kinship connection between two people tells one nothing of the actual *content* of that relationship, at least in a Western context. Friendship, on the other hand, is defined solely on the basis of the social contact which really exists and is continually worked upon: participation depends on the relationship created over time between the particular people involved, while what *brings people together* in friendship may not be what *keeps* them together (cf. Rawlins 1992:2). Pitt-Rivers seeks a slightly different form of contrast from his anthropological analysis of relevant literature. He notes: 'Friendship, far from being commonly regarded as the essence of kinship is usually opposed to it [. . .]' (1973:89) before illustrating his point with Fortes's data on the West African Tallensi and Ashanti. Pitt-Rivers concludes that, for many writers: 'The concept of friendship is an invention of soi-disant "civilised society" which has abandoned kinship as an organising principle' (90).

The sense that friendship has little chance to flourish where kinship structures remain strong is reinforced by other ethnographic evidence. In studying the Ndendeuli of Tanzania (also discussed by Aguilar, p.169), Gulliver (1971) reports that he actively looked for ties of friendship among men but found (63) that only one among seventy-three hamlets contained household heads who were not close kinsmen. In the single exception the two men were close friends of many years' standing, ever since their labour migration together as youths. In practice, these friends treated each other like kin, and their associates assumed that they were closely related. Such long-lasting and firm friendship appeared uncommon among the Ndendeuli, who generally preferred to use recognized channels provided by kinship links: 'Where friendship was important it was mutually between particular kinsmen, strengthening their relationship' (63). Personal friends were few as it was felt that unrelated men were likely to suffer conflicts of loyalties.

Gulliver's ethnography and the wider argument that it represents are persuasive. However, one of the points that this book seeks to make is that clear distinctions between friendship and kinship, if sometimes analytically useful and ethnographically very evident, are not always easy to sustain. The power of kinship as an idiom through which to express the power of all social relations considered to have binding qualities cannot be denied. Indeed, Gulliver's example demonstrates how two friends come to be seen by others as related by blood, given the strength of their association. Herman (1987) describes another example of how the idiom of kinship is applied to friendship in his analysis of ritualized friendship in ancient Greece. 'Xenoi', or partners located abroad, with whom élite members of a city could establish alliances, came to resemble kin in terms of displays of affection, the use of courtesy terms derived in part from kinship idioms and the assumed perpetuity of their relationship. Kinship and friendship were partially overlapping, rather than mutually exclusive, classificatory terms (19). Pitt-Rivers himself points out that variants of social relations exist, partaking of the properties of both kinship and friendship, so that 'non-kin amity loves to masquerade as kinship' (1973:90). Mystical analogies with parenthood can also be constructed in some social relations, such as *compadrazgo* (godparenthood) (93).

Deborah Reed-Danahay argues in this volume (pp.137–154) that anthropologists tend to think of friendship and kinship as binary opposites because of their disciplinary preoccupation with kinship. However, the villagers she studied in the commune of Lavialle in rural Auvergne chose most of their friends from distant kin or relatives of other natives of their local community (a case perhaps of kinship being transformed into friendship, in contrast with the Ndendeuli and Greek cases of friendship taking on the guise of kinship). Both kin and friends were placed by villagers in opposition to the category of 'outsider'. Reed-Danahay demonstrates how kinship and friendship cannot easily be separated in a context that is highly endogenous. Both promote attachment to the locality and its farming way of life in the face of economic problems and the lure of the city. Both, in other words, contribute to processes of cultural production, and friendship in this region cannot be seen as the mere 'hand-maiden' of kinship.

If Lavialle demonstrates certain parallels with many non-Western contexts in terms of its social world of face-to-face contacts and widely encompassing kin networks, Paul Durrenberger's and Gísli Pálsson's depiction of the Iceland of the sagas (pp.59–78) looks initially and rather surprisingly like contemporary middle-class culture in one particular aspect: its valorization of voluntary ties of friendship and relative lack of emphasis on kinship. Their thesis is that friendship constituted an important social institution in the context of a stateless, loosely-knit society that encompassed constantly shifting political alliances. In some ways, friendship could be seen as more important than kinship and affinity, with the former often activating the latter rather than the reverse. Informal friendship was akin to 'big-man' systems in the way it was achieved through exchanging gifts and favours on a dyadic basis, although alongside it there existed the highly formal institution of blood-brotherhood which sometimes involved several men. As Durrenberger's and Pálsson's chapter develops, therefore, we realize that saga friendship is ultimately rather different from Western ideals of a form of intimacy removed from the public sphere. Furthermore, it combines its elements of choice with a strong and brooding sense of inevitability.

In many parts of the contemporary world kinship is itself being transformed as a means of expressing relationships under increasingly optative conditions of contact with relatives. A sense of the interconnections on this level between categories of friendship and kinship is certainly evident in urban, Western examples. Brain claims (1976:15) that Western boundaries between friendship, kinship, affinity and loving are disintegrating – a wife is ideally her husband's best friend and vice versa, for instance. Gurdin's (1996:162) work on urban Canadians concludes: 'It was difficult for Montrealers to relate friendship to kinship and vice versa in large part because the language, thought, and emotions of friendship and kinship are experienced as intersecting and complementary, often at the same time.' Firth and Djamour's much earlier study (1956) of London kinship systems argues that a prime characteristic of such systems is selectivity on the basis of emotional attachments. In 'open' societies, where kinship is organized multilaterally, the number of possible kin to be drawn upon beyond the elementary family is very large. Kinship becomes like friendship in that it is personal and to some extent a matter of choice (cf. Reed-Danahay's discussion in this volume [p.146] of Bourdieu's [1972] analysis of *cousinage*). However, as we have seen, the principle of optation need not be evident only in contexts of Western modernity. The Cameroonian Bangwa described by Brain (1976:108), recognize a clear difference between chosen/achieved allies ('friends of the heart') and ascribed ones ('friends of the road'). People choose from a large network of kinship ties those persons who provide practical and emotional satisfaction: 'They found kin to be friendly with' (17).

Assessing Western Models of Friendship

If rigid distinctions between friendship and kinship do not always hold in the West or indeed elsewhere, what can we make of specifically Western models of friendship? In what sense, if any, might they provide a useful basis for comparative study? Certainly, some consistent trends can be discerned in the literature. Many writers present friendship in ideal terms as interstitial, private and absolutely voluntary. From the perspective of philosophy, Deutsch (1994:17–18) argues that the primary condition for friendship is personal autonomy, involving self-control, moral self-governance, authentic self-making and a post-Enlightenment commitment to free choice. In the same volume (1994:95), Parekh characterizes the fragility and informal nature of friendship by arguing that it is entirely voluntary, not embedded in a network of other relations or reinforced by social sanctions. According to this view friendship becomes a special relationship between two equal individuals involved in a uniquely constituted dyad. The argument echoes that of Pitt-Rivers's (1973:96) analytical distinction between friendship and formal, jural, social relations combined with the claim that friendship is ideally founded on sentiments, not rights or duties. According to this view, once reciprocal relations are subject to calculation the amity essential to friendship disappears. Similarly, Paine's 1969 paper discusses the role of sentiment in Western friendship within middle-class culture and argues that such friendship is relatively structurally unencumbered, with this characteristic being reflected in its affective content (1969:507). Part of Paine's point is to note the distinctiveness of our society in its permissiveness in granting such autonomy to interpersonal relations. He asserts that Western friendship is the one that exists in greatest independence from kinship and other institutional arrangements. Friendship thus becomes 'an institutionalised non-institution' (514).

These ideas contrast in certain respects with assumptions informing classical Western models of friendship. Aristotle (1976) famously distinguished between those friendships based on utility, those based on the pursuit of pleasure, and those (true, perfect, longer-lasting) alliances founded on virtue. The last and purest form of friendship illustrates his conviction that such individual relationships can provide a basis for all societal bonds (McGuire 1988:xxx; cf. Moltmann 1994). Friendship and community become complementary rather than opposed, so that Aristotelian (and subsequent Ciceronian) perspectives idealize a situation where 'good men' make good alliances for the benefit of the community. This ideal of friendship was sustained by the development of Christian monasticism. As Collins remarks (1988:112) it is not surprising that monks, being 'essentially "outside" reproductive-kinship relations, should emphasise friendship as their appropriate form of affection and reciprocity'. Nevertheless, strong dyadic friendship could also threaten the communitarian establishment of the 'heavenly city' on earth. McGuire (1988:xiii) notes that early Christian monks sometimes perceived friendship and community not as complementary, but as potentially rivalrous, given that exclusive personal bonds could threaten communal fellowship.

The virtue of monastic friendship also features strongly in the history of Buddhism. But Buddhist monastic ideas about friendship did not permeate lay society and nurture communitarian ideologies as they did in Christian culture because of the radical, unworldly orientation of Buddhist spiritual liberation. Unlike Buddhism, in Christianity 'the mundane world constitutes at least one arena for activities which are relevant to salvation' (Collins 1988:120).

Contemporary versions of the classical model persist as utopian ideals for some writers. Bellah et al. (1985) lament the decline of friendship as an expression of moral commitment (one might almost say 'covenant' in this north American context) in relation to the community and describe how it has become heavily influenced by a therapeutic, individualistic attitude. The Aristotelian view – whether or not it was ever actually realized in practice – has seemingly been privatized in the modern era (as recommended by Deutsch and Parekh), being replaced by the notion that virtuous friendship should be isolated and protected from such aspects of public life as politics and power. Such a perspective, at least in its contemporary variants, relies partly on a nineteenth-century romantic view according to which 'society' is no longer an ideal but rather becomes a social culprit, separating humans from each other. Devotion to personal friendship as opposed to the social good is epitomized by E. M. Forster's well-known statement that if he had to choose between betraying a friend or his country he hoped that he would choose to betray his country.

If Western and particularly middle-class friendship is characterized in romantic, post-Aristotelian terms as involving autonomy, voluntarism, sentiment and freedom from structural constraints, it can more readily be distinguished from other social forms. It should be untainted by the inequalities of patron-client relations, the constraints of kinship, the pragmatism of certain forms of balanced exchange and the commitment to the group as found in religious fellowship (Paine 1969). In our volume, Carrier's contribution (pp.21–38) begins with a deliberately polemical outline of this view. One of the arguments of his chapter is that friendship's emphasis on spontaneous and unconstrained sentiment depends on the presence of distinct conceptions of the self. In Melanesia, he finds 'situated' selves that are enmeshed in and constituted by relations with others, so that interior sources of sentiment are lacking. By way of contrast, those people who are seen as capable of being true friends are the notionally free and independent actors of modern, Western, liberal thought, who live in social contexts where person and society are seen as distinct rather than meshed entities. (Giddens's Reith lecture echoes this point in his description of a potentially 'pure relationship' that is entirely constituted by 'emotional communication'.) Drawing on Parry's (1986) discussion of the gift, Carrier points out that the altruistic giver and morally autonomous friend are products of the same ideological perspective – one in which purity of purpose and spontaneity can explicitly be contrasted with the assumptions of the market-place.

Silver (1990) and Bliezner and Adams (1992:30–1) similarly contrast the impersonality of market exchange with the sympathy and affection expected of Western personal relations. Resonances can also be discerned between this argument and what Allan (1996:9) calls 'the privatisation thesis'. The latter has made headway since the publication of *The Affluent Worker* by Goldthorpe et al. (1969), though it draws on models of modernization reaching back to Tönnies. The claim is that Western/modern life is becoming more segmented into different spheres (for instance separating home and bureaucratically organized work) and increasing the amount of behaviour removed from the public gaze. People are more committed to private than to public spheres of life with inevitable consequences for patterns of social involvement and the significance of informal relations.

Such ideal-typical models of social development provide useful tools 'to think with' but cannot be regarded as straightforward ethnographic reflections of the politics and ambiguities of Western social relations. Carrier concludes that: 'The emergence of the autonomous self was as much a device through which an emerging élite justified the cutting of old relationships and denying the claims made on them by others as it was a warrant for making new friends among polite society.' Here, the political aspect rather than the romance of autonomy is highlighted. In the same vein, Paine describes his contribution to the current volume (pp.39–58) as a complement to the 'idealized' approach taken in his 1969 paper: while the earlier piece depicted the middle classes as giving without expecting equivalent return and creating relationships that depended on good faith rather than the jural sanctions of 'bond' friendships, his current essay looks at such aspirations as they venture out into the real world. Paine now finds it necessary to question the candidness and autonomy of the private universe of middle-class friendship. He depicts the complexities and inherent contradictions involved in the exercise of such friendship and the creation of trust. For instance, treachery within a given set of contacts can be relational since the same act can involve somebody in being a friend to one person and a traitor to another.

One of the clearest attacks on de-contextualized notions of freedom and autonomy as applied to friendship is provided by Allan (1989). He demonstrates how relations conventionally depicted as voluntary, informal and personal can be seen to operate within the still considerable constraints of class, ethnicity, age, gender and geographical location. Allan thus attempts to counter 'claims implicit in much of the literature, and indeed, even in everyday notions, that friendship is a matter of choice' (47). The tendency towards homophily even in the West (the fact that friends are so often of the same age, gender and class) further illustrates the implicit but powerful constraints on choice, while (99): 'There may be no clear-cut rules governing friendship, but there are cultural scripts about the ways in which friend relationships should be structured.' Allan's work forces us to consider Western friendship's connections with and influences from other networks of social relationships as well as its insertion into wider institutional and ideological frameworks, despite the prevalence of representations (also evident in the romantic love complex) of friendships as private, self-governing dyads.

In this book, Rezende's discussion of fieldwork carried out in London (pp.79–98) shows how relations in the work place interact positively and negatively with those constructed in leisure time. Her piece illustrates a further challenge to the notion of Western friendship as pure and unfettered autonomy by noting how unreserved exposure of the 'true' self can be interpreted by involved parties as imposing unwarranted feelings too much on others. Rezende juxtaposes such conclusions with observations on how, by so-called Western standards, Brazilians tend to personalize work relations and the public sphere in general. The result in

Brazil is a relationship between people of different classes, such as mistresses and maids, that is more one of affinity than equality, and moreover one that challenges Western conceptions of public and private.[4]

Rapport's chapter (pp.99–118) approaches issues of freedom and restraint by looking at a specific social activity. He shows how playing dominoes with friends in a rural part of the north of England can be both distillation of and ambiguous escape from other social and institutional contexts of village life. Dominoes is a leisure time pursuit and yet requires of its players that they uphold strict norms of propriety. The outcome of any game (in terms of deciding winners and losers of a particular contest) is uncertain, and yet as a ritualized form of sociability its effects in bringing people together are more predictable. Rapport's contribution therefore indicates ways in which the form of amity expressed by dominoes-players involves a kind of intimacy that is precisely contingent on its physical expression; it is both constructed within a set-apart, ludic genre of sociality and dependent on the wider context of the game and the pub for its character.

Rapport's observations highlight the potentially labile and shifting nature of friendship and its creative but not unconstrained use by participants to configure degrees of amity that shade into intimacy. The ambiguities of closeness remain, allowing exact degrees of revelation and reserve to remain unexamined: we are therefore led back in a less dramatic but equally important way to Paine's discussion of the articulation of trust between friends. 'Nigel' the ethnographer, as one of his fellow players tells him, is a man who lives 'many lives', not all of which are (or ever can be) evident to his friends and informants in the village.

The creativity of friendship need not be confined to issues of self-representation. Friendship also provides a critical site for anthropologists to study identity formation, to pose new questions about the articulation of personal and social identities, or to question the validity of such a distinction for those they study. These themes are vividly evoked by Allison James (1993) in her ethnographic account of British childhood. If Western, middle-class, male, adult friendship is portrayed as frequently fragmented, brittle, poorly anchored and only weakly institutionalized (Paine 1969), children's friendships appear all the more fragile. Yet, the patterning of these interrelations, often so momentary as to appear frighteningly vacuous to adult onlookers (James 1993:212), enact and encode potent forces in the culture of children. The performance of friendship and 'the power to personify which [it] unleashes for children' (234) stands out as a primary medium for composing identity. Satisfying the demands of being a friend entails cultivating a familiarity with the prevailing moral economy of friendship in its ideological and experiential aspects. By paying attention to the performance of friendship and to children's commentaries on that performance, James obtains evidence for the manner in which cultural knowledge about friendship is generated, as well as the kinds of skills that British children practise, or fail to practise, in the management of friendships.

Any consideration of the potential effects of wider ideological frameworks on friendship must take into account not only the subject's position in the life-cycle (see also Hess 1972) but also include consideration of gender. Although none of the papers in the volume focuses specifically on this issue, it emerges at various points as authors assess the extent to which gender has an impact on assumptions regarding the validity of society-wide generalizations about friendship. Carrier draws on the work of Hartsock (1985) to note how the household work and child-rearing predominantly carried out by women involves them in a 'relational' rather than an 'autonomous' social world. Reed-Danahay critically discusses research that examines friendship in the context of differential access to public spheres of society, and in particular looks at the impact of marriage on female opportunities or desires for friendship beyond the possible tensions of family life. Describing rural Chinese contexts, Smart (pp.119–136) invokes some of the same themes by noting the importance of loose and unofficial networks of specifically female friends and neighbours for young brides who seek the means to resist the patriarchal nature of official kin structures (cf. Wolf 1972).

Other authors assess the significance of the apparent lack of female participation in official or 'public' realms of society. Abrahams (pp.155–168), describing the situation in Estonia during a period of rapid economic change, notes the greater mobility of men than women outside the domestic sphere, at least in rural contexts. Yet he also points to the importance of women as links in the development of chains of connection by entrepreneurial husbands. For Durrenberger and Pálsson, the relevant issue is more how to explain the striking absence in the Icelandic sagas of sustained references to friendship involving women. One explanation they put forward is that female friendship, seemingly divorced from the exercise of overt political power, was simply taken for granted. It may seem from both the Estonian and Icelandic ethnography that female friendship is (or has been) liable to belong to the more 'informal' or at least non-public spheres of society; yet such a tendency does not diminish from its practical significance in sustaining wider social structures and processes.

A number of studies produced over the past twenty years have approached the issue of gender by focusing on the quality of same-sex friendships in the West. They have reflected general agreement that men are inclined to share *activities* with their male friends whereas women prefer to share *feelings* with female friends (Davidson and Duberman 1982; Allan 1989). McWilliams and Howard (1993) maintain that 'gender schema and stereotypes are particularly likely to influence the solidarity and hierarchy of cross-sex friendships':

> If women's behaviour is more likely to be interpreted as solidarity-oriented because of stereotypes about women's communal, nurturing, and prosocial nature, then the recipient of advice from a woman may be less likely to interpret that behaviour as being hierarchical.

In contrast if gender stereotypes make it more likely that men's behaviour will be characterised as agentic, instrumental and status asserting, then the recipient of advice from a man will likely interpret that behaviour as being more hierarchical (McWilliams and Howard 1993:196–7).

Overall, our characterizations of both lay and academic concepts of friendship imply that a powerful, Western (and in particular a middle-class) ideology of freedom, flexibility and creativity, that is sometimes shared by the researcher, must be tempered by the sociological realities of institutional constraint and cultural scripts, such as that cited above – even if these scripts are always changing and under dispute. We need to acknowledge the significance and uniqueness of an ideology that is the product of a specific set of historical circumstances; however, the (hardly surprising) presence of economic, social and even geographical constraints make Western friendship seem more like its non-Western counterparts than such an ideology would at first suggest.

Conversely, anthropological observations on social relationships in non-Western contexts could usefully be subjected to the opposite intellectual treatment, with assumed inflexibility and rigid structure being nuanced by taking account of social process and ambiguity. We should beware of crudely depicting Western societies as infinitely open and progressive in contrast to others that are putatively walled in by linguistic and social barriers (Brain 1976:148). Abrahams (in this volume pp.155–168) briefly discusses the ambiguities associated with seeing friendship in linear, monochrome terms as a harbinger of Western modernity. He juxtaposes the view that sees friendship, like patron-client relations, as enabling escape from the stranglehold of traditional kinship ties with the alternative perspective that contrasts such social forms with the impersonal structures of modernity. Perhaps Abrahams' conclusions to his discussion can be quoted as a suitably balanced approach to the debate: 'Both viewpoints are, of course, defensible, since typologically such ties lie somewhere in between the polar opposites of kinship and bureaucracy'.

Abrahams' specific characterization of Estonia in relation to such issues has significant parallels with Alan Smart's discussion in this volume of friendship and *guanxi* in Chinese societies. Both contributors conclude that apparent movement from socialist redistribution to market models need not produce impersonal approaches to the deployment of critical resources. Rural entrepreneurs in Estonia find that anonymous transactions and the workings of the market cannot provide solutions to the organization of life in a context of economic uncertainty. More significant is the cultivation of expectations of trust and mutual commitment combined with forms of gift-giving and reciprocity that recognize the importance of people rather than cash. Referring to Chinese contexts, Smart observes that practising the art of *guanxi* – an institution that sometimes overlaps with friendship and which involves the invoking of pre-existing social relations – is critical to getting things done in everyday life. As in Estonia, the use of cash to reward favours is often risky, not least since it implies that purely material interests are involved.

Smart uses his ethnography to make many wide-ranging points about Western assumptions concerning personal relations (and, like Carrier and Rezende, he draws on Silver's [1990] useful work to do so). He argues, for instance, that we should avoid the ethnocentric evolutionism involved in seeing *guanxi* as part of a pre-modern, premarket form of social organization. An Asian critique of Western capitalism is founded, indeed, on rejection of Western assumptions of the need for strictly separate domains of economy, polity and society. *Guanxi* incorporates both genuine sentiment and a series of techniques for getting things done in contexts where instrumentality and expressivity are not seen as inherently opposed dimensions of a relationship. Generally, Smart argues for an approach that does not search for a pure, distilled 'essence' of friendship but rather acknowledges the importance of friendship-like relational idioms based on shared identities in a culture where even sibling relationships are hierarchically ranked by age. In line with other contributors, he takes into account the concept of the person in the context he describes. If the Chinese version of the self is formed and reformed through the fluid construction of relationships then information concerning these relational webs becomes critical: selves and relationships are seen as much more contextual and situational than is common in Western styles of social interaction. Here, then, we are journeying far from Enlightenment and Post-Enlightenment representations of the autonomy of the person.

Constructing an Agenda

Observed as a set of sociological practices rather than as pure ideology, Western friendship may have more affinities than is often assumed with social processes evident in other societies and cultures. Even so it should not simply be reproduced as the basis of an 'etic' model that could putatively be deployed in cross-cultural comparison and analysis. In fact, we argue that there is little pragmatic sense in attempting to construct a rigid, globally applicable, definition of friendship. Such a project would serve little purpose other than to set up boundaries of inclusion and exclusion that themselves would become catalysts for heated and probably fruitless debate. Certainly, we cannot claim that all the contributors to this volume have employed exactly the same conception of friendship in defining an object of study. For instance, Smart uses his Chinese material to challenge Carrier's distinction between the spontaneous affection required of friendship and the kinds of social relationships inherent in the world of work. Durrenberger and Pálsson see friendships as strategically cultivated in a way that does not fit easily with Carrier's standpoint.

Nor is it possible, in many cases, to say where the conceptual 'West' ends and the 'non-West' begins. Even to talk of a Western or Northern European perspective is frankly problematic: Abrahams, for instance, contrasts Finnish and British ideas of the relationship between friendship and kinship. Moreover, it is clear that considerations of class and ethnicity (Donnan 1976) as well as sexual orientation (Nardi and Sherrod 1994) may affect attitudes to personal relationships.

We propose that a more positive agenda in the ethnographic study of friendship is to use micro-analyses of particular social contexts in order to address a broad package of questions relevant to our discipline and to wider societal concerns. The study of friendship can be used as a means of examining social relations that may include but are not reducible to kinship; that are sustained beyond single or short-term encounters; that involve the search for some form of sentiment or at least empathy and common ground between persons. To phrase the aim of the project in another way, we wish to locate and analyse the social space that exists once such factors as kinship, territory and fixed hierarchies have been accounted for. Related to this aim, an analytical thread running through the book as a whole refers to friendship as a site of identity-formation that mediates, often ambiguously, between constraint and creativity (or at least relative flexibility) in the formation of social ties. Such ties help define how a given person is to be perceived, by him/her self as well as by others.

We are not searching for cross-cultural generalizations about supposed pan-human needs for intimacy and emotional compensation as responses to the rigidities of ascribed social relations or impersonal bureaucracies. Nor do we propose the foundation of a new subdiscipline of 'friendship studies' that would elevate the topic into a fetishized category whilst, in all probability, artificially excluding messy gradations of relationship between close bonding, familiarity, acquaintanceship, etc. Rather, we suggest that a focus on the notion of friendship encourages us to look at old data in new ways, to challenge some academic and lay stereotypes about the constitution of social relationships and to be ready to observe the construction of new types of sociality in a globalizing but complex and contradictory world whose cultural and social boundaries are constantly being transformed.

Notes

1 The Reith Lectures are a series of public lectures delivered annually by a distinguished scholar under the auspices of the BBC. The lecture we are quoting from is the fourth in the series, entitled 'Family'. Giddens's global message

was reinforced by a global medium: the lectures were published on the Internet on the BBC's web site <http://news.bbc.co.uk>.

2 The first three are all regions that have played a strong role in anthropological writings about patron-client and unilineal kinship relations.

3 Many ethnographers have removed evidence of personal involvement from published texts (including the affect displayed by informants themselves). As Grindal and Salamone point out (1995:1), when writers have displayed their own emotions they have sometimes even used pseudonyms (cf. Laura Bohannan's *Return to Laughter* [Bowen 1964]).

4 In a rather different way, Aguilar's chapter on East Africa challenges Western notions of intimacy and the public/private divide by noting that Boorana letters are part of public knowledge.

References

Allan, G. (1996), *Kinship and Friendship in Modern Britain*, Oxford: Oxford University Press.

—— (1989), Friendship: Developing a Sociological Perspective, Boulder and San Francisco: Westview Press.

Aristotle (1976), *Nichomachean Ethics*, revised edition, trans. J.A.K. Thompson, Harmondsworth: Penguin.

Bellah, R., Madsen, R., Sullivan, W., Swidler, A. and Tipton, S. (1985), *Habits of the Heart: Individualism and Commitment in American Life*, New York: Harper and Row.

Bliezner, R. and Adams, R. (1992), *Adult Friendship*, London: Sage.

Bourdieu, P. (1972), 'Les Stratègies Matrimoniales dans le Système de Reproduction', *Annales*, 4–5:1105–25

Bowen, E.S. (1964), *Return to Laughter*, Garden City, N.Y.: Doubleday.

Brain, R. (1976), *Friends and Lovers*, New York: Basic Books.

Cohen, Y.A. (1961), 'Patterns of Friendship', in Y.A. Cohen (ed.), *Social Structure and Personality*, New York: Holt-Rinehart-Winston.

Collins, S. (1988), 'Monastacism, Utopias and Comparative Social Theory', *Religion*, 18:101–35.

Davidson, L. and Duberman, L. (1982) 'Friendship: Communication and Interactional Patterns in Same Sex Dyads', *Sex Roles*, Vol.8, No.8.

Deutsch, E. (1994), 'On Creative Friendship', in L. Rouner (ed.), *The Changing Face of Friendship*, Notre Dame: University of Notre Dame Press.

Donnan, H. (1976), 'Inter-Ethnic Friendship, Joking and Rules of Interaction in a London Factory', in L. Holy (ed.), *Knowledge and Behaviour*, Papers in Social Anthropology, Vol. 1., Queens University of Belfast.

Duck, S. (1983), *Friends For Life: The Psychology of Close Relationships*, Brighton: Harvester Press.

Fabian, J. (1983), *Time and the Other: How Anthropology Makes its Object*, New York: Columbia University Press.

Firth, R. and Djamour, J. (1956), 'Kinship in South Borough', in R. Firth (ed.), *Two Studies of Kinship in London*, London: The Athlone Press.

Fortes, M. and Evans-Pritchard, E. (1940), *African Political Systems*, London: Oxford University Press.

Goldthorpe, J. H., Lockwood, D., Bechhofer, F. and Platt, J. (1969), *The Affluent Worker in the Class Structure*, Cambridge: Cambridge University Press.

Grindal, B. and Salamone, F. (1995), *Bridges to Humanity: Narratives on Anthropology and Friendship,* Prospect Heights: Waveland Press.

Gulliver, P.H. (1971), *Neighbours and Networks: The Idiom of Kinship in Social Action among the Ndendeuli of Tanzania*, Berkeley: University of California Press.

Gurdin, J. (1996), *Amitié/Friendship: An Investigation into Cross-Cultural Styles in Canada and the United States*, San Francisco: Austin and Winfield.

Hartsock, N.C.N. (1985), 'Exchange Theory: Critique from a Feminist Standpoint', in S.G. McNall (ed.), *Current Perspectives in Social Theory*, Vol.6, Greenwich, Conn.: JAI Press.

Herman, G. (1987), *Ritualised Friendship and the Greek City,* Cambridge: Cambridge University Press.

Hess, B. (1972), *Aging and Society*, Vol.3., New York: Russell Sage Foundation.

James, A. (1993), *Childhood Identities: Self and Social Relationships in the Experience of the Child*, Edinburgh: Edinburgh University Press.

Jacobsen, D. (1973), *Itinerant Townsmen: Friendship and Social Order in Uganda,* Menlo Park, California: Cummings.

McGuire, B. (1988), *Friendship and Community: The Monastic Experience 350–1250*, Kalamazoo, Mich.: Cistercian Publications.

McWilliams, S. and Howard, J.A. (1993), 'Solidarity and Hierarchy in Cross-Sex Friendships', *Journal of Social Issues*, 49 (3):191–202.

Moltmann, J. (1994), 'Open Friendship: Aristotelian and Christian Concepts of Friendship', in L. Rouner (ed.), *The Changing Face of Friendship*, Notre Dame: University of Notre Dame Press.

Nardi, P. and Sherrod, D. (1994), 'Friends in the Lives of Gay Men and Lesbians', *Journal of Social and Personal Relationships*, 11 (2):185–99.

Paine, R. (1969), 'In search of friendship: an exploratory analysis in "middle-class" culture', *Man* 4 (4):505–24.

—— (1974), 'Anthropological Approaches to Friendship' in E. Leyton (ed.), *The Compact: Selected Dimensions of Friendship*, New Foundland: University of Toronto Press.

Parekh, B. (1994), 'An Indian View of Friendship', in L. Rouner (ed.), *The Changing Face of Friendship*, Notre Dame: University of Notre Dame Press.

Parry, J. (1986), 'The Gift, The Indian Gift and the "Indian Gift"', *Man*, 21:453–73.

Pitt-Rivers, J. (1973), 'The Kith and the Kin', in J. Goody (ed.), *The Character of Kinship*, Cambridge: Cambridge University Press.

Rabinow, P. (1977), *Reflections on Fieldwork in Morocco*, Berkeley: University of California Press.

Rawlins, W. (1992), *Friendship Matters: Communication, Dialectics, and the Life Course*, New York: Aldine de Gruyter.

Silver, Allan (1990), 'Friendship in Commercial Society: Eighteenth-Century Social Theory and Modern Sociology', in *American Journal of Sociology* 95(6):1474–504.

Wolf, E. (1982), *Europe and the People Without History*, Berkeley: University of California Press.

Wolf, Margery (1972), *Women and the Family in Rural Taiwan*, Stanford: Stanford University Press.

2

People Who Can Be Friends:
Selves and Social Relationships
James G. Carrier

Friendship is not just a relationship between people, it is a kind of relationship, one based on spontaneous and unconstrained sentiment or affection. After all, if the relationship is constrained we confront something very different from what we call 'friendship', something like bureaucratic relationships, kinship relationships or patron-client relationships. Similarly, if the sentiments displayed are forced or bought, we confront dissimulation of the sort that Arlie Hochschild (1983) describes for airline cabin crew and that we associate with a range of occupations from that of sales staff to courtesans.

I do not mean that co-workers, kin, patrons and clients feel no affection towards each other. If they do, however, we see them as people who are also friends. Although it may have begun because their work, family gatherings or the like brought them into contact with each other, their mutual affection is added to their other relationship with each other, it does not constitute it. To speak of friendship between two co-workers, then, is to speak of something construed as distinct from the relationship defined by their respective locations in the organization that employs them. Thus, to speak of friendship at all is to speak of a particular kind of relationship, one based on spontaneous sentiment.

A friendship is between the people who are friends, the unconstrained people who come to feel spontaneous affection for, and so befriend, each other. To speak of friendship, then, is to speak of people as responding to an internal spring of motive, their sentiments. Without the presence of people construed in this way, the sort of people who are capable of friendship, we must speak of co-workers who get on together, of kin who feel the bonds of their relationships and the like. Without people who can be friends, in other words, we can not speak of friendship.

What I have laid out is an uncompromising view of friendship, one that sees friendship in its purest form. In its uncompromising idealization it brings to the fore elements that are common, even central, to the idea of friendship. A study of friendship among middle-class American women, by Helen Gouldner and Mary Symons Strong (1987), illustrates some of these points. To begin with, the women they interviewed made a clear differentiation between amicable relationships based on propinquity, common interest or the like, and friendship. Thus, the authors quote one woman distinguishing between neighbours in her apartment building on the one hand and friends on the other:

> Even though you meet the same mothers and children over and over again and spend hours on end talking, you don't necessarily meet with people you want to become friends with [. . .] The relationship between the mothers is not based on who you are, but on how close you live to each other and whether the kids get along. It's a matter of convenience more than being attracted to someone and choosing them as friends (Gouldner and Strong 1987:65).

The idea that people who are only neighbours, however amicable, are not friends, echoes my point that friendship springs from a spontaneous affection, unconstrained by things such as geography. For the women Gouldner and Strong studied, spontaneity is an important feature of friendships. Thus, these women

> [. . .] conceived of themselves as not planning or even cultivating the growth of a relationship – much less maneuvering to forward its development. 'I don't like to think of our friendship in that crass way',was the reply of a successful real estate broker. 'It spoils it for me' (Gouldner and Strong 1987:23).

My purpose in this chapter is to describe this way of speaking about, and hence of thinking about, the sentimental relationships we call friendship. Even though I will be focusing on the thought and the talk, it is important to remember that friendship is more than just thought and talk, is not just 'an ensemble of texts' (Geertz 1973:5, 452). It is more because we act and shape our world in terms of it. When bank tellers are admonished to act in a friendly way towards customers, when children are told not to sit around the house but to go out and find some playmates, when advertisements portray people happily spending time with each other, the talk and the thought are made flesh and people are assessed in terms of their conformity to the notion.

My attention to the talk and the thought about friendship means I set aside the affection that people we call friends feel towards each other. I ignore it, not because I think it is unreal or unimportant, but because it is the talk and the thought that constructs as friendship the relationship in which the affection occurs, that makes it different from other relationships in which people feel affection towards each other. I see no reason to doubt that all people in all sorts of relationships can feel affection towards each other. But not everyone talks of the affection and the relationship as friendship.

I said that speaking of friendship entails thinking of people who respond to their internal, spontaneous sentiments rather than the demands or expectations placed upon them by the ties of kinship, trade, propinquity, interest or the like. In other words, the idea of friendship entails a distinct conception of what people are like, of the self. One important stream in the anthropological consideration of the self emerged out of the study of gift exchange in Melanesian ethnography, and I will use exchange as the frame for my discussion of the selves who can be friends.

Jonathan Parry (1986:466) provides a useful point of entry to the link between exchange and the self, when he refers to the 'ideology of the "pure gift"', one in which the giver and the gift are 'free and unconstrained'. This freedom and lack of constraint are the essence of friendship. It is, after all, only through freedom and lack of constraint that the independent individual can be motivated by the spontaneous affection that makes real friendship.

This conception of the free, spontaneous individual is not just a part of popular thought. It is common in social scientific writing on modern gift giving, a key element of friendship. Thus, Russell Belk says (1979:100) of the gift 'that (a) it is something voluntarily given, and that (b) there is no expectation of compensation'. Similarly, for David Cheal (1988:12) gift-giving occurs when 'the incumbents of roles go beyond their recognized obligations and perform gratuitous favors'. Seen from this perspective, the self of friendship is the free and independent actor who is a key feature of Western liberal thought (see Ouroussoff 1993).

In this chapter I want to make the notion of friendship problematic. I have begun this process already by noting that our conception of friendship entails a corresponding notion of the self. I continue this process by considering other ways that selves can be conceived. Doing so is no assertion that these other sorts of selves are bereft of relationships that are affectionate. Rather, I introduce these other selves precisely to make the point that our term 'friendship' seems little applicable to their affectionate relations.

The first way I present these other selves is through a sketch, necessarily stylized, of changing conceptions of the person, the self, in Western thought over the past few centuries. This sketch will show that the kind of self associated with relations of friendship is a relatively recent phenomenon. I then turn to conceptions of the self and social relations in a very different place, Melanesia. While these conceptions are interesting in their own right, my purpose in presenting them is only to point to the existence of scholarly descriptions of selves and social relations that are very different from the modern Western form that I present.

Although I said that I will sketch the emergence of the modern Western conception of the self, it is important to recognize that this conception hides, as well as reveals, notions of the self and social relations. I conclude, then, by considering more fragmented, but none the less suggestive, evidence that indicates that what I have called the modern Western conception of the self needs to be seen as less widespread than it might appear, less an expression of human nature and more a reflection of some people's beliefs and experiences.

Changing Western Selves

This conception of the autonomous self capable of real friendship has a history, one that helps show alternative conceptions. Marcel Mauss (1985) has argued that the seventeenth and eighteenth centuries saw a marked change in the notion of the self in Western Europe, and in light of my observation that the friendly self looks like the liberal's independent actor, it is worth noting that this period also saw the rapid spread of capitalism. Mauss argues that it was during this time that some intellectuals began to propound the modern idea of the individual.

It appears that prior to this time the self commonly was seen to be situated rather than autonomous, based in and shaped by the relationships within which it exists, and hence a self to which 'friendship' is not really appropriate. In other words, and in spite of the arguments made by Alan Macfarlane (1978), in this older view people are locations in structures or webs of relationships. As a result, people's motives, or perhaps their only valid motives, are to be explained by their locations. With such an understanding of the self, a person's identity is defined in terms of his or her position in the social frame, and each person is concerned that others be 'sincere', to use Lionel Trilling's (1972) term, concerned that they do not hide or be misleading about that position.

Gradually, however, this view of the self as springing from its situation gave way to one in which individual consciousness was seen as the autonomous and irreducible being that defines the essential nature of the person. Under such a construction of the self, each of us is a self-contained individual, 'equal, identical and separate monads' (Barnett and Silverman 1979:73), an individual who can be a friend. And under such a construction, our irreducible beings are the source, or perhaps the only valid source, of motive. In this newer view, then, people identify each other in terms of individual predispositions and wills, and they are concerned that others, again in Trilling's terms, be 'authentic', not hide or be misleading about that will. While this new view of the self gained in importance in the seventeenth and eighteenth centuries, before 1800 in England it was important primarily among capitalists and larger land owners (Abercrombie, Hill and Turner 1986:104–10).

I want to put some flesh on the skeleton that I have described, flesh that bears more directly on the modern notion of friendship. I do so through a consideration of emerging understandings of the nature and bases of moral behaviour. According to Colin Campbell (1987), around 1700 there began to appear in England a morality that demonized constraint and that justified the spontaneous expression of the unfettered self, the sort of expression that exists in modern constructions of friendship. Campbell points to the emergence of the idea that people had an intuitive moral sense of the right and the wrong, and that they had an innate desire to do the right and avoid the wrong. With this moral calculus, constraint is evil because it hinders this innate, moral desire. As Campbell (1987:150) puts it, 'virtuous behaviour can only be conduct which is freely chosen, arising directly out of one's very being'. Campbell illustrates this new morality with Shaftesbury's *Characteristics of Man, Manners, Opinions, Times*, published in 1711. There, Shaftesbury says of the good man:

> He never deliberates [. . .] or considers the matter by prudential rules of self-interest and advantage. He acts from his nature, in a manner necessarily, and without reflection; and if he did not, it were impossible for him to answer his character (in Campbell 1987:150).

Because of the innate desire to do the good and avoid the bad, moral behaviour is encouraged when the will is free and unconstrained, best able to operate.

The idea that people have an innate desire to do the good and avoid the bad is justified by what one might call an aesthetic of morality. The good and the true were attractive because unfettered people recognized their beauty, just as the bad and the false were repulsive because people innately recognized their ugliness. This aesthetic strengthened the case for autonomous spontaneity, because of its corollary that public standards of taste and external criteria of judgement are suspect, if only because they are not spontaneous. The unconstrained pleasure the free individual experiences with the true, like the unconstrained displeasure experienced with the false, count for more than conformity to any articulated aesthetic, ethical or logical criteria (Campbell 1987:154–60). Personal feelings, then, cease to be merely idiosyncratic reactions that are suspect. Instead, they become the best and most valid moral judgements. In terms of friendship, this meant that individuals, autonomous in their being, spontaneously relate to those around them, being attracted by the good and repulsed by the bad. They were unfettered by the constraints of interest, whether of mutual service as in some Chinese relationships (see Smart in this volume, pp.119–136) or of patronage and protection as in the Iceland of the Sagas (see Durrenberger and Pálsson in this volume, pp.59–78).

As Campbell describes him, then, Shaftesbury offers a sort of Friend's Charter, one that is echoed almost three centuries later by the women that Gouldner and Strong (1987) studied. The relationship that is most moral is that which reflects the spontaneous affection that two autonomous, unconstrained people feel towards each other. Prudence, reflection and self-interest are poor guides for establishing relationships with people, as is the desire to conform to common opinion by seeking to befriend the popular. These are poor guides because they do not allow the innate moral sense to operate, the sense that leads us to see the good people as attractive and the bad as repellant. Thus it is that spontaneity and affective sentiments, the bases of friendship as we commonly use the term, are not just good in their own right. In addition, they lead to the good relationship, the friendship of and with the good person.

Later in the eighteenth century, according to Allan Silver, this changing conception of the self appeared in a somewhat different form, in the Scottish Enlightenment and especially in the work of Ferguson, Hume and Smith. These writers argued that previously people had seen themselves in terms of one manifestation of what I have called a location in a structure of relations, their position in structures of faction or patronage, of the sort found in areas of English commerce in the eighteenth century (McKendrick, Brewer and Plumb 1982:ch.5) and in the Iceland of the Sagas. According to these writers, a location in such a structure gave people their identity, just as it shaped expectations of how they ought to behave. In other words, it was the source of people's motive.

These writers, however, said that there was emerging a new form of sociality and social identity, that of the independent individual free of the structure of faction, patronage and interest. Among these independent individuals, strangers were 'authentically indifferent co-citizens' (Silver 1990:1482), not defined by their position in an encompassing structure of allegiance. Whether such people would become friends depended upon the operation of 'natural sympathy', which Adam Smith, in *The Theory of Moral Sentiments*, described as 'an involuntary feeling that the persons to whom we attach ourselves are the natural and proper objects of esteem and approbation' (in Silver 1990:1481). Here is something very like what Shaftesbury described, an innate moral sense that manifests itself in the expression of spontaneous and individual likes and dislikes.

Thus, a new conception of the self was emerging at the beginning of the eighteenth century and established solidly at the end. This new self was seen to exist free from the external constraints of alliance, faction and patronage, as it was seen to be free from the internal constraints of prudential calculation and self-interest. With these new selves, moreover, proper and moral sociable relationships took a new form as well. No longer was it expected that one would consort with those appropriate to one's social location. Instead, people were expected to consort with those who appealed to their innate sense of the good, those for whom they felt a natural sympathy; in short, those for whom they felt spontaneous affection. With this new model self, then, morally acceptable affectionate relationships arise unbidden and are based on nothing but the spontaneous sentiments of the autonomous people involved.

People who espoused this view of the self and who, one supposes, liked to think of themselves in this way, were Shaftesbury's 'good men' and they formed what the Georgian English called 'polite society'. According to Mark Girouard, people in polite society saw themselves as dispensing with the interests and factions that they thought had marred the preceding era. Instead of interest and faction they wanted 'polish' (cf. Hirschman 1977:56–63): 'A polite man was someone polished, in the sense that he had no angularities which limited his contact with other people' (Girouard 1990:76). In 1711, John Toland said that in polite society,

'A Tory does not stare and leer when a Whig comes in, nor a Whig look sour and whisper at the sight of a Tory. These distinctions are laid by' (in Girouard 1990:78).

The self-concept of polite society was enshrined in the spacious and unified architecture of the theatres, coffee houses, assembly rooms and public promenades that were so pronounced in Georgian architecture and town design. Girouard (1990:77–8) says that resort towns like Bath were the quintessential polite Georgian place. People from many different places and occupations went to these towns, though all were genteel of course. As they travelled from home to resort, these people shed the normal obligations of estate, profession or trade and became more fully unconstrained than they had been at home, more fully able to give play to the spontaneous, and therefore moral, sentiments, in the greeting of old friends and the meeting of new.

As my invocation of the Scottish Enlightenment implies, the appearance of the disinterested stranger, the self not enmeshed in a web of prior relationships, was linked conceptually to changes in society, and especially the differentiation of a social and an economic realm. For instance, Ferguson argued that in the old order economic survival depended upon the manipulation of interpersonal relationships and people's relationships were motivated, or at least tainted, by their desire for gain. The result, says Silver (1990:1484), was that 'one has no choice but to be, in Ferguson's disapproving phrase, "interested and sordid" in all interactions, concerned only with whether they "empty [or] fill the pocket" '. The growing differentiation of economy and society, however, meant the emergence of what many saw, and lauded, as an impersonal market sphere devoted to material self-interest, leaving the social sphere free to be ruled by matters of the heart. As Parry (1986:466) summarizes the emerging differentiation of market and social life: 'Free and unconstrained contracts in the market also make free and unconstrained gifts outside it.' However, it is important to remember that, as with the modern notion of friendship, here it is the thought and the talk that are important. I consider below the degree to which this new notion of the self and its relationships accurately depicts people in modern Western societies.

Social Selves in Melanesia

I have sketched the emergence of the most visible and articulated Western notion of the self, one suited to the idea of friendship, and the ways that it differed from the older notion of the self, one seen as being constituted and motivated by the social relations in which it is embedded and hence unsuited to the idea of friendship. I want to illustrate what such a situated self might be. I do so by drawing on material from Melanesia, where the notion of the self has been a topic of scholarly interest recently. In presenting this material, I do not mean to imply an equation between a Melanesian 'far away' and a Western 'long ago'. I mean, instead, only to point out that in both Melanesia and the pre-modern West, conceptions of the self appear to have a more clearly social dimension than they do in the modern West.

The predominant anthropological treatment of identity in Melanesia springs from Marilyn Strathern's *The Gender of the Gift* (1988), an investigation of Melanesian thought intended as a reflection on Western thought, explicitly including the notion of the autonomous self. A central point is that Melanesian selves do not resemble the Western model of the autonomous person. Rather, people are constituted by social relations, are activated through social relations, realize themselves through social relations. I need to explain what each of these phrases means.

The idea that Melanesian selves are constituted through social relations means that the self emerges from the people and relationships which brought the person about. Strathern says (1988:13) that these selves: 'Contain a generalized sociality within. Indeed, persons are frequently constructed as the plural and composite site of the relationships that produced them.' At the simplest level, this means that the child is constructed as the embodiment of its two parents and of the relationship between them. This is not construed as the passing of a detachable endowment from generation to generation, but instead as a more encompassing notion that the child contains the parents and their relationship.

A Hagen child is created through a metonymic transaction between parents, each contributing a part of their substance while retaining their distinctiveness. The relationship is reified in the child who substitutes for it, and who duplicates the identity of neither parent but combines them both within itself. Its androgyny symbolizes a completed transaction (Strathern 1988:262).

Because the Melanesian self is social, it 'is not axiomatically "an individual" who, as in Western formulations, derives an integrity from its position as somehow prior to society' (1988:93). And because there is no individual prior to social relations, so it is difficult to conceive of the spontaneous affections that emerge from internal sources that characterize the Western notion of friendship.

I have explained briefly what I mean by the idea that Melanesian selves are constituted through social relationships. It is important to join this to my second point, that Melanesian selves are activated through social relationships. Thus, the self that is social in its origin remains social, in the sense that people's conceptions of who they are and how they are moved to behave varies with the social relations in which they find themselves.

One way in which this situated self is manifest is through kin relationships, which are construed in situational terms. Put simplistically, a man is an affine in the presence of his wife's brother, an agnate in the presence of his father's brother's son, a son in the presence of his mother, and so on. And as one is an affine, agnate, son or whatever, so one is expected to behave accordingly. A corollary of this perspective is that there is no 'real you', no stable self that endures from situation to situation, or at least none that is very important. There is no basis for Smith's natural sympathy or Shaftesbury's unreflective nature, and hence no basis for friendship of the sort I have described.

One consequence of this view of the self is what looks, to modern Western eyes, like insincerity. Indeed, one young, educated and reflective man from Manus, in Papua New Guinea, made such an observation about his own people to my wife and me while we were doing fieldwork: 'We Manus are so insincere.' In saying this, he was not only reflecting upon his experience of Manus life, he was reflecting his own position, that of a man brought up in a Melanesian society yet also exposed to the Western conceptions of self that are implicit and explicit in formal education and in much of the media in Papua New Guinea, and that are an important element of the evangelical Protestant religious movements in the country (Gewertz and Errington 1996). What I have described as the plasticity of identity and expectation found in the relational Melanesian model of the self becomes an insincerity when considered from the modern Western perspective, which assumes that all people have an autonomous self.

This case illustrates how Melanesian selves both resemble and depart from the old Western self, and particularly the self of faction and patronage that was criticized by writers of the Scottish Enlightenment. In both cases, the self, one's pertinent identity, motives and expectations, derives from one's social location rather than from interior sources. However, for Ferguson and the rest, that location is one's relatively stable place in a structure of social groups. To borrow Toland's example, one is a Whig or a Tory, and one is so wherever one goes; until, of course, one enters polite society. For the self-reflective young Manus man, however, one's social location was much more fluid, for it was likely to vary from circumstance to circumstance, depending upon one's relationship to those with whom one is interacting at the moment.

What I have described thus far indicates the degree to which identity in Melanesian societies is constructed as reflecting the person's social situation, and thus lacks the autonomy required for friendship. Strathern, however, takes an even more radical position. Notably, she argues that aspects of identity that Westerners see as fairly basic and as existing across situations, aspects that even the sceptical would tend to agree constitute the real you, are in fact treated as situational in Melanesia. The most striking of these is gender, and because her argument is an extension of the points made already, I will discuss it only briefly (see Strathern 1988:119–32, 182–7). Likewise, I will follow the primary ethnographic focus on men and their identities.

To say that Melanesian people see themselves as containing those who produced them, is to say that each person contains both mother and father, female and male.

At different times, a person's male or female component will be predominant, and at yet other times neither will predominate. Thus, for example, a man who feels obligated to spend money on his domestic household rather than a clan activity may stress his female component in relation to the set of his clan agnates, who are construed as predominantly male. On another occasion that same man may stand with his fellow clansmen in a unitary male assemblage that is opposed to other men whose female identity is important. In a sense, this is one way of conceiving the tension men can feel between their membership in masculine agnatic groups and their membership in androgynous or even feminine domestic groups.

I said that the third element of Strathern's argument is that Melanesian selves realize themselves through social relations. This point is made most clearly in Strathern's discussion of power. She says that the predominant Western view is that power is 'a resource to the possessor', something that is there to be exercised (1988:104). However, the Melanesian view is different. There, it would not be correct to say that power *per se* exists. It is better to speak of agency, affecting the people around one. One realizes oneself, you know what sort of person you are, by the effects one has on others. In terms of gender, men become men because they lead women to act in certain ways, just as women become women because they lead men to act in certain ways. '[E]ach sex elicits the acts of the other, for those counteracts are the evidence of its own efficacy'(Strathern 1988:299). Mark Mosko (1992:203) puts this in a somewhat different way when he says that Melanesian 'persons evince and anticipate the knowledge or recognition of their internal composition and capacities in the responses of others.'

It is important to note, however, that this is not an automatic process with a sure outcome: 'There is nothing automatic about elicitation; it is effected under [. . .] conditions of uncertainty and anxiety' (Strathern 1988:299). Were this process automatic, eliciting the counteract would be just the affirmation of a pre-existing identity. Rather, because the counteract is problematic, identity is discovered or defined through interaction, rather than celebrated through it. You do not know if you have power, or are female or a father until the appropriate others respond in the appropriate ways in the appropriate settings. And if they do not, then you are not, at least in that situation.

As Strathern and others describe things, the Melanesian self differs clearly from the Western. Where the Western self is an autonomous, irreducible entity that springs from a person's very being, the Melanesian self is constituted by and embodies others. In the Western conception, the unfettered self is the key source of motive, the seat of Smith's natural sympathy and Shaftesbury's moral judgement. In Melanesia, on the other hand, motive and even sentiment spring from the relationships of which one is a part. Indeed, one's very sense of who one is comes not from one's self, but from the effects one has on others, the ways they respond to one's actions.

The Melanesian self as I have described it is not one that can have friendships of the modern Western sort, for it lacks the autonomous, interior source of sentiment. This does not mean that Melanesians have no affective relationships. However, anthropological descriptions do indicate that they are unlikely to think of those relationships in terms of friendship. If the lessons of my own fieldwork are any indication, those who are close to each other are likely to speak about the relationship not in terms of sentiments or distinct personal attributes, but in terms of a common situation or structure of relationships that encompasses the people involved.

Thus, a common way of speaking is in terms of kinship. A person gets on so well with another because they stand in a certain kin relationship with each other. The observation that the speaker gets along rather poorly with a third person who stands in exactly the same kin relationship is beside the point, which is how people talk and think about amicable relationships. There are cases, of course, where the idiom of kinship will not serve, as when two people from different parts of the country meet at work or university. In this circumstance, the relationship commonly is explained in terms of shared situation: We two worked together; We two went to school together, as Smart (in this volume, pp.119–136) describes for China. Even here, then, personal sentiments and attributes are muted and situational factors are stressed. These examples suggest that the anthropological rendering of selves that are situated is indeed matched by an indigenous understanding of amicable relations that is not couched in the terms by which Westerners distinguish friendship from other sorts of relationships.

Whose Western Self?

Thus far I have discussed friendship in terms of an associated conception of the sort of people who are capable of being friends, the autonomous, unconstrained and spontaneous self endowed with the sort of sentiment that is associated with friendship. I have indicated that this is a modern Western understanding of the self. However, it is important to recognize that this understanding, although highly visible, is an occidentalist over-simplification and stylization of Western society and Western selves.

It is true that the predominant notion of the self in Western society is of the autonomous actor of liberal thought. It is also true that this notion has some validity: Nancy Hartsock (1985) suggests that this self reflects reasonably well the experience of those in dominant positions in society. But saying this is the same as saying that such selves do not reflect the lives of all those in the West. In effect, as Michèle Lamont (1992:180) observes of analogous American conceptions of the self, such notions 'universalize to the population at large the culture of [. . .] upwardly mobile Americans working in the for-profit sector'.

Nancy Hartsock points to one group of Western people who are not likely to experience autonomy and are, hence, not likely to have autonomous selves: women. She notes that, in addition to their wage work, women commonly maintain the household and rear its children. In this household labour, women are enmeshed in relationships that are more complex and constraining than those experienced by middle-class men. As she puts it, women commonly experience 'a complex, relational world' rather than one of autonomous selves, one in which their inter-actions are not voluntary: '[T]hose in charge of small children have little choice' (1985:65, 66). Here Hartsock comes to a conclusion anticipated somewhat earlier by Nancy Chodorow (1978), who argued that because sons repress their early identification with their mothers while daughters do not, so women are less likely to see themselves as autonomous individuals.[1]

I invoke Hartsock to make the point that the predominant Western notion of the autonomous actor, while doubtless a reflection of the experiences of some Western people, applies to some people more than others. Those for whom the notion does not fit may still espouse it, but, one imagines, they are likely to see themselves as lacking friends. While Hartsock singles out gender as a pertinent factor in this regard, class is another one. Long ago, Max Weber pointed out that while some economic actors can be autonomous, autonomy generally is restricted to the dominant, propertied classes. On the other hand, those without property have no such leisure. They are constrained by the need to sell their labour, 'in order barely to subsist' (Weber 1946:182). Here Weber speaks of class in his own technical sense. Others have also addressed the relationship between class and understandings of the self, and hence say things that can help show the degree to which the predominant Western construction of the self applies to only a limited section of the population. However, while these writers speak of class, they do so in a loose sense, for what they describe is a set of practices, experiences and beliefs that, while they may be associated with class, ought perhaps to be kept distinct from it analytically.

One of the more interesting writers who has addressed conceptions of the self and their relationship to class in this loose sense is Basil Bernstein, especially in his description of Bethnal Green's working-class families around 1960 (especially Bernstein 1971; see also Willmott and Young 1960). These families were in the lower working class, but what is more pertinent for my discussion is their social milieu and practices. They lived very localized and common lives. Wage-earners among them overwhelmingly had the same sorts of occupation, their jobs and social lives were circumscribed with the immediate, densely populated area of Bethnal Green. Consequently, people shared a high proportion of their experiences with each other: co-workers, neighbours, social companions and kin overlapped, in the way that they do for many Chinese workers (Smart in this volume, pp.119–136). One consequence of this social order is that people had what Bernstein called a 'positional orientation'. They saw their selves as locations in an encompassing web of social relations. Bernstein distinguished this from something that looks much more like the predominant view of the autonomous self, what he called the 'personal orientation'. Those with this orientation saw their selves as independent entities, and Bernstein said this was characteristic of the wealthier and more mobile English middle class.[2]

One corollary of Bernstein's argument is that middle-class people, with their personal orientation, are prone to see themselves as having a self that transcends the different areas of their lives. Alternatively, people in the lower class, with their positional orientation, are prone to see their identity as a function of specific contexts. On the assumption that the pertinent experiences and orientations are related, albeit loosely, to class in the more restricted sense, it follows that middle-class people would be more willing to develop sociable relationships among co-workers than would those in the working class. Evidence that supports this argument comes from John Goldthorpe's study of Luton in the 1960s. Goldthorpe and his colleagues found that generally there was little likelihood that anyone would identify co-workers as friends: fewer than a fifth of those they studied did so. However, they also found that those of different classes differed in this regard: 'White-collar couples draw more heavily on friends made through work' than do blue-collar couples (1969:90; see also Hunt and Satterlee 1986).

The core of the point that I have drawn from Bernstein is that people with different experiences and forms of interaction are likely to construe their selves in different ways. The autonomous, unified self that researchers associated with the middle classes is particularly suited to the notion of friendship, a relationship that links people because of their spontaneous affection. On the other hand, those of the working classes would be likely to see themselves as enmeshed in, defined and constrained by a web of social relations, a notion of the self unsuited to the notion of friendship. This is not to say that working-class people have fewer amicable relationships, that they live lives that are emotionally impoverished. Rather, it is to say that their relationships are organized, thought about and talked about differently, in terms of mates, neighbours and kin rather than friends.

The idea that members of the working-class structure their sociable relationships differently than do members of the middle class is supported by Graham Allan. Drawing on published studies and his own work, he (1979:70) concludes that people in the working class tend to 'limit their sociable relations [to] particular social contexts and structures'. The idea that members of the working class see themselves as being more constrained by their relationships than do members of the middle class is supported by J. Bussey and his colleagues. In their study of the ways that people in Bradford gave presents, they found that higher-class respondents were prone to explain the giving by saying it was the spontaneous expression of autonomous sentiment, emotion and affection. On the other hand, lower-class respondents were more likely to refer to the expectations of others and the dictates of the situation in which they found themselves (Bussey et al. 1967:61, 67). As Helga Dittmar (1992:182) concludes, '[A] congruence exists between the Western dominant construction of identity as self-determined agency and the reality of belonging to affluent circles.'

Evidence that the idea of the autonomous self is related to class in the loose sense is apparent from the early emergence of that idea. Shaftesbury, Toland and the writers of the Scottish Enlightenment rejected the older notion of the situated self. But in their descriptions of the new model self they were not describing a society made of autonomous individuals devoid of constraining structures. For Smith and Shaftesbury, the sentiments were not, it seems, free and unconstrained. It is true that Whigs may not have looked sour at the sight of a Tory. However, it is also true that both were ready to 'distinguish the polite Gentleman from the rude Rustick' (1737 etiquette manual, in Girouard 1990:77). In an important way, then, the new model self was a situated self. However, this was not the inter-personal situation of faction or kin, but the more impersonal situation of taste and class, for polite society 'was made up of the people who owned and ran the country' (1990:77).

Historically, then, it is plausible to suggest that the emergence of the autonomous self was as much a device through which an emerging élite justified the cutting of old relationships and denying the claims on them made by others as it was warrant for making new friends among polite society (on this process more generally, see Errington and Gewertz 1997). This suggestion is embodied in a contradiction contained in Georgian architecture. At the same time that grand and orderly public spaces were appearing, where polite society could meet, people were devoting more of their effort to creating private spaces, within which people lived more and more of their lives (see Rybczynski 1988: especially at 105–21), lives increasingly free of the intrusion of rude Rusticks.

Conclusions

I have had one, simple purpose in this chapter. That is, to point out that the notion of friendship is a way of thinking about affective relationships, and that this way of thinking has as its unspoken corollary a notion of the self, the autonomous person who is capable of friendship. This means that it may be unwise to see friendship as a human universal or, to say the same thing somewhat differently, as a product of human psychology. In saying that friendship is a way of thinking, I do not mean it is only that. It is expressed directly and indirectly in many of the public and private messages that modern Western people send each other. It is a standard against which people judge themselves and others. It is a norm that many people seek to emulate or reject. Whether emulated or rejected by individuals, it is a central aspect of the ways that modern Western people think of and act toward each other.

I have pursued my purpose in three ways. First, I traced the historical development in Western thought of the idea that the self is an autonomous being capable of unconstrained affection. Second, I used Melanesian material to illustrate what an alternative idea of the self might look like, and I argued that those who have this idea of the self are unlikely to speak and think in terms of friendship in the modern Western sense. Finally, returning to the West, I suggested that the idea of the autonomous self is not just an historical development, but is likely also to be more common among some segments of the population than others. In particular, I said that there is evidence that the idea that the self is autonomous is more common among males and the middle classes, while the idea that the self is defined and constrained by situation is more common among females and the working classes.

To consider friendship as I have is to point out the way that the idea of friendship is part of a larger cluster of social and cultural practices. This in turn encourages a consideration of the factors that encourage the development of the modern notion of friendship and that are associated with it. I want to end by touching on these, and I do so by returning to my point of entry into a consideration of friendship, the topic of exchange.

At the same time that the new model individual was emerging in Western thought there was, as I have noted, a change in the ways that people ordered their relationships with each other. With the development of a distinct and impersonal sphere of economic transaction, it became increasingly possible and increasingly proper for people to gain their economic necessities through transactions with those who are relative strangers: the clerk, the employer and so forth. People were less obliged to enter into personal relationships in order to secure their subsistence and many economic relationships were re-cast, became more transient and impersonal (see generally Carrier 1994:chapter. 7). At the same time, and to echo a point I made regarding polite society, those with substantial resources, increasingly able to gain protection from the state rather than from bodies of retainers, were less likely to want to enter into durable personal relationships with their inferiors, of the sort found in Iceland of the Sagas (Durrenberger and Pálsson in this volume. pp.59–78). A large household or affinity was decreasingly a source of prestige, power and even security, while it remained a substantial drain on material resources. So, it appears that for the élite at first and increasingly for ordinary people, durable personal relationships were losing their importance in economic and political terms. With this change, it seems that personal relationships became more purely optional and expressive, which facilitated the spread of the notion of the autonomous self and the modern idea of friendship.

It seems likely, then, that the modern notion of friendship, with its stress on involuntary sentiment unclouded by calculation or interest, is particularly congenial to those in certain socio-economic situations. This has a number of corollaries. The first and simplest is that what I have said is a prerequisite of friendship, the autonomous sentimental self, is likely to exist only among people who can pursue political and economic survival and success through relatively impersonal mechanisms, of which the capitalist market and the state are eminent examples.

The second corollary is that friendship as a norm or standard, part of people's taken-for-granted universe, is likely to emerge only where a significant proportion of the people in a society think that they can pursue their survival in the appropriate way or that they ought to be able to. Put in other words, when political-economic conditions are right and the autonomous and sentimental self becomes the norm, even people to whom it applies only poorly are likely to see themselves and their fellows in those terms. The result of this may be conformity to the norm, or it may be the decision that they are inadequate, that they lead lives that are impoverished emotionally, that they need to get out of their ruts, go out and make some friends.

The third corollary is implicit in my discussion of the historical emergence of the autonomous self in Western thought. Were the nature of political and economic structures and processes in Western countries to change to resemble more the sort of relational system that Smart (this volume) describes, the notion of the self would likely change, and with it the nature and importance of the idea of friendship. The inverse applies as well. But to say this is only to say that the idea of friendship and of the autonomous sentimental self are cultural elements that do not exist on their own, but exist in a broader social, political and economic context.

Notes

1 Though Hartsock's point is pertinent, the situation is obviously more complex than this. For instance, some argue that, at least in the United States, the very notion of affection is becoming gendered and, more particularly, feminized (Cancian 1986, 1987). At the very least, this indicates that the notions of friendship and affection need to be clarified further.
2 Alexandra Ouroussoff (1993) echoes Bernstein's point without using his terminology. In her study of a pseudonymous British multinational corporation, she found that managers saw themselves as autonomous, while ordinary workers saw themselves as defined by their position in a web of social relationships.

People Who Can Be Friends

References

Abercrombie, N., Hill, S., and Turner, B.S. (1986), *Sovereign Individuals of Capitalism*, London: Allen and Unwin.
Allan, G.A. (1979), *A Sociology of Friendship and Kinship*, London: Allen and Unwin.
Barnett, S., and Silverman, M. (1979), 'Separations in Capitalist Societies: Persons, Things, Units and Relations', in S. Barnett and M. Silverman, *Ideology and Everyday Life*, Ann Arbor: University of Michigan Press.
Belk, R.W. (1979), 'Gift-Giving Behavior', in J.E. Sheth (ed.), *Research in Marketing*, Vol.2, Greenwich, Conn.: JAI Press.
Bernstein, B. (1971), 'A Sociolinguistic Approach to Socialization', in B. Bernstein, *Class, Codes and Control*, Vol.1, London: Routledge & Kegan Paul.
Bussey, J., Banks, S., Darrington, C., Driscoll, D., Goulding, D., Lowes, B., Phillips, R., and Turner, J. (1967), *Patterns of Gift Giving: Including a Questionnaire Survey of Bradford Households*, B.Sc. (Hons) thesis, University of Bradford.
Campbell, C. (1987), *The Romantic Ethic and the Spirit of Modern Consumerism*, Oxford: Basil Blackwell.
Cancian, F. M. (1986), 'The Feminization of Love', *Signs*, 11:692–709.
—— (1987), *Love in America: Gender and Self-Development*, New York: Cambridge University Press.
Carrier, J.G. (1994), *Gifts and Commodities: Exchange and Western Capitalism since 1700*, London: Routledge.
Cheal, D.J. (1988), *The Gift Economy*, London: Routledge Books.
Chodorow, N. (1978), *The Reproduction of Mothering*, Berkeley: University of California Press.
Dittmar, H. (1992), *The Social Psychology of Material Possessions: To Have Is To Be*, Hemel Hempstead: Harvester Wheatsheaf.
Errington, F. K., and Gewertz, D.B. (1997), 'The Rotary Club of Wewak', *Journal of the Royal Anthropological Institute*, 3: 333–53.
Geertz, C. (1973), *The Interpretation of Cultures*, New York: Basic Books.
Gewertz, D.B., and Errington, F.K. (1996), 'On PepsiCo and Piety in a Papua New Guinea "Modernity"', *American Ethnologist*, 23: 476–93.
Girouard, M. (1990), *The English Town*, New Haven: Yale University Press.
Goldthorpe, J. H., Lockwood, D., Bechhofer, F. and Platt, J. (1969), *The Affluent Worker in the Class Structure*, Cambridge: Cambridge University Press.
Gouldner, H. and Symons Strong, M. (1987), *Speaking of Friendship: Middle-Class Women and their Friends*, Westport, Conn.: Greenwood Press.
Hartsock, Nancy C. N. (1985), 'Exchange Theory: Critique from a Feminist Standpoint', in S.G. McNall (ed.), *Current Perspectives in Social Theory*. Vol.6, Greenwich, Conn.: JAI Press.

– 37 –

Hirschman, A. (1977), *The Passions and the Interests*, Princeton: Princeton University Press.

Hochschild, A. R. (1983), *The Managed Heart: The Commercialization of Human Feeling*, Berkeley: University of California Press.

Hunt, G., and Satterlee, S. (1986), 'Cohesion and Division: Drinking in an English Village', *Man*, 21:521–37.

Lamont, M. (1992), *Money, Morals, and Manners: The Culture of the French and the American Upper-Middle Class*, Chicago: University of Chicago Press.

Macfarlane, A. (1978), *The Origins of English Individualism*, Oxford: Basil Blackwell.

Mauss, M. (1985 [1938]), 'A Category of the Human Mind: The Notion of Person; the Notion of Self', in M. Carrithers, S. Collins and S. Lukes (eds), *The Category of the Person*, Cambridge: Cambridge University Press.

McKendrick, N., Brewer, J. and Plumb, J.H. (1982), *The Birth of a Consumer Society*, Bloomington: Indiana University Press.

Mosko, M.S. (1992), 'Motherless Sons: "Divine Kings" and "Partible Persons" in Melanesia and Polynesia', *Man*, 27:693–717.

Ouroussoff, A. (1993), 'Illusions of Rationality: False Premisses of the Liberal Tradition', *Man*, 28:281–98.

Parry, J. (1986), 'The Gift, The Indian Gift and the "Indian Gift"', *Man*, 21:453–73.

Rybczynski, W. (1988), *Home: A Short History of an Idea*, London: Heinemann.

Silver, A. (1990), 'Friendship in Commercial Society: Eighteenth-Century Social Theory and Modern Sociology', *American Journal of Sociology*, 95:1474–1504.

Strathern, M. (1988), *The Gender of the Gift: Problems with Women and Problems with Society in Melanesia*, Berkeley: University of California Press.

Trilling, L. (1972), *Sincerity and Authenticity*, Cambridge, Mass.: Harvard University Press.

Weber, M. (1946), 'Class, Status, Party', in Hans Gerth and C. Wright Mills (eds), *From Max Weber*, New York: Oxford University Press.

Willmott, P. and Young, M. (1960), *Family and Class in a London Suburb*, London: Routledge & Kegan Paul.

3

Friendship: The Hazards of an
Ideal Relationship

Robert Paine

. . . if I had to choose between betraying my country and betraying my friend, I hope I should have the guts to betray my country.

E.M. Forster, *Two Cheers for Democracy*

The Self and Two Worlds of Value

Understandings of friendship are surely predicated on understandings of self, and it is there that I begin (Cohen 1994; Taylor 1994; Trilling 1972). My question is, how, sociologically, does one verify one's own self? There are of course a variety of ways of doing that, all of which impart cultural nuances to the meaning and handling of friendships; I suggest, though, that behind the variety are two radically different value orientations. They are seen in the questions: Am I true to the self others see in me, the self that society has 'given' me? Or, am I true simply to my own self, the one that I 'made'? For the moment, consider them as though they experientially mutually exclude each other, and that there is only one of each.

The one has everything to do with the importance of the total social person in all social relations. Or as Tord Larsen puts it, '[T]he individual discovers his true identity in his roles, and to turn away from the roles is to turn away from himself' (1987:6). Thus in Ambéli, the Greek village studied by Juliet Du Boulay, 'It is to the village that the villager looks to confirm his identity' (1974:13). Or there is Stevens, the butler in Kazuo Ishiguru's *The Remains of the Day*: 'Like the silver he polishes so skilfully, the man's whole identity has been a reflection of others' (Wigston 1989: C17).[1] Both, the villagers and Stevens, are locked into rules of conduct that virtually compose their very being. This, we may say, is the world of 'tautological' value (Larsen 1987) or better, in Alfred Schuetz's formulation, the world of 'common sense' with its currency of 'of course' assumptions (Schuetz

My sincere appreciation for critical readings and insightful comments to my inter-disciplinary colleagues Mike Aronoff, Bill Barker, Anne Hart, Peter Harries-Jones, Stuart Pierson, and volume editors Simon Coleman and Sandra Bell.

1944:499, 502). Here, individuality may even be seen 'not as the expression of identity but as the loss of it' (Du Boulay 1974:80).

The other value orientation emerges in situations where there is no unfragmented total social person and where '[w]e live in a continual competition with society over the ownership of ourselves' (Arnold Simmel 1971:72) and where '[f]aith is no longer socially given, but must be individually achieved' (Berger *et al.* 1973:81). This I call the world of idea-value. It is at the centre of this essay. For it is there that the hazards of friendship as an ideal relationship are especially notable. First, though, I return to Du Boulay's portrait of Ambéli for a portrait of a culture governed by tautological value, to better secure the contrast between these 'worlds'.

'Idealness?' Of course the people of Ambéli know it, but in a muted and impersonal way. Here, for example, is their view of the conjugal bond: '[Two people] embark upon marriage, not as a result of a deep affinity of character, nor because they see in each other any unique personal significance, but in order to form a social and symbolic unit – to set up house together and to procreate children' (Du Boulay 1974:90). This is wholly in accord with the ethos in which 'identity' (in the singular) – the sense of self – is imparted through membership rather than by one's 'own essential individuality' (202); it leaves friendship 'almost by definition, impermanent' (213). Where there is a conflict of interest, loyalty to the family prevails over friendship of course; yet even in everyday circumstances, friendships are especially unsafe (190) for confidentiality between friends is not upheld – kinship loyalty intervenes.[2] Still, there is a need for friendship; it is a need of mutual aid. Thus friendship becomes – instrumentally without deepening a friend's sense of self – a commodity of exchange: 'friendships are exchanged among the community rather than actually destroyed' (215). Perhaps the important point for us is that, in Ambéli, the self is the fulfiller of roles with but the minimum of independent self-awareness, and the personal and private friendship is an impossibility – 'for where you do not know yourself you cannot know others' (Du Boulay 1974:84).[3]

Illuminating comparisons are at hand from two other classical anthropological studies from the Mediterranean. In Alcala (Pitt-Rivers 1961), an Andalusian pueblo and a larger community (population: over 2,000) with a more diversified social structure, the situation is, accordingly, a modified version of that in Ambéli. There is place for the cultivation of individuality and with that a general importance attached to friendship. Even so, there are few 'true friendships, founded upon esteem and affection, which approximate to the ideal and endure a lifetime': calculations of interest intervene and interfere (140). And, added to that, outsiders by birth are distanced: '[T]he system of nicknames in the townships of Andalusia seldom recognises any outsider by any identity other than the place of his origin' (Pitt-Rivers 1968:16 n.1).

The situation among the pastoralist Sarakatsani of highland Greece (Campbell 1964), on the other hand, is more extreme than in Ambéli. Here, too, 'the solidarity of the family resides in its exclusiveness and opposition to those who do not belong', but this is carried to such lengths that 'any relationship with an unrelated person would be regarded by other members of the family as a form of *betrayal*' (205; my emphasis).[4]

In contrast to the foregoing, the world of idea-value is one of high individuation that draws deeply on friendship. It is the various joinings of these two qualities, individuation and friendship, that particularly engage me. I think Suttles is just about right when he says 'friendship' (in the world of idea-value) 'demands a verifiable self [that] cannot be one that complacently complies with public propriety' (Suttles 1970:107). Still, that is only half the story. What of the 'demand' inside the relationship? In some measure or another, the intimacy of friends serves the need of each for emotional and cognitive security; even to the extent of reproducing an environment of 'predictability', 'expectation', and 'assured anticipation' (Deutsch 1958:265). In short, a closed environment of trust and confidences. Significantly, it also has some tautological cadence.

The emergent point, then, is that the two 'worlds' are dominant orientations where the one does not wholly exclude the other – we all live with some of *both* of the two kinds of value (this increases rather than reduces the tension between them). However, I suppose this situation is truer of life for citizens of Athens, say, than it is for Ambéli villagers who, to a great extent, are guided through life by one clear set of ('problem-solving': Douglas and Wildavsky 1982:80) institutions.[5] The difference here between these two 'worlds' is that, in the one, trust is likely to be a 'prescriptive' matter between kin or bond friends (Du Boulay 1974; Paine 1970), whereas in the personal and private relationship there is no such prescription: just as these friends choose each other so they choose to offer trust – or to betray. That said, though, there can be (as we will show) anomalous intrusions of 'of course-ness' in the idea-value world.

The 'Idealness' of Friendship

Still in preparation for the particular ethnographic material that follows later, I now suggest three essential features of the ideal relationship in an idea-value world.[6] The three are its rules of relevancy, its standard of equivalence and its privacy. Rules of relevancy refer to what is permissible and/or desirable in a relationship, and friendship (from now on, all references are to the ideal form within the idea-value world) is remarkable in that those rules appear not to be imposed from the outside, and, furthermore, they may be largely hidden from view to all outside the relationship. Hence the 'secret code' of which Ingmar Bergman speaks: giving 'you the confidence to reveal yourself in true fellowship' (Bergman 1988:261).

A standard of equivalence is essentially about what is a bargain within a relationship, and here friendship is an exception to the general notion that a 'good' bargain for a person is one in which the value received is greater than that which is given (cf. 'transaction', Barth 1966). Instead one expects what R.D. Laing has called 'reciprocal interiorization' (1968:72). Yet the ideal of friendship rests not on the compulsion of reciprocity; rather, one gives freely of oneself and hopes to receive in the same spirit.

Thus it follows that this ideal of friendship – in contradistinction to what the anthropological literature describes variously as 'bond friendships' (Paine 1970:146–8.) – is a private as well as a personal relationship. And as Wilson (1974) reminds us, privacy refers to 'the state of relations between relationships' (101), that is to say, privacy insulates relationships from one another. Thus friendship is constituted and maintained on the basis of good faith rather than jural sanctions.

Woodstock; Traitors

I think it important to recognize that the cadences of the 'idealness' we are talking about have been very much on the minds of sociology writers, especially American, beginning with Kaspar Naegele in 1958 and picking up a head of steam with Gerald Suttles and Peter Berger and his colleagues in the early 1970s.

I am tempted to view the Naegele-Suttles-Berger construction of friendship ethnographically as a 'Woodstock' phenomenon[7] of which I see Charles Reich's best-selling *The Greening of America* (1971) as a programmatic declaration. The book heralds 'a revolution of the new generation' (2) and 'offers us a recovery of self' (3). 'The commandment is: be true to oneself' (242) – not to the ethics of 'the Corporate State of the 1960s' (2) which work against the autonomy of a personal self.[8]

The 'founding' sociological text of this reading of friendship (actually preceding Woodstock itself by a decade) is, I think, Naegele's, where he writes that by the logic of the senior class of high school students he interviewed, 'friendship becomes an *exemption* from society' (1958:244; my emphasis). With Suttles this becomes: 'The logic of friendship [. . .] is a simple transformation of the rules of public propriety into their opposite' (1970:116). This means that the portrayal of friendship as a social 'exemption' becomes one of aggressively counter-engaging the norms of public social life. And the quest for a 'verifiable self' that does not complacently comply with public propriety comes front stage: 'What is required is that each person disclose something about himself that would be embarrassing or damaging in a less restricted audience' (107). Perhaps the quintessential point from Berger *et al.* in this connection is that such an individual is '"interesting" to himself' (1973:78).

At the same time, as one recognizes how Naegele and company contributed to an understanding of friendship, I think we should read them less as ethnography and more as moral texts.[9] There is ground for scepticism as to what they put into the exceptionality (which there is) of the friendship relationship; for example, the across-the-board assumption of intimacy and – much as night follows day – of trust. Ingmar Bergman is nearer the truth when he writes: 'Friendship demands honesty, the only demand, but difficult' (Bergman 1988:261).

As to what friends must 'disclose' (Suttles) as part of a verification process, essential to that is familiarity with particular 'of course' codes (Schuetz). 'Exemption' (to varying degrees) from the outside and conversant familiarity within the relationship: these, between them, constitute the tension in the construction of friendship. And the balance that is struck may be expected to change.

At much the same time as Naegele and company were exploring (and positing), sociologically, the contemporary liberation of the self, public attention, particularly in Britain, was being drawn as well to something in quite a different key to Woodstock: real-life episodes of espionage and treachery. British biographers, political commentators and, not least, novelists began to excavate, through the context of espionage, entanglements of the self with matters of loyalty and betrayal, and the places subterfuge and mendacity have inside a web of friendship.

Taken together, Woodstock and entanglements ('fictional' and 'real') with espionage provide, I suggest, a broader ethnographic and imagined base from which to understand friendship and the lengths to which idea-value may be taken within it. Yet a recurrent theme is still that of the tension between those two kinds of self: those 'given' me and those I 'make': 'What a strange love (it will be thought) that thus conforms to laws whereby it stands condemned in order the better to preserve itself' (de Rougemont 1956:35).

Foregrounding

As I have said, the particular concern of this essay is with the perilous placing of these ideal attributes out in the world, and the extent to which they are honoured in practice. So, in relation to the discussion thus far, let me now foreground some of the issues that lie ahead. First, there is reason to question (as already noted) the extent of candidness between intimates and also whether the private universe is all that autonomous. Alternatively, what of 'unscripted' implications of their practice? Here I have particularly in mind their abuse. For perhaps especially in today's 'disembedded' society (Giddens 1991), a friendship may be perceived as a sanctuary – and this has its hazards. An individual may 'nest' in the special relationship of friendship so as better to pursue and protect from surveillance her/ his own separate agenda, even as emotive comfort is drawn from the relationship. This may lead to treachery.

Now, words such as 'treachery' and 'traitor' – or 'stranger' or 'intimate' or 'hero' – all indicate a relational and highly contextual state of affairs: a friend, my friend, may be a hero to me while a traitor to you. Or, my friend becomes a traitor in my eyes (though perhaps not in yours).[10] Moreover, what one took to be mutually exclusive connotations sometimes become conjoined as in 'intimate stranger'. Such is the perceptual environment of friendship: itself a relational condition, it has its own politics.

However, the conundrum is 'verifiable self'. Given the plurality of 'self' it is, first of all, not a matter of 'the' verifiable self but 'a' verifiable self according to occasion and context. Even then, one may expect 'competition' between more than one or a movement from one to another. Anyway, *who* is the verifier and against what others? And at what cost? Cost to oneself and/or to others – especially friends?

Loyalty

The ideal of the personal and private relationship is acutely dependent on there being no moral separation between friends, and yet it is essentially defenceless against that eventuality. The dilemma is one of loyalty – or, more to the point, of loyalties. Loyalty is one of the ways in which to express and experience self; yet loyalty reduces options, so while the idea of distributive loyalties is oxymoronic, as a social practice, within the 'world' of idea-value, it is near ubiquitous. 'Betrayals' of some loyalties in favour of others follow. And there may be due cause to ask how much weight should be attached to any 'verifiable self' across such shifting sands (Paine 1989a).[11]

Any of this can ravage a friendship, for of course it is these exact same persons, our friends, in whom we deposit our trust and some of our confidences, who are in a position to put our own notions of self and our self-esteem at risk. Here is Ingmar Bergman again, this time on this dark side of friendship, the relationship devoted to 'the truth' (1988:261): 'On the whole I have no illusions about my own talent for friendship. I am indeed faithful, but extremely suspicious. If I think I am betrayed, I am quick to betray. If I feel cut off, I cut off, a dubious and very Bergmanlike talent' (263). So where there should be trust suspicion may creep in, precisely on account of putting oneself 'in trust' to another. But what might Bergman, or any of us, put into the notion of being betrayed? Or rather, why does the notion occur in the first place? How does it sit with the acknowledged pluralism of 'our' world of idea-value, even allowing that an individual can have different biographies (cf. Berger *et al.* 1973:69)?

The answer is, I suppose, that each of our friendships is seen by us as touching the self in a unique way (its own rules of relevancy) – each friendship, one may say, is a biography of the self. Perhaps, then, to feel 'betrayed' (Bergman) is to feel one has lost some part of oneself – that part which one 'gave' to the friend.[12] And to betray? Here we hear an echo from Tod Hoffman: 'We constantly define and refine our loyalties. And in so doing we commit our share of treasons' (1997:32–3).

As viewed by the putative 'offender', though, all that may have happened is in accord with the endowment of the friendship: its rules of relevancy are its own to make and unmake. This echoes Larsen's argument that 'individuals may change their social identities and preserve their individual authenticity' (1987:13). But, if there is offence to the principle of privacy and confidences that were passed between friends now journey further, then there is 'treason'.

One way of handling a conflict of loyalties of one's own making is not to perceive it as such. The all-important and durable friendship of Harold Nicolson and Vita Sackville-West offers an example. They were husband and wife and parents together, yet not only did each have their own many 'islands of personal privacy' they also had independent homosexual lives (Nicolson 1971).[13]

Sometimes, of course, the contradiction is dissolved at the cost of an open betrayal. This we find in le Carré's *The Little Drummer Girl* (1983). However, such a resolution belongs more to the 'blind' passion of sexual love (and that is the case with Charlie) than to friendship – the 'blindness' is without balance; among the things it doesn't see are alternatives.[15]

So often, though, the conflict between loyalties is not resolved even when it has the surface appearance of having been so. Issues of verifiable self may be hidden, and not just from others but also from oneself. Perhaps there is an element of this in the Harold-Vita relationship, but I see it most strongly and interestingly in T.S. Eliot's/ Thomas Becket's musing in *Murder in the Cathedral*. Becket, erstwhile friend and confidant of the King, has resolved the ostensible conflict of loyalties, that between Crown and Church, but then:

> The last temptation is the greatest treason:
> To do the right deed for the wrong reason . . .
> For those who serve the greater cause may make the cause serve them (Eliot 1962:30).

Then there are those cases in which the contradiction is *not* to be resolved. For its resolution would destroy a value while letting the contradiction live generates value; and the value has all to do with verifying the self. Perhaps the classic case is the story of Tristan and Iseult and (its presentation as a love story aside) its historical affinity with the case of Becket (Crown vs. Church), along with its different resolution, is striking. The epic is grounded in 'the antagonism which grew up in the second half of the twelfth century between the rule of chivalry and feudal custom'; hence there arose 'a conflict between two kinds of *duty*', between being 'the vassal of some chosen Lady' (chivalry) and 'the vassal of a lord' (feudalism) (de Rougemont 1974:32–3). The culture of that day placed 'obstructions' in the way of any resolution (54 and *passim*). And today? Friends can reach a similar impasse (whatever the issues may be) but, in an effort to bypass a betrayal of one loyalty in favour of another, the silence of secrecy may be kept (cf. Shils 1956).

'Nesting'

On account of its making its own rules of relevancy, including those of privacy, friendship can become a sanctuary of inestimable value to the self. However, on this same account it can be an ideal 'cover' for someone in need of an alibi. The required credential is a veritable self. But the catch is – from the point of view of the accepting friend – the plurality of 'veritableness'. It is this clandestine use of – even motivation for – a friendship that I refer to as 'nesting'. I draw on Kim Philby, one of the Cambridge spies,[16] as well as fictional characters in Graham Greene and le Carré novels to highlight some of the issues of 'nesting'.

Let me begin, in keeping with many a real-life story, with 'friendliness' (Kurth 1970; Naegele 1958) rather than friendship. Friendliness is one remove from friendship even though it may be mistaken for it. The difference is crucial. Naegele reports from his field research among high school students:

> Friendliness stood for a pleasant recognition of the other and a response to his right to be recognized. It hid as much as it gave [. . .] It was expressed in passing – in the corridor, between classes [. . .] This way it stood both for disengagement and acceptance. To value it, is to disvalue intensity (including moodiness). As such it becomes an asset [. . .] in the endless maneuvers [sic] of getting along with people (Naegele 1958:241).

Philby, we are told, 'said as little as possible, and allowed people to assume [. . .] things they thought they knew about him' (Page et al.1968:151; emphasis in the original). What they found was a 'straightforward [. . .] genial drinking companion and reliable friend' (271). And the Secret Intelligence Service (SIS) brass conflated loyalty and patriotism with social class and upbringing.

So already behind 'friendliness' there is likely a culture of 'of course-ness' (Schuetz). This was true in the case of Philby; as le Carré put it: '[our] social attitudes and opinions [. . .] account as much for Philby's survival as for his determination to destroy us' (le Carré 1968:9). So the Philby of 'pipe, flannels and old tweed jacket' was verified (Page et al. 1968:139); but this was not a verifiable self of an individual, rather, it was the verified self of a social category.[17]

Yet friendliness may slide into 'true' friendship with its privacy and confidences. All the more the shock then when the duplicity of a friend (cf. E.M. Forster: 'friend or country?'), such as Philby, is laid bare for all to see: 'You took me in for years [. . .] I once looked up to you, Kim. My God, how I despise you now [. . .] ' raged a long-time colleague in the SIS (Penrose and Freeman 1986:397). Similarly with a professorial colleague of Anthony Blunt's at the Courtauld Institute: 'He had deceived me [. . .] all those hours we had spent talking had meant nothing. Nothing at all. He had been playing a game with his friends.' (520)

What is being exposed here, once again, is the cosy – falsely cosy – notion of 'the verifiable self'. This doesn't simply have to do with spies and their duplicities, so let me return for a moment to Stevens, Ishiguro's creation. Why the adage 'no man is a hero to his valet'? Presumably because the valet has back-stage access (Goffman 1959). Now this is quite often what friends (or lovers) suppose they have, and yet, they may really be 'seeing' themselves more than they 'see' their friend; or they 'see' themselves and the friend through the prism of their relationship. But Stevens does not see himself, simply the man he serves. 'Why, Mr. Stevens why, why, why do you always have to pretend?' Kate, the housekeeper, asks Stevens in despair (Ishiguro 1989:154). For Stevens himself, however, it is not pretence but imitative devotion that he sees as the necessary vehicle of loyalty *vis-à-vis* his employer. But it means that Stevens loses not only Kate but seemingly any verifiable self: 'You see, I trusted [says Stevens] *I can't even say I made my own mistakes.*' (243; emphasis added).

The irony is that this description of Stevens – the compliant and loyal, genuflecting and guileless servant – fits how some of the supporting cast in le Carré's *A Perfect Spy* (1986) feel about Magnus Pym:

Axel: 'Magnus is a great imitator, even when he doesn't know it. Really I sometimes think he is entirely put together from bits of other people, poor fellow' (le Carré 1986:501).

Kate: 'He's a shell . . . All you have to do is find the hermit crab that climbed into him. Don't look for the truth about him. The truth is what we gave him of ourselves' (248).

Magnus, however, *has* a verifiable self (hidden away), it is simply that Axel and Kate (le Carré's) and others had to deny it in order to distance themselves from him.[18] Perhaps our perplexity in being deceived inclines us to ascribe weak knowledge of self to the treacherous 'friend'?[19] And the issue quickly becomes 'not merely a matter of differing loyalties, but of moral absolutes' (Hart 1998:294) where 'loving the enemy, Proffy, is worse [even] than betraying secrets' (Oz 1997:69).

Needed here is the notion of intimate stranger. This is a person quite different from the 'stranger' (Bauman 1990; G. Simmel 1971) who 'comes today and stays tomorrow' (G. Simmel 1971:143) who 'disturbs the resonance between physical and psychical distance' (Bauman 1990:150) and with whom it is impossible to have a relationship of 'inner and exclusive' quality (G. Simmel 1971:148). Indeed, the 'journey' of the intimate stranger is a reversal of the stranger's, who, belonging to 'the outside,' moves 'into the inside' (Bauman 1990:146). Instead, beginning on the inside the intimate stranger moves to the outside while still seen as belonging. Thus in her account (1968) Eleanor Philby, wife of Kim Philby, speaks of the 'real horror of discovering that my husband was not the man I thought he was' (1): 'I had always felt that one of the most precious things which bound us together was that we had no secrets from each other' (78).

And Philby himself? Pitt-Rivers (1961:139) writes of his Andalusian pueblo that '[t]he criterion which distinguishes true from false friendship flees from the anthropologist into the realms of motive'. This can be said equally, if differently, of Philby's life. Philby may well have needed friendship as much as anyone, perhaps more than most of us; not just as a 'cover' for his life as an agent but also emotively on account of his 'double life'. Here is Eleanor Philby again: 'He was able to pour into our relationship all the sensitivity and love a human being could possibly give to another. It probably was his only outlet and the only way he could have survived the strain of those thirty years' (1968:xiv). So Kim Philby *qua* individual perhaps found the sanctuary that friendship offers even as he 'nested' there. What he had to do — and did — was to avoid open conflict between that personal imperative and his other loyalty (cf. K. Philby 1968). Hence the surety secrecy offered.[20]

Adversarial Culture

Here I return to the ideal relationship, friendship, in the shadow of the politics of the verifiability of self: after all, the very notion of idea-value suggests politics, just as the tautological with its codes of 'of course-ness' expectedly dampens political ardour. I take the term 'adversarial culture' from Lionel Trilling (1967) for whom it exists to 'liberate the individual from the tyranny of his culture [. . .] and to permit him to stand beyond it in an autonomy of perception and judgment [. . .] and perhaps revise [it]' (12). There is a premonition of Woodstock in this of course; but much of the same comes from the pen of Isaiah Berlin (1969:131) and, years earlier, from Keynes. In connection with the Cambridge Apostles' circle of his youth and of the Bloomsbury group that followed, Keynes wrote: 'We [between friends] entirely repudiated a personal liability on us to obey general rules. We claimed the right to judge every individual case on its merits, and the wisdom, experience and self-control to do so successfully. This was a very important part of our faith and for the outer world our most important and dangerous characteristic' (cited in O'Faolain 1956: xxxvi). Of course Keynes exaggerated. But I think the point stands that the Apostles and Bloomsbury did help to shape a contemporary adversarial culture, as did Woodstock, and in doing so influenced a culture of friendship (cf. Becker 1962; Podhoretz 1969; Rutherford 1978). So E.M. Forster wasn't so alone after all.

The worth of adversarial culture is its readiness to challenge moral and social contradictions, and the ideal friendship relationship with its own rules of relevancy is made for that. However, the practice of adversarial culture (beyond its hortatory rhetoric) introduces argument and beyond argument, fundamental differences.[21] What, then, when friends find themselves on opposing sides? Can a person afford to win when there's a friend on the other side? How should, and do, friends fight? In C.P. Snow's novel of electoral politics within a Cambridge college, those most hurt in the political in-fighting are, exactly, two friends: Eliot and Getliffe. Eliot to Getliffe: 'I can't begin to explain the colour red to a man who's colour blind. You'd better take my word for it;' Getliffe to Eliot: 'It will be hard for me to think you reliable again' (Snow 1956:69, 72; cf. Paine 1977). In short, adversary culture depends on the support of the idea-value culture found in the ideal code of friendship and yet, on occasions, it may wound, even destroy, such friendships. The likely causes of these casualties are of a different nature to those in the world of tautological value: not the exhaustion of the utility of a friendship nor the intervention of an ascriptive claim such as kinship; but, quite simply, disagreement, more often than not of an ethical or ideological kind.

Adversary culture circles may well spawn public heroes (as they do traitors), or at the very least an 'heroic' ambience 'out there', and this is not without significance for the image-making of friendship. Heroes bolster the verifiable selves that individuals claim for themselves; heroes bring to public attention the value for which an individual strives; heroes thus give vicarious force to the (perhaps otherwise unsung) poetry of individual lives. In this sense, you don't have to know a hero at first hand for he/she to be a 'friend' – or to be led to a friend through your hero.

Conservatively, Sean O'Faolain tells us that the hero, is 'a purely social creation [. . .] He represents [. . .] a socially approved norm' (1956:xii).[22] But what when heroes' values are a source of public controversy? When the heroic puts societal norms in contention? This posits the need for a distinction between heroes who are simply meritorious and others who are adversarial, perhaps complexly so. The meritorious hero is conformist, the symbolic embodiment of the (supposed) collective will, perhaps even to the extent of his being publicly invented as a hero. The adversarial hero is non-conformist – the innovator, visionary, rebel.[23]

Where simply meritorious heroes may seem to be little aware of the 'meaning' of what they are doing (cf. tautological value), the adversarial hero speaks, writes, and otherwise acts in a self-conscious absorption of 'meaning' (cf. idea-value). Yet the meritorious, played as a role, is of itself a useful 'cover'. Indeed, before he was exposed as a traitor, Kim Philby (of pipe, flannels and old tweed jacket) was, to many in SIS, a hero – not of the rebel kind but as one embodying the socially approved norm.[24] Friendship, then, or at least friendliness, was an appropriate relationship with him.

Own Allegiances

The issue before us is still the verifiability of self. In this closing section, though, I switch the perspective from the 'political' and manipulative to the 'subjective' (inasmuch as they are separable); for ultimately, perhaps, friendship has to do with the 'credibility' of our personal lives along with our 'anxieties' on that account (Trilling 1972:93). My chosen way into this is the paradox buried in *The Homeless Mind* (Berger, *et al.* 1973), an inquiry into 'modernization and consciousness'.

Peter Berger and colleagues saw the 'modern' predicament as, on the one hand, the loss of 'traditional' loci of security and verities, and, on the other, the impersonalization of life through the pervasive intrusion of bureaucracies (cf. Suttles 1970). The situation was characterized as one of generic 'homelessness' (82) from which emerges 'a quest for new ways of "being at home" in society' (214; cf. adversary culture).[25] It is a quest 'to plan and fashion one's life as freely as possible' in which '[i]ndividual freedom, individual autonomy and individual rights come to be taken for granted as moral imperatives' (79); and crucially, 'a subjective realm of identity is the individual's main foothold in reality' (78) – all so different from life in Ambéli. The paradox is simply that 'homelessness,' viewed in this way as a process, opens the way to a condition of relative *freedom* from institutional constraints, and possibly, as Susan Sontag (1970:185) would add, 'a harsh purification of "self"'. I will now briefly review each of our principal characters in this light – not least among them Graham Greene and le Carré.

First, though, allow me to introduce Maurice, the hero in *The Human Factor*. A white in South Africa, morally degraded by government apartheid policies, he is also in love with a black South African: 'I became a naturalized black when I fell in love with Sarah', he says (Greene 1978; 119). Through his close relationship with Sarah he exorcises some of the self that was 'given' him as he 'makes' (re-makes) his own self. A traitor for some, an adversarial hero for others: Maurice discloses secrets to the USSR; and a key (and recurring) dialogue in *The Human Factor* is this:

> 'You haven't said a word of blame, Sarah.'
> 'What sort of word?'
> 'Well, I'm what's generally called a traitor.'
> 'Who cares?' she said. . . . 'We have our own country. You and I and Sam [their child].
> You've never betrayed that country, Maurice'
>
> (Greene 1978:187).

Maurice, then, is not 'nesting' in his relationship with Sarah. Nor is he 'a shell' for the truth about which you have 'to find the hermit crab that climbed into him', as we heard Kate saying of Magnus Pym.[26]

To return to Stevens: it might be thought that he had found a sanctuary in the home of Lord Darlington, his employer; and so perhaps he had – in the way Ambéli is that for its villagers. However, the subjective realm of his identity he squashed and he was friendless (and lonely) – he had forfeited the freedom to fashion his life: his self was in a 'given' of sorts.

And Philby? We have already spoken of how his relationship with Eleanor was possibly a sanctuary even as he 'nested' there. The seductively suggestive theme behind the Philby story is how life histories (particularly in their formative phases) may influence the turns that loyalty – and with it, friendship – takes. In the Philby case it is not homosexuality or even the English class system (that was simply an assistance in his quest); rather, it is what I label as the 'natal expatriate' experience – and one does not have to leave one's natal country for it to happen.

Leaving Philby for the moment, listen to Graham Greene on his experience of school in England: 'I had left civilization behind and entered a savage country of strange customs . . . a country in which I was a foreigner and a suspect . . . Was my father not the headmaster? I was like the son of a quisling in a country under occupation' (1971:74). Here neither school nor home offered a sanctuary (and the young boy feared that he would be seen as 'nesting' should he strike up a friendship). It was, apparently, a childhood of cognitive dissonance out of which, however, would come, once adolescence was behind him, the 'quest for new ways of "being at home" in society' (Berger *et al.*). Remarkably, so it was with le Carré too: 'I was, so to speak, born into an occupied country, because the catastrophes in our family were so great and there were so many things that I couldn't reveal that I seemed to go about in disguise' (Masters 1987:231).

And so back to Philby. Here the 'expatriate-ness' includes the conventional context; in his own words: 'I was born in India, brought up in various parts of the Arab world, and I was at school in England . . . I don't feel that I have any nationality' (Page *et al.* 1968:274).[27]

The point that I want to draw from this is how each of these men 'see' (or 'saw') – as do, assuredly, many heroes of the adversarial kind – England and English life neither wholly from the inside nor wholly from the outside, but with 'side vision' from some in-between place. Being born on the edge of things in these ways[28] makes possible moral critique of our own society from points external to it (Bock 1980:949). For some, their situation becomes an invitation to live (in Graham Greene's phrase) on the 'dangerous edge of things' (Masters 1987:118); and this, as we have seen, has everything to do with the making and unmaking of personal and private friendships; secondarily, it explains something about some spies.

Without fail, a life such as Philby's evokes polarized responses – traitor or hero? deceiver or friend? – and le Carré's and Graham Greene's perceptions of Philby follow this pattern. John le Carré sees moral degeneracy driven by deceit – 'deceit, as I understand it, [is] his nature' (1968:15); Greene broods over 'the dilemma of the foreign agent with moral principles' (Masters 1987:116). In the one view the motivation of a man such as Philby is reduced to a crude and derisive deprivation thesis.[29] In the other, the question becomes 'should each individual be condemned to blind allegiance?' (Hoffman 1997:39); should friends?

However, we have seen that idea-value and the friendships within it are anything but blind (even as there is always an 'Ambéli factor'). Further, the notion of verifiable self is portable. In *The Human Factor* an SIS officer, avoiding the word 'traitor' concerning Maurice, comforts Sarah: 'Let's say – he chose a different loyalty' (Greene 1978:243).

Notes

1 Du Boulay is an ethnographer and Ishiguru a novelist, yet I give equal credence to both – and I use other 'fiction' in this essay too. Is this justified? asks one of my readers. In this instance of Ishiguru's Stevens, my reader wonders 'does he conceal an identity which the narrative allows to be revealed?' If so, does this mean we are presented with a different realm of 'truth' from that one finds in an ethnography? While aware that there may be a problem here that I don't acknowledge, my answer is ethnographers worth their salt (such as Du Boulay) do 'reveal'; yet precisely in the study of friendship, the insights of anthropology (for good reasons) are meagre compared to those offered by some novelists. The 'truth' question? Let each reader judge.

2 'Not only do people love to gossip, but they are also, in a sense, obliged to, since the prescription for loyalty between kin means not only that one kinsman should preserve the secrets of another, but also that he should not exclude such a kinsman from his confidence' (Du Boulay 1974:156).

3 It is worth noting that the friendships, so often of brief duration, are 'unencumbered – one might say, undefended – by ritual of any sort' (Pitt-Rivers 1961:32). Of itself, this could be taken as a hallmark of the personal and private friendship; however, friends in Ambéli, far from making their own rules for their relationships, are constrained by the rules of kin groupings.

4 Of course were that the whole story it would be hard to imagine a family could cope with the vicissitudes of life; in fact – and this holds for each of the three cultural groups – personal bonding (e.g. spiritual kinship, patron-client relations) occurs with persons outside. These relationships tend to be 'marked' ritually and are thus public knowledge and are likely to have greater longevity.

5 The idea-value orientation recognizes not just the presence of contradiction

but its importance in the making of meaning; in the tautological orientation, however, such contradictions as occur are not recognized as that and are treated in a self-validating way (Paine 1989b).

6 See Paine (1969) for a fuller exposition. I called this ideal relationship a 'luxury' that perhaps few cultures enjoy; one that does, I said, is the Western middle class.

7 For three days in August 1969, 400,000 young people were drawn to Wood-stock, in Bethel NY, for an open-air music festival cum love-in cum peace rally. The occasion was one of 'exemption' from the rules and conventions of mainstream society. Margaret Mead was there and wrote a celebratory piece for *Redbook Magazine*.

8 At the time of publication, Reich was a member of the Yale University Law School.

9 Even so, the worry of another reader stands: the implicit transfer of this kind of data to the British scene. I take his point, even as I suppose there are cross-cultural relevancies (and important clues) in the cited writings. Meanwhile, what a challenging enquiry for someone!

10 'Treason doeth never prosper, what is the reason? For if it prosper, none dare call it treason' (Sir John Harrington, *Epigrams,* Book IV, No.5, 1612).

11 Similarly, the disclosure of a 'dark secret' (Goffman 1959) may be a pretence – a piece of posturing – with the 'secret' carefully selected.

12 It is as well that we remind ourselves of the cultural specifity in these matters. For example, Bergman on the one hand and on the other: Octavio Paz's view of the Mexican (male?) as a 'hermetic being' for whom 'to confide in others is to dispossess oneself' (1961:31).

13 Harold writes to Vita: 'How I have missed you! I am a bivalve, and don't function properly when I am forced to be unicellular' (Nicolson 1973:127).

14 'Charlie [the drummer girl] was transported from her beliefs, driven to betray what she once thought she had stood for, thus recreating her loyalties' (Hoffman 1997:45).

15 On sexual love and love in relation to friendship, see Brain (1976) and de Rougemont (1974).

16 Along with Burgess, Maclean, and Blunt (and a 'fourth man'?). Philby has exercised the imagination of both Greene and le Carré: 'Haydon' in le Carré (1974), 'Harry Lime' in Greene (1950) and 'Maurice Castle' in Greene (1978). Both have also written about Philby himself – condemnation (le Carré 1968) and with sympathy (Greene 1968).

17 The story of George Blake (Blake 1990) – like Philby, a KGB agent while working with SIS, but unlike Philby, not an Englishman by birth – confirms that when it comes to the social category of 'outsider', the Establishment, along with SIS, 'thinks' much the same way as the villagers of, say, Ambéli.

18 I may be wrong about this. At any rate, Myron Aronoff, whose research readings into the le Carré novels far surpasses mine (and who generously let me see the manuscript of his forthcoming book on the subject), believes I am. We both agree that Pym is le Carré's paradigmatic 'chameleon', in Aronoff''s view this signifies 'a hollowness, a lack of a centered personality . . . [a lack of] a fixed repertoire' (Aronoff [1999]).

19 Notably, Hugh Trevor-Roper and Rebecca West speak of 'traitors' as 'moral and mental automata' unable 'to choose between good and evil' (Trevor-Roper 1968:7; West 1947:180).

20 Its management remains something of a mystery (cf. Sherry 1994). Certainly the notion of Philby having 'two separate sides to his head' with one of them being 'the real Philby . . . a lifelong Communist' (Page *et al.* 1968:26) gets us nowhere (cf. Narayan 1993). A cardinal message in Graham Greene's oeuvre is that a life such as Philby's belongs to both sides (of the head), and Noel Annan's comment on Pym, the central figure in le Carré's *A Perfect Spy*, is acutely suggestive of possible psychodynamics in such cases: 'Whoever he loves he betrays and then wants them all the more to love him' (Annan 1986:3).

21 For example, both Blunt and Burgess (of the Cambridge spies) were Apostles in their time; the likes of Hugh Trevor-Roper and Rebecca West would have been Apostles, we may suppose, had they been at Cambridge, and both placed the spies outside of all moral bounds (see note 19).

22 This view is variously embroidered in the literature: A hero may be no more than a central character of a story – 'simply someone who is worth talking about' (Zweig 1974:84) or 'a man who deserves to live in the imagination of his time' (Howe 1962–63:364) or 'one of humanity's ideals, like the saint and sage' (Rutherford 1978:1).

23 Of course, the life of a person may well embrace both the meritorious and the adversarial (perhaps along with a measure of complication); I suppose Homer's Achilles is the classical example.

24 If Hugh Trevor-Roper and Malcolm Muggeridge didn't see him quite as 'hero', they were, nonetheless, taken in by him.

25 Giddens (1991) with particular attention to the interrelation of 'disembedded-ness', risk, and intimacy may be read as an 'up-date' on *The Homeless Mind*.

26 Along with 'Maurice', George Blake, of real life, warrants notice (see note 17). On his decision to work for the KGB, he writes: 'I now felt a great relief. My inward struggle was over [. . .] I had purpose. Everything fell into place' (Blake 1990:146). He regrets he had to practise deception, but argues that 'the contribution I could make to the cause' as a double agent 'would be significantly greater' than had he come out into the open and joined the Communist Party (141).

27 He was called 'Kim' after the hero of Kipling's novel of that name – an Irish

boy who grows up among Indians and becomes involved in intelligence exploits. The father, St John Philby, left India for Arabia where he became a prominent Arabist and close adviser of Ibn Saud; born of the English ruling class, St John maintained throughout his life an excessively ambivalent attitude to it and to England. The son, Kim Philby, was of course sent 'home' to school in England – Westminster.

28 As George Blake also recognizes that he was (Blake 1990:44).
29 To wit: 'Philby grew up with the idea that he was born an empire baby – to rule; and he was born in a world where "all his toys were being taken away by history"' (Masters 1987:253). And the same is said of 'Haydon' (le Carré 1974; Masters 1987:229).

References

Annan, Noel (1986), 'Underground Men', *The New York Review of Books*, May 29:3–5.

Aronoff, Myron J. (forthcoming in 1999) *John le Carré's Spy Novels: Balancing Ethic and Politics*, New York: St Martin's Press.

Barth, Fredrik (1996), *Models of Social Organization*, London: Royal Anthropological Institute.

Bauman, Zygmunt (1990), 'Modernity and Ambivalence', in Mike Featherstone (ed.), *Global Culture*, London: SAGE Publications.

Becker, Ernest (1962), *The Birth and Death of Meaning*, New York: Free Press.

Berger, Peter and Berger, Brigitte, and Kellner, Hansfried (1973), *The Homeless Mind*, New York: Random House.

Bergman, Ingmar (1988), *The Magic Lantern*, New York: Viking Press.

Berlin, Isaiah (1969), 'Two Concepts of Liberty', in *Four Essays on Liberty*, London: Oxford University Press.

Blake, George (1990), *No Other Choice: An Autobiography*, London: Jonathan Cape.

Bock, Philip K. (1980), 'Review', (Kenelm Burridge Someone No One: An Essay on Individuality) *American Anthropologist* 82:949–50.

Brain, Robert (1976), *Friends and Lovers*, New York: Basic Books.

Campbell, John (1964), *Honour, Family and Patronage*, Oxford: Clarendon Press.

Cohen, Anthony P. (1994), *Self Consciousness: An Alternative Anthropology of Identity*, London: Routledge.

de Rougemont, Denis (1974), *Love in the Western World*, New York: Harper and Row. First published in 1956.

Deutsch, Morton (1958), 'Trust and Suspicion', *Journal of Conflict Resolution,* 2:265–79.

Douglas, Mary and Wildavsky, Aaron (1982), *Risk & Culture*, Berkeley: University of California.

Du Boulay, Juliet (1974), *Portrait of a Greek Mountain Village*, Oxford: Clarendon Press.

Eliot, T.S. (1962), 'Murder in the Cathedral' in *Collected Plays*, London: Faber & Faber.

Forster, E.M (1951), *Two Cheers for Democracy*, London: Edward Arnold.

Giddens, Anthony (1991), *Modernity & Self-Identity,* Stanford: Stanford University Press.

Goffman, Erving (1959), *The Presentation of Self in Everyday Life,* New York: Anchor Books.

Greene, Graham (1950), *The Third Man,* London: William Heinemann.

—— (1968), 'Introduction', in Kim Philby, *My Silent War*, New York: Grove Press.

—— (1971), *A Sort of Life*, New York: Simon and Schuster.

—— (1978), *The Human Factor*, Harmondsworth: Penguin Books.

Hart, Peter (1998), *The IRA and its Enemies*, Oxford: Clarendon Press.

Hoffman, Tod (1997), 'Treasons and Loyalties', *Queen's Quarterly,* 104:31–45.

Homer (1990), *The Iliad*, translated by Robert Fagles, New York: Viking Penguin.

Howe, Irving (1962–63), 'T.E. Lawrence: The Problem of Heroism', *The Hudson Review*, 15:333–64.

Ishiguru, Kazuo (1989), *The Remains of the Day*, London: Faber and Faber.

Kurth, Suzanne B. (1970), 'Friendships and Friendly Relations', in George J. McCall *et al.* (eds) *Social Relationships*, Chicago: Aldine Publishing.

Laing, R.D. (1968), *The Politics of Experience*, Harmondsworth: Penguin.

Larsen, Tord (1987), 'Action, Morality, and Cultural translation', *Journal of Anthropological Research* 43:1–28.

le Carré, John (1968), 'Introduction', in Bruce Page, David Leitch and Philip Knightley, *Philby: The Spy Who Betrayed A Generation*, London: Andre Deutsch.

—— (1974), *Tinker, Tailor, Soldier, Spy,* New York: Bantam Books.

—— (1983), *The Little Drummer Girl*, New York: Alfred A. Knopf.

—— (1986), *A Perfect Spy*, London: Hodder and Stoughton.

Leyton, Elliot (ed.), (1975), *The Compact: Selected Dimensions of Friendship*, St John's: Institute of Social and Economic Research, Memorial University.

Masters, Anthony (1987), *Literary Agents: The Novelist as Spy*, Oxford: Basil Blackwell.

Naegele, Kaspar D. (1958), 'Friendship and Acquaintances: An Exploration of Some Social Distinctions', *Harvard Educational Review*, XXVIII:232–52.

Narayan, Kirin (1993), 'How Native is a "Native" Anthropologist?', *American Anthropologist* 95:671–86.

Nicolson, Harold (1971), *Diaries and Letters, 1945–62*, ed. Nigel Nicolson, London: Fontana Books. First published in 1968.

Nicolson, Nigel (1973), *Portrait of a Marriage*, New York: Atheneum.

O'Faolain, Sean (1956), *The Vanishing Hero*, Freeport: Books for Libraries Press.

Oz, Amos (1997), *Panther in the Basement*, translator, Nicholas de Lange, New York: Harcourt Brace.

Page, Bruce, Leitch, David and Knightley, Philip (1968), *Philby: The Spy Who Betrayed A Generation*, London: Andre Deutsch.

Paine, Robert (1969), 'In Search of Friendship: An Exploratory Analysis in "Middle-Class" Culture', *Man*, 4:505–24. Reprinted in Leyton (1975).

—— (1970), 'Anthropological Approaches to Friendship', *Humanitas*, VI:2. Reprinted in Leyton 1975.

—— (1977), 'Furor Academicus. What There's to Learn from C. P. Snow', in Richard Salisbury and Marilyn Silverman (eds), *A House Divided? Anthropological Studies of Factionalism*, St. John's: Institute of Social and Economic Research, Memorial University.

—— (1989a), 'Our Friends, Our Heroes, Our Traitors' (The Kaspar Naegele Memorial Lecture), University of British Columbia, Department of Anthropology and Sociology, Occasional Paper No.1.

—— (1989b),'High-Wire Culture: Comparing Two Agonistic Systems of Self-Esteem', *Man*, 24:657–72.

Paz, Octavio (1961), *The Labyrinth of Solitude*, London: Evergreen Books.

Penrose, Barrie and Freeman, Simon (1986), *Conspiracy of Silence: The Secret Life of Anthony Blunt*, London: Grafton Books.

Philby, Eleanor (1968), *Kim Philby: The Spy I Loved*, London: Hamish Hamilton.

Philby, Kim (1968), *My Silent War*, New York: Grove Press, Inc.

Pitt-Rivers, Julian (1961), *The People of the Sierra*, Chicago: University of Chicago Press.

—— (1968) 'The Stranger, the Guest and the Hostile Host', in J-G Peristiany (ed.), *Mediterranean Rural Communities and Social Change*, Paris and The Hague: Marton & Co.

Podhoretz, Norman (1969), 'Synge's Playboy: Morality and the Hero', in Theodore R. Whitaker (ed.), *The Playboy of the Western World: A Collection of Critical Essays*, Englewood Cliffs, NJ: Prentice-Hall.

Reich, Charles A. (1971), *The Greening of America*, New York: Bantam Books. First published in 1970.

Rutherford, Andrew (1978), *The Literature of War: Five Studies in Heroic Virtue*, London: MacMillan.

Schuetz, Alfred (1944), 'The Stranger: An Essay in Social Psychology', *The American Journal of Sociology* 49:499–507.

Sherry, Norman (1994) *The Life of Graham Greene, Volume Two: 1939–1955*, London: Jonathan Cape.

Shils, Edward A. (1956), *The Torment of Secrecy*, Melbourne: Heinemann.

Simmel, Arnold (1971), 'Privacy Is Not An Isolated Freedom' in J. Roland Pennock and John W. Chapman (eds), *Privacy*, New York: Atherton Press.

Simmel, Georg (1971), 'The Stranger', in Donald N. Levine (ed.), *On Individuality & Social Forms*, Chicago: University of Chicago Press. First published on 1908.

Snow, C.P. (1956), *The Masters*, Harmondsworth: Penguin Books.

Sontag, Susan (1970), 'The Anthropologist as Hero', in Hayes E. Nelson, and Tany Hayes (eds), *Claude Lévi-Strauss: The Anthropologist as Hero*, Cambridge, Mass.: MIT Press.

Suttles, Gerald D. (1970), 'Friendship as a Social Institution', in George J. McCall *et al.* (eds), *Social Relationships*, Chicago: Aldine Publishing .

Taylor, Charles (1994), 'The Politics of Recognition', in Amy Gutmann (ed.), *Multiculturalism,* Princeton: Princeton University Press.

Trevor-Roper, Hugh (1968), 'The Philby Affair', *Encounter* XXX(4):3–26.

Trilling, Lionel (1967), *Beyond Culture*, Harmondsworth: Penguin Books. First published in 1963.

—— (1972), *Sincerity and Authenticity*, London: Oxford University Press.

West, Rebecca (1947), *The Meaning of Treason*, New York: Viking Press

Wigston, Nancy (1989), 'The Culture Shock of the Discreet Butler', (Review of *The Remains of the Day*), *Globe & Mail, June 3.*

Wilson, Peter J. (1974), 'Filcher of Good Names: An Enquiry into Anthropology and Gossip', *Man*, 9:93–102.

Zweig, Paul (1974), *The Adventurer: The Fate of Adventure in the Western World*, New York: Basic Books.

—4—

The Importance of Friendship in the Absence of States, According to the Icelandic Sagas

E. Paul Durrenberger and *Gísli Pálsson*

In anthropology, friendship has usually taken a back seat to kinship. A pertinent example is Turner's article on the Icelandic sagas (1971). While Turner acknowledges the importance of the 'diverse ties of kinship, affinity, neighbourhood, political affiliation and friendship', arguing that 'politics, or better, politicking, rather than kinship alone, seems to play a major role' (365), he tends to over-emphasize the role of kinship when outlining the 'fields' and 'arenas' within which 'social dramas' take place. Indeed, for him one of the sagas, *Njáls saga*, is an 'anthropological paradise' because of the wealth of information it contains on genealogies and family memoirs:

> Of course, anthropologists, with their practical immersion in small-scale societies with 'multiplex' social relationships [. . .] attach great importance *precisely* to genealogical connexions, for kinship as such, in societies of this type, is often the spine or main trunk of articulation of many kinds of social relationships, economic, domestic, political, and so on (361–2, emphasis in the original).

This article explores the nature and dilemmas of medieval Icelandic friendship in the context of big man-follower relationships, focusing on the constraints and characteristics of voluntary ties in the absence of a state. As we will see, Turner's emphasis on kinship hardly does justice to the 'ethnography' of the sagas; friendship was a central social institution during the time of the so-called Commonwealth period, a social formation which lasted for roughly four centuries, from the late ninth century to the imposition of the Norwegian state in the late thirteenth century.

In medieval Iceland, friendship was more important than kinship in the sense that often the former activated the latter rather than the vice versa. Kinship was

We thank Eiríkur Rögnvaldsson and Óðinn Gunnar Óðinsson (both at the University of Iceland) for their help in searching for information on friendship in a computerized database containing the Icelandic sagas. Also, we appreciate the comments of Sigríður Dúna Kristmundsdóttir and Haraldur Ólafsson (both at the University of Iceland) regarding some of the ideas presented in the paper.

one means among several to develop friendship and sometimes it did not work. We shall argue, on the basis of sketches from the sagas, that Commonwealth friendship ensured mutual trust and support in a loosely-knit social structure at a time of shifting political alliances. The sagas provide evidence for the idea (if not practice) of spontaneous or 'pure' friendship. More often, however, saga accounts relating to friendship concentrate on the rather opportunistic aspects of crafting a friendship by gift exchange or sometimes by 'buying' relationships. This supports Paine's critique (1969:507) of the idea that friendship is simply 'the act of proffering the outstretched hand'. Mauss, one may note, opened his essay on exchange and reciprocity (1954:xiv) with a citation from a medieval Icelandic document on gifts and friendship. The practice of crafting a friendship with gifts resonates with Smart's argument (in this volume, pp.119–136) that instrumentality and unconstrained sentiment represent potentially interrelated phases in the nurturing of friendship. There is relatively little evidence of female friendship, but this may be due to the patriarchal bias of the sagas and the impact of the literary genres and rhetoric of medieval Europe which focused on male bonding.

The sagas reflect social life in the stateless society of the Icelandic Commonwealth. Despite their rather objective style, they offer a wealth of ethnographic information about what we now tend to classify as 'personal' matters – including the concepts and practices of friendship (*vinátta, vinfengi*). Saga scholars usually distinguish between several genres of sagas. The so-called 'family sagas', or 'the sagas of Icelanders', describe the period from the time of settlement, between A.D. 874 and 930, when the General Assembly (*Althing*) was founded, to sometime after the introduction of Christianity, in the year 1000. They comprise about one hundred sagas and shorter stories that were compiled in several large manuscripts at various times after they were written.[1] *Sturlunga saga* (named after one powerful family), on the other hand, largely concentrates on near contemporary events from 1230 to 1262.[2] While it is both necessary and legitimate to speak of different genres of sagas, we should be aware of the difficulties of definition involved. The notion of literary genre has been subject to many debates; as Todorov points out (1990:16), to define genre as a 'class of texts' is mere tautology.

Traditionally, anthropologists have used several rather rigid 'typological' schemes to deal with the multiple forms of political systems. Typologies obviously have their drawbacks. In particular, they do not facilitate an adequate understanding of processes of change, nor do they satisfactorily deal with 'intermediate' cases and the range of variation found in the ethnography. And some schemes have been challenged for their ethnographic hollowness, for shortage of actual cases or illustrations. Thus Carneiro claims that Fried's notion of 'stratified non-state' society, a notion that may be applied to the Icelandic Commonwealth (Durrenberger 1992), is a 'phantom concept' (Carneiro, cited in Gledhill 1988:11). Indeed, Fried himself suggested that 'stratified societies lacking political institutions of state level are almost impossible to find' (Fried 1967:185). Some classification, however, seems essential to identify similar social formations, to indicate what kind of comparison would make most sense. Whatever the Icelandic Commonwealth was, it was definitely *not* a collection of bands, an egalitarian society, a family-level group, or a state (Pálsson 1995:chapter 4).

Generations of saga scholars have extensively studied saga texts as literary and historical documents. For some literary scholars, there is no medieval Icelandic culture outside the sagas; the sagas *constitute* medieval culture. Thus Meulengracht Sørensen suggests 'there are no longer any roads to reality outside the actual sagas' (1992:28). The literary tradition has remained silent on social and comparative approaches to medieval Iceland. For two decades or so, however, several anthropologists, archaeologists, literary scholars, and social historians have been identifying and exploring the value of an approach which reverses the priority of text over life (see Hastrup 1985; Durrenberger 1992; Pálsson 1995; Earle 1997). From this point of view, the sagas are potentially valuable ethnographic documents. Even if the saga accounts were mostly fictive, they would not be devoid of ethnographic value. Baxter remarks, with respect to many areas of modern life, that 'it is difficult, often impossible, to observe at all, let alone as a participant observer [. . .] so it seems sensible to use the published observation of those who have participated' (1991:123). This applies, of course, especially to students of the past. We simply have not got much else to work with. Combining saga readings, modern ethnography, and archaeology in a kind of Bakhtinian dialogue between the past and the present may significantly add to what we know about the Commonwealth.

'A Century of Friendship': A Problem of Chronocentrism?

To what extent are we able to understand medieval realities in terms of concepts derived from modern societies? Generally, the 'historical anthropology' advocated by Gurevich and the French '*Annales* school' warns against the imposition of modern criteria on the minds of people of earlier centuries. To paraphrase the substantivist argument in economic anthropology, the medieval world and the modern one represent quite different systems of literary production. Beside the obvious difference in technology between the 'age of ink' and the 'computer era', there are differences in concepts of historiography, writing, and literature as well as social relations of literary production. There are grounds, on the other hand, for resisting the popular claim that the past is inevitably a 'foreign country' (Lowenthal 1985). O'Brien and Roseberry (1991) suggest that a form of historical theory which is based on the foundation of cultural relativism necessarily fetishizes the past, exaggerating its distance from an unproblematic present. Evidently, in exaggerating difference and denying agency, the modern chronocentric discourse of alterity, whether it be in history or anthropology, is just as ethnocentric as the earlier

Eurocentric view of the primitive. Perhaps we should refrain from indulging in the 'critical cold war' of modern scholarship (Patterson 1987:39) and adopt an intermediate position, assuming that something happened in history and questioning nevertheless any notion of privileged access to it.

Writings about friendship vary from one age to another, in both content and scale. In medieval Europe, there was a renewed interest in the issue of friendship. A number of poets and intellectuals returned to early classical works – in particular, Cicero's *De amicitia* (44 B.C.):

> The Latin works on *amicitia* which the Middle Ages received asserted that friendship contributes fundamentally to the good life and that its ideal embodiment is possible [. . .] While producing and adding to their own corpus on *amicitia*, religious writers of the Middle Ages maintained much the same beliefs as they redefined true friendship on a spiritual plane. In this continuity of values and consciousness of tradition, they could conceive of themselves as true friends of the giants of antiquity (Hyatte 1994:41).

Thus, friendship was a central theme for the European intellectual community – a kind of medieval Latin-based cyberspace operating with ink and vellum, cultivated in monasteries and courts and based on readings of classic Greek texts. A recurrent theme in a variety of literary genres (treatises, philosophical dialogues, personal recollections) was the idea of 'one soul in bodies twain', usually applied to courtly love and the ideal of 'perfect' friendship between two males. This friendship revival was particularly evident in the twelfth century. An historian of the Middle Ages suggests that although the twelfth century is 'popularly viewed as the century of love, it can equally properly be called "the century of friendship"' (Ziolkowski 1995:81).

The affective and voluntary ties we nowadays classify as 'friendship' do not, therefore, seem to be restricted to 'modern' society as Carrier suggests (in this volume, pp.21–38). On the other hand, one needs to keep in mind (along with Carrier) that the concepts of individual, self, person, and society, all of which are central to the discussion of friendship, vary from one context to another. Thus, the meaning of the English term 'individual' has undergone fundamental changes in the course of history. In the middle ages, it referred to an 'indivisible' relational whole – that which cannot be divided, like the unity of the Trinity. Nowadays, in contrast, the concept of the individual suggests the very opposite, namely distinctions and discontinuities. The change in the meaning of the English concept of the individual, Williams points out, 'is a record in language of an extraordinary social and political history' (1976:133). The 'indivisible', medieval European concept of the individual echoes the relational perspectives emphasized in the ethnography of New Guinea (Carrier, in this volume, pp.21–38) as well as recent studies of hunter-gatherers (Bird-David 1999). More importantly, for our purposes, it resonates with the concepts of medieval Scandinavians. As Gurevich has shown,

Scandinavians regarded themselves as indissolubly linked to each other, their possessions, and the land they cultivated:

> The categories of possession, nobility and inherited qualities were closely connected, undivided in the minds of the ancient Scandinavians [. . .] And the fact that a man was [. . .] personally linked with his possessions found reflection in a general awareness of the indivisibility of the world of men and the world of nature (Gurevich 1992:178).

These considerations about the historicity of the concept of the individual and the timing and context of saga writing make any discussion of friendship in the Icelandic Commonwealth somewhat problematic.

Many of the sagas were composed in the turmoil of thirteenth-century Iceland and later copied in monasteries. Sagas that purport to focus on pre-Christian Icelandic realities sometimes clearly add to their indigenous accounts 'alien' material, presumably borrowed from European texts. Thus, exotic themes as well as a range of classical literary devices, plots, styles, and metaphors are occasionally borrowed from abroad. Scholars have, therefore, debated the relative importance of the pre-Christian period and the early Commonwealth, on the one hand, and, on the other, the later society of state hegemony and Christianity. The issue is unlikely to be settled once and for all, given the limited evidence available. The European connection and the timing of the writing of the sagas do not, however, necessarily detract from the ethnographic value of the sagas. Every saga contains echoes from a distant discourse. If any text or utterance is necessarily a collaboration of generations of writers and speakers, the boundary between literary studies, on the one hand, and anthropology and history, on the other, is not as important as is often implied. The factual and fictive necessarily go hand in hand.

The European ideal of friendship emphasized the necessarily egalitarian relations of friends. According to the sagas, however, friendship was an integral part of the hierarchical relations of the Commonwealth. This provides additional support for the view that the sagas were the products of the political system of the Commonwealth, and not simply artefacts of literary movements in Europe, lending sociological credibility to the sagas as ethnographic documents. Inequality is built into any entourage system and many sagas, indeed, dwell on how to establish claims to dominance. The friendship bond implied precisely that, despite potential inequality among them, the people involved would not indulge in 'the comparison of men', ensuring a certain amount of ambiguity regarding power differentials. Friends, by definition, did not contest each other. With increasing consolidation of power by the end of the period, the tensions and ethical dilemmas of the friendship bond became increasingly apparent. Ceremonial friendship or blood-brotherhood probably played an important role in this context, publicly notifying mutual commitment among the parties involved, under conditions of escalating hierarchy and dominance.

While the saga authors may have depended extensively on foreign texts and rhetoric, sometimes producing 'mere' translations of European texts, their works must somehow mirror their own needs and circumstances and, therefore, the reality of early Iceland. Many saga narratives about big men, warfare, and exchange, to mention a few issues, parallel ethnographic descriptions from non-European contexts, and these parallels are too consistent to be simply a coincidence. Several anthropologists, including Turner and Durrenberger, have been struck by the similarities of their own ethnographic experience and saga accounts: 'Because I had lived in a society in which witches, sorcerers, ghosts, feuds, hauntings, factions, and vengeance were daily realities, the sagas seemed true and believable to me' (Durrenberger 1992:4). In Turner's words, the sagas 'read like exceptionally well-filled ethnographic records and diaries' (1971:371). Even if events did not occur exactly as they are written, the assumptions of how the social context works (how it is represented) is reflective of the writer's own history and realities. While the emphasis which the sagas place on 'pure' friendship may echo the ideology of the scribal culture of twelfth-century Europe, many accounts of friendship clearly resonate, as we shall see, with what we think we know about the dynamics of medieval Iceland and similar social formations at other times and places.

The Social and Historical Context

In the Commonwealth, power was vested in local big men, *goðar* (singular *goði*). While *goðar* occupied a formal position and there was a fixed number of political units or *goðorð* in the country (thirty-six at first, thirty-nine later on), the bond between a *goði* and his followers was both personal and contingent. A *goðorð* did not necessarily imply authority over a well-defined territorial unit, nor was it necessarily associated with a single individual. Thus, the inheritors of a *goði* might share the power and responsibilities of a *goðorð*. From early on there were local assemblies. Each big man was obliged to attend the annual meetings of a General Assembly (*Althing*, founded in 930) where law was made and cases were adjudicated according to intricate procedures. Violence was an important mode of dispute-processing. Plaintiffs had to enforce legal judgements by holding courts of execution at the farms of the defendants. These often led to violent clashes. The *Althing* was not primarily a legal institution but an arena for building coalitions, for making, breaking, and testing connections, including those of friendship. If one were not a big man, he had to select some big man to follow. Relationships among big men were equally voluntary. There were two sorts of group: the entourage of a big man and the coalition of big men. Parties to either kind of relationship had to see some advantage to maintaining it. Kinship played very little role in this context and sagas detail feud relationships among members of what would be bilateral kindreds, had they existed (Phillpotts 1913).

The social system rested on concepts of property, of unequal access to resources, but there was no state to defend claims to ownership. One could maintain such claims only through coalitions of force which depended on being a member in good standing of some big-man entourage or developing some personal power base for oneself by trying to head an entourage. Being a member or leader of an entourage was primarily a matter of social manoeuvre, generosity to one's following, arranging good marriages and foster relationships, holding feasts, winning important law cases at the *Althing,* and winning fights. Important exchanges of wealth within Iceland were in this social context not a separately defined economic sphere.

Inattention to maintaining a sufficiently strong following or other social miscalculation could cause great losses of fortune. *Hrafnkel's saga*, for instance, describes how a big man lost his power-base through inattention to his following and only regained it by carefully building it anew. Wealth was accumulated and lost in social manoeuvre. *Íslendinga saga* (the saga of Icelanders), in the *Sturlunga* compilation, relates many incidents during the thirteenth century of people gaining wealth by marriage and force, even poetry, but not by trade. Big men consumed such goods as timber for houses and churches, grain for brewing, imported weapons and clothing to support their friends and followers and to indicate, by the level of their generosity and consumption, their ability to support others. These functions are integral aspects of the institution of big-manship which persisted from the first settlement until 1262. Those who had access to sufficient resources to support a household were legally defined as tax-paying farmers (*bændur*). After 965 each of them had to be the follower of a big man. Big men were dependent on farmers for support – to feed their increasingly large personal followings or armies, to support them at assemblies, to accompany them on raids on other big men or their followers, and to defend them from such raids. Without such support and the ability to amass force, claims to ownership of land had no force.

Relations between big men and farmers were not smooth. Big men had their 'own' estates to support their establishments, and some maintained followings of armed men, but this was a difficult proposition, since it added consumers to the household without adding production (Durrenberger 1992). The big men had to rely on their followings of farmers to support them with both arms and supplies. This was one component of any farmer's household fund, his 'rent' so to speak, his expenditures for travel and support for his big man, without which his big man or another would take his land and livestock. In addition, expeditions took labour from the farm and put the farmer's life at risk. Even so, a farmer's claims to land were not secure, since his big man might abandon him, another more powerful big man might claim his land, or simply take it, or a farmer might lose his land in a realignment of alliances among big men, which were frequent.

Each big man had to attempt to muster overwhelming force. It was therefore not possible to maintain any balance of power among big men. In order to gain overwhelming force, each big man had to expand, and on an island such as Iceland, with limited resources, any expansion was at the cost of other big men. Such attempts at expansion on behalf of all the big men provide much of the dramatic action of the *Sturlung* period. The alternative to expansion was to lose influence, the ability to make good one's claims, one's followers, and one's power as a big man. The resources for expansion came from the householders' funds, from the production they appropriated from the landless workers as they replaced slaves. The 'social cost' of the system was the creation and maintenance of a large class of poor and landless people.

By the thirteenth century, the institution of big-manship became exaggerated, the demand for luxury goods increased just at the time when the foreign trade was falling off and the Norwegian traders came less and less frequently. Whereas big men had gone overseas to obtain luxury goods in the early part of the Commonwealth, few did in the later period. It was more important to stay in Iceland in order to manage the entourages and coalitions necessary to insure enough force to maintain claims to land ownership on which the extraction of value rested. At the same time, and for the same reasons, the necessity of foreign goods increased. For a while Norwegian traders came to Iceland but by the end of the twelfth century the Norwegian trade diminished because the traders had no use for Icelandic wool and had no grain to sell. As the use of force increased, so did the necessity to maintain overwhelming force and the necessity to build and maintain entourages and coalitions through the social manoeuvre that was facilitated by the consumption, gift, and display of imported goods (Durrenberger 1992).

When the ceiling on the size of holdings was removed by the availability of hired labour (around year 1000), large landholders began to expand their holdings. There was no state to guarantee differential access to resources and individuals had to enforce their own claims to ownership by force. As they began to expand their holdings these claims more and more frequently clashed and force was more frequently used. There had been burnings, betrayals, and mutilations before, but the violence of the *Sturlung* period was unique in its ferocity, frequency, and intensity. In 1262 when the chieftains agreed to cede their authority to the king of Norway, the Icelanders demanded that the Norwegians send trading ships to Iceland in return. To get the luxury goods they needed to be chieftains individuals had to give up being chieftains and the fundamental contradiction of stratification without a state. Unwilling to relinquish stratification, they were absorbed into a state system, thus ending a nearly 400-year-long history of a stratified society without a state. There is abundant internal evidence that the writers of the family sagas, set in a past of 200 to 300 years before, appreciated legal, linguistic, and religious differences between their time and the time they wrote about (Durrenberger and Durrenberger 1987; Pálsson 1995: Chapters 4 and 5).

The Concepts and Practices of Friendship: Sketches from the Fieldnotes

There are numerous references in the sagas to the concepts of 'friendship' (*vinátta*, *vinfengi*), 'friend' (*vinur*), and 'being happy in one's friends' *(vera vinsæll)*. Friendship is clearly a major theme, involving relations with and among both ordinary farmers and wealthy big men. Not only do references to friendship frequently appear in the margin of the saga accounts in a variety of contexts, some sagas revolve around the issue. Many accounts are rather formulaic, indicative of a literary style as well as of a social reality; phrases such as 'they departed in friendship' and 'they were great friends' occur again and again with identical or near-identical wording. Also, there are several references to 'perfect friendship' (*fullkomin vinátta*), echoing the romantic ideal of medieval Europe. Furthermore, there are many examples of courtly love, usually involving foreign kings. Most accounts, however, seem to suggest that friendship was grounded in the tension and shifting context of Commonwealth politics.

Often the sagas contrast relations among friends, on the one hand, and, on the other, relations among kinsfolk (*frændur*) and affines (*tengdir*): 'Then Þórir and Björn took up friendship in addition to affinity' (*Egils saga* 35:410); 'There was great friendship between them beside kinship' (*Bárðar saga* 1:46).[3] 'From then on', *Bandamanna saga* comments about the relations of a father and a son (12:25), 'their friendship was maintained in addition to good kinship'. While kinship and affinity, the sagas suggest, were important relationships, they did not necessarily imply a close personal bond and often they seem to have been secondary to friendship: sometimes there was clear hostility, the *absence* of friendship, among close relatives ('The relatives departed without any friendship' [*Þorgils saga skarða* 388:592]). Often the knowledge of friendship, of rumours regarding who were 'said to be' friends, was no less important for the understanding of events and potential responses than knowledge of kinship and affinity.

Some accounts indicate that friendship was a spontaneous development, as if no action or deliberation was involved: the saga simply states that 'a great friendship happened [*gerðist*]' (*Egils saga* 81:502). Far more often, however, the sagas suggest that friendship was intentional, informed by self-oriented, sometimes clearly opportunistic, motives. Thus, there are frequent references to the 'crafting' or 'tying' (*binda*) of friendship. Friendship is frequently initiated by a particular speech-act, by 'offering' (*bjóða*) or 'speaking to' friendship (*að mæla til vináttu*), associated with gift exchange, often involving horses, silver (money), and weapons: 'There was good friendship between them and the exchanging of gifts' (*Gisla saga Súrssonar* 8:858). The importance of gift exchange is underlined by the native concept of 'gift of friendship' (*vinargjöf*). Sometimes there were huge gatherings with the consumption of luxury goods: 'There was a nice feast with many people, and there was no shortage of good drinks. As the feast was over, the guests received gifts and departed in friendship' (*Íslendinga saga* 485:749). Gifts and favours are 'offered' and 'accepted' 'in return to' (*i mót*) friendship. Sometimes the vocabulary of 'buying' (*kaupa*) and money is unashamedly employed: 'Geitir [. . .] goes to see Geirmundur and offers him to take money for friendship' (*Vopnfirðinga saga* 10:1997).

In addition to the rather informal friendship already discussed, which was usually dyadic and achieved by exchanging gifts and favours, there was the highly formal institution of blood-brotherhood (*fóstbrœðralag*, literally 'foster-brother-hood'), secured by means of vows and swearing, and sometimes involving several men: 'I can think of a good means for this, that we bind our friendship with more firm agreements than before and swear to blood-brotherhood, the four of us' (*Gísla saga Súrssonar* 6:857). Often the formal bonds of blood-brotherhood are put to the test in a context of conflicting loyalties. In *Egil's saga* a man named Björn visits Skalla-Grímur having committed a crime against Skalla-Grímur's blood-brother Þórir. Skalla-Grímur says in an 'angry' mood on his arrival, puzzled by the visit: 'How do you dare to come to me; didn't you know of the friendship between me and Þórir?' to which Björn responds: 'I know well that between you and Þórir there is blood-brotherhood and good friendship' (34:409).

In Commonwealth Iceland there were different kinds of friendship, with different degrees of permanence and intensity. Given the competition among big men, the shifting alliances of the Commonwealth, and the absence of a state, friendship bonds were subject to intense pressures. Not only are there frequent references to 'young' and 'old' friendship, the relative strength and stability of friendship is a common theme. Friendship is said to 'increase' (*aukast*), to 'stay' (*haldast*), to 'decrease' (*réna*), or to 'end' (*ljúka*), sometimes with enmity: 'You have failed in this case Ketill and thus our friendship is ended' (*Vopnfirðinga saga* 5:1992). Some friendships are characterized by ebbs and flows, successively rising and falling according to the micropolitics of the groups involved.

In some cases, a friendship bond is created to achieve a dubious, hidden motive: 'I would not have become your friend if I had known that this was behind it' (*Vopnfirðinga saga* 5:1991). As a result of increasing concentration of power in the hands of the major chieftains, growing tension within the Commonwealth generally, and the escalation of warfare, cheating and exploiting friends seem to have become more prevalent by the end of the Commonwealth. Significantly, the *Sturlunga saga* compilation, which provides near-contemporary descriptions of political change during the last years of the Commonwealth, has more to say on betrayal and the misuse of friendship than the family sagas focusing on earlier times. In the former, trust is an important theme: 'I advise you [. . .] that you maintain your friendship with Gissur, but you should not count on considerable friendship' (*Þorgils saga skarða* 390:595). One scene involving the confrontation of the armed groups of two friends has the following account: 'Then Árni Bjarnason said: "Let us not fight since we have spoken to friendship." Then Árni Bjarnason lowered his shield from his face. But as Árni Bjarnason saw that, he raised the axe with both hands and gave him a blow' (*Sturlu saga* 64:79). There are even occasional references to the 'selling' of friends: 'I fear that my brother Snorri has exchanged friends and sold the friendships of Sighvatur and Sturla in return to that of Kolbeinn' (*Íslendinga saga* 238:346).

There is a striking relative absence in the sagas of references to friendship involving women. Out of a total of several hundred accounts of friendship, only a few relate to women. The term for 'female friend' (*vinkona*) occurs only a dozen times, and in most cases in the context of courtship between a man and a woman. Accounts of friendship between women are not totally absent (*Laxdæla saga* has one example [53:1618]), but they are clearly exceptional; there are some extensive accounts of the *absence* of friendship between women, notably the account of *Njáls saga* (see below) of the enmity between Bergþóra and Hallgerður. Also, the indigenous term for blood-brotherhood only allows for males, that is 'brothers'. In at least two cases a female friend is said to be a witch, which may suggest that female friendship was different from the friendship between males: 'Þórdís was a witch. There was great friendship between Þorgrímur and Þórdís' (*Gunnars saga keldugnúpsfifls* 1:1144). Clearly, judging from saga accounts, friendship was mostly a male affair.

Some Extended Cases: The Sagas of Njáll and Gísli

Njáls saga is the longest and most intricately wrought of the family sagas. One of its central characters, Gunnar, is handsome, accomplished, well travelled, very athletic, somewhat modest, and not very clever: the archetype of the saga hero. After he returns from successful travels abroad, he goes to a meeting of the General Assembly where he meets the tall, blonde, and beautiful Hallgerður, the daughter of Höskuldur and niece of his half brother and friend Hrútur. Hallgerður has had a series of previous unfortunate marriages, unfortunate because her husbands have been killed by her over-sensitive foster father for what he took to be insults to her.

Gunnar's advisor in all matters is the wise and prescient Njáll, who advises against the marriage. Gunnar does not listen, and Hallgerður gets him involved in disputes with others, including Njáll himself. He is able to keep his relationship with Njáll on good terms because Njáll knows about his problems, but he gets involved in feuds with others, which end in his being outlawed. At one point he slaps Hallgerður, something that has caused the death of a former husband. Outlawed, he refuses to leave his farm, and, since he does not leave, anyone can kill him with impunity. His many friends offer him help, which he refuses. His enemies attack him in his house, but he holds them off with his bow and arrows until an attacker leaps up and cuts his bow string. Then he asks his wife to cut a length of her long hair and plait it into a bowstring for him. She reminds him of the time he slapped her and refuses to help. He defends himself valiantly, but his enemies kill him in the end. Then the saga shifts to Njáll and his sons, who fall under the influence of a scheming and jealous big man, Mörður. This leads to a series of events that culminate when the enemies of Njáll burn him and his family in their house. One son-in-law escapes and the remainder of the saga details his vengeance, how he hunts down the burners and kills them.

Much of *Njáls saga* is a consequence of the unfavourable relationship between Gunnar and his wife. Because of their friendship, Gunnar and Njáll took turns hosting each other for a winter visit. At such a visit, their wives argued, exchanged insults, and became enemies. While the men are at a meeting of the General Assembly, Gunnar's wife has a slave kill one of Njáll's slaves. When the news reaches the assembly, Gunnar allows Njáll to assess the compensation, and pays it. The next year, Njáll's wife has the killer killed, and Njáll returns the money he had previously received from Gunnar. The next year, his killer is killed, and Gunnar pays compensation. There is another round of reciprocal killings, and the foster father of Njáll's sons is killed. At this they take vengeance and kill the killers themselves, but Gunnar asks for no compensation. When Njáll mentioned it, Gunnar said Njáll should assess the settlement himself and the two pledged that they would always settle matters between themselves and remained friends. The friendship between Gunnar and Njáll was stronger than the relationship of either man to his wife.

The central figure of *Gísla saga* is far from the model hero. The saga starts in Norway, where a disappointed suitor of Gísli's sister tries to burn his family in their house. Gísli and his family escape, burn the burners, and go to Iceland. The parents die and the three siblings get married. The brothers work the same farm, just next to that of their sister's husband, Þorgrímur. Gísli travels abroad with his wife's brother, Vésteinn, while Gísli's brother, Þorkell, travels with their sister's husband, Þorgrímur. After they return, Þorkell overhears his wife telling Gísli's wife that she loves Gísli's wife's brother, Vésteinn. Þorkell divides the family wealth and moves in with Þorgrímur next door. Vésteinn comes to Gísli's place for a feast, but someone sneaks into the house and stabs him to death in his bed. Gísli knows the killer is Þorgrímur, because Þorkell is related by marriage to Vésteinn and cannot kill him but Þorgrímur is not, so Þorkell has got Þorgrímur to kill his rival. Gísli waits until there is another feast at his brother's farm, then sneaks into the house at night and kills Þorgrímur with the same spear he used on Vésteinn. Gísli's sister marries Þorgrímur's brother, Börkur. A sorcerer casts a spell on the killer of Þorgrímur, that he will receive no aid. Gísli's sister figures out that Gísli killed her husband when he makes a careless verse about it. When she tells her husband, he gets Gísli outlawed and begins to hunt him down. Gísli evades his hunters for years by clever tricks and finally Gísli and his wife settle in an out of the way valley in the West Fjords, but Börkur's followers find Gísli and attack him. He makes a valiant defence, aided by his always loyal wife, but his attackers kill him.

The central event of Gísli's saga is the mutual killing among the group of friends and siblings. The early structuring of the relationships among the four men sets up the dynamics of the remainder of the saga. The two brothers, their sister's husband, and Gísli's wife's brother are at a local assembly together when a man comes into their booth and accuses them of neglecting the business of the assembly because they would rather sit and drink with each other. When the four go to the meeting of the assembly, a big man informs them that the cases are of no import- ance, that the big men will call the friends if anyone needs their help. Now people begin to say that these four are overly bold, offering their help when no one has asked for it. One big man, known for his prescience, predicts that in three summers, they will no longer be so close. When word of this prophecy reaches the friends, Gísli suggests that they defy it by making their friendship stronger by swearing blood-brotherhood, which they do in a ritual performance. When they came to all shake hands on the oath that each would avenge the other as a brother, one, the sister's husband, refuses to bind himself to Gísli's wife's brother, Vésteinn, because it is sufficient burden for him to be so sworn with the two brothers. Gísli then refuses to bind himself to his sister's husband, Þorgrímur. Thus, he knows it was Þorgrímur who killed Vésteinn; thus it is that Gísli can kill Þorgrímur. This episode illustrates the importance and closeness of friendship. Þorgrímur will commit a dastardly deed, and secretly kill Vésteinn, at the behest of his friend Þorkell. Likewise, Gísli, is bound to avenge his friend by killing his brother's friend. The ties between the brothers and their friends are much stronger than the ties between the two brothers themselves. Friendship is stronger here than brotherhood.

Typically, a saga has an abundance of genealogical material to situate all of the principles relative to one another with respect to descent and marriage. As events occur, and as people make choices that determine other events, things are 'laid down' until the conclusion is inexorable and inescapable. Thus the sagas convey a strong sense of inevitability but also of choice and decision. Gunnar decides to marry his wife against Njáll's advice, and the rest follows. While kinship and history provide the starting point, people's actions lay down new events upon those foundations. Among the things that can be so 'laid down' and determine future events are prophecies, predictions, and curses, such as the prediction of the big man that the friends in *Gisla saga* would not long remain friends. Thus each action a person takes to make, break, or strengthen a friendship or an enmity contributes to the inevitability of the outcome. One could make enemies as well as friends, usually by reversing any of the processes of making friends. For instance, a scurrilous verse could make an enemy as quickly as a killing. Both had the same impact of diminishing honour. Likewise, one could make enemies by belittling them with inferior seating arrangements at a feast or by not inviting them at all, by withholding support in disputes, or by supporting a rival.

Discussion

Given the evidence of the sagas, we are able to throw some anthropological light on the 'foreign' world of the Icelandic Commonwealth. The move from Norway to Iceland seems to have disrupted the kinship system that was in place (see Phillpotts 1913). In spite of the fact that the law-books detail elaborate kinship schemes for reckoning compensation, such a system was never operative in Iceland. The important relationships were those of alliance and entourage, both of which relied on friendship rather than kinship. The sagas mention when a kinship connection is involved, that friendship went with kinship to explain the relationship. Friendship rather than kinship was assumed to underlie such important associations. People were careful to develop, maintain, and sustain the friendships that underlie their entourage and alliance relationships. Some of the means for doing this were through fostering children, usually of a superior; supporting a person in a dispute; hosting a feast for subordinates or people of more or less equal standing; composing laudatory verses about someone, often a king of another Norse land; and giving gifts.

Many saga accounts of friendship resonate with ethnographic descriptions of personal relationships in other stateless societies 'governed' by big men and chieftains. In such contexts, it seems, informal friendship is a particularly important social institution, ensuring mutual support in a context of ever-changing political alliances. The self-account of Ongka, a Hagen big-man in New Guinea, is a case in point. Ongka held no position as of right of birth, instead he had to depend on a personal alliance established through gifts and the force of his arguments: 'Orators, especially the big men themselves, enumerate the gifts they are making, recite the political background of alliance and enmity underlying the occasion, and stake their claims to fame' (Strathern 1979:xx). The more formal institution of *fóstbrœðralag* or blood-brotherhood also has a series of ethnographic parallels; for instance the 'friends to the death' among rural Thai (Piker 1968) and ceremonial friends among the Jivaro of the Amazon forest (Descola 1996). As Descola remarks of the latter, ceremonial friendship 'introduces an order of its own that sometimes contradicts the sociological principles that govern ordinary relations' (1996:154). It would be more appropriate to say, however, with respect to the Icelandic Commonwealth, that friendship constituted the 'ordinary' relations of big men and followers, in some cases activating the more secondary or dormant relations of kinship and affinity. Affinal relations mirrored or followed from relations of friendship in the sense that it was not uncommon to marry a daughter to secure (*treysta*) an existing relationship or to initiate friendship. Friendship, whether ceremonial or informal, can be viewed as an adaptation to situations of fundamental insecurity, the necessity of surviving in a context of shifting alliances and chaotic political manoeuvres. Indeed, one of the main terms used for friendship (*vinfengi*) suggests that friendship is acquired through some form of payment. Perhaps a suitable ethnographic parallel in a *state* society would be the friendship relations of urban gangs and drug users in urban Western society, for here too it is vital, because of the absence of more formal means for protection, to have someone to count on; a recent study of drug users in the United States suggests that despite the chaotic context people 'viewed themselves as involved in "safe" networks which offered social support' (Sterk-Elifson and Elifson 1992).

As we have seen, there are very few accounts in both the sagas themselves and saga scholarship of female friendship. Sigurðsson appears to take the gender bias at face value, arguing that it is 'tempting to conclude that friendship was reserved for men alone' (1993:215). Not only is Sigurðsson's claim an exaggeration, since, as we have seen, references to female friendship are not totally absent, there may also be more to the story. The literary genre of medieval Europe, with its focus on male bonding, may help to explain the relative absence of female friendship in saga accounts. Just as indigenous voices have spurred students of 'great men', 'big men' and 'chiefs' to emphasize the political leadership of male personalities, so the sagas have invited a biased, patriarchal discourse emphasizing the notion of the *goði*. While formal leadership is usually dominated by males, even though in some cases women may 'choose to play the "big person" game' (Lepowsky 1990:35), there are other avenues to power, some of which may be open to women. Careful comparative reading of the sagas may allow one to read between the lines, to reveal the popular culture of early Iceland. Perhaps, female friendship is taken for granted and therefore not related.

Claims about the absence of female friendship are not restricted to the saga world. Uhl points out with respect to Andalusia, that anthropologists, and informants, 'may actually be involved in an unintentional "conspiracy" to portray friendship as public, male, and important, while minimizing or denying the existence of adult female friendship' (1991:92). Relations of friendship among female adults, she suggests, are systematically suppressed or cognitively 'veiled' because they compete with domestic relationships (101). Interestingly, the implicit essentialism of the ethnography of Southern Europe, medieval scholarship, and the sagas, emphasizing male bonding, is diametrically opposed to the essentialism of much recent literature on gender and moral development, including the works of Carol Gilligan and Nancy Chodorow; in the latter case, the capacity for intimate bonding, for friendship and love, is seen as the privilege of women. Women 'connect' while men rule and divide. An alternative, 'androgynous perspective' (Cancian 1991), which abandons such a gendered polarization, may be needed to deal with the realities of gender and friendship in both history and ethnography.

Not only do the saga authors suppress or edit out important evidence by simply remaining silent, no doubt they also add to their material. One of the problems of using the sagas to elicit ethnographic information on friendship relates to the fact that most of them – the family sagas in particular – were written long after the events they purport to describe. Medieval European intellectuals were influenced by Greek texts on the ideals of friendship, and this is likely to be somehow reflected in saga accounts. One example, perhaps, is the account of the saga of Njáll of the virtues of the relationship between Gunnar and Njáll; despite all the tensions involved they remain loyal to each other. While medieval Icelandic texts may have been rooted in European discourse, they are also saturated with ethnographic information on Commonwealth Iceland. Whatever fictionalizing of dialogue and chronology that may have occurred in saga writing does not indicate that their depictions are unreliable; the texts gain sociological credibility to the extent that they report the same kinds of events that anthropologists have witnessed as characteristic of other societies which are stateless, on the margins of states, have big men or chiefs, or are otherwise similar to the Icelandic Commonwealth. The issue of friendship is one example.

Anthropologists have a tendency to take the role of kinship for granted and to force such 'structural' relations upon their ethnography, anxious to see order in, and make sense of, the seamless flow and chaotic nature of everyday life. Thus, the formal traditions of anthropology, focusing on the ways in which social life is embedded in relations of kinship and affinity, have informed one generation of anthropologists after another, turning the ethnographic gaze away from the realities of the concept and practices of friendship (Paine 1969). The ethnography of *modern* Iceland provides one striking example. Pinson, an ethnographer who spent thirty-four months in Iceland in the 1970s, has argued at some length that the notion of lineage (*ætt*) is 'the key to the Icelandic psyche' (1979:189); not only does she suggest that the kinship system 'structures most social relationships', friendship, she goes on, 'is virtually nonexistent in Iceland' (191). Pinson's strong thesis about the absence of friendship seems to have less to do with the realities of Icelandic ethnography than her tacit acceptance of the theoretical hegemony of kinship in anthropological discourse. Indeed, there is ample evidence of the importance of friendship in modern Iceland; much of which indicates that, in references to kinship, relations are opportunistically selected from a large repertoire of overlapping and contradictory terms. Rich suggests that the consensus about Icelandic kinship is shifting and that new studies may indicate 'whether the apparent complexity and latent contrasts in the system are a product of the systematizing gaze of anthropology, a product of Icelandic history and culture, or an apparition' (1989: 76–7). Modern Icelanders continue to talk about personal relationships in terms of medieval ideals of friendship – ideals, as we have seen, for which there is evidence in the Icelandic sagas. It is important, however, not to take the 'evidence' at face value; the rhetoric of friendship – informed by the literary conventions of the authors of the sagas and, more recently, nationalistic readings of the early texts – may bias our analysis of friendship in Iceland, in both the present and the past.

Notes

1 The entire corpus of the family sagas and shorter stories is now available in coordinated English translation (*The Complete Sagas of Icelanders Including 49 Tales*, 1997).

2 Other categories of medieval Icelandic prose include the kings' sagas, *Fornaldarsögur* or quasi-mythological 'Sagas of the past', and legal texts, notably *Grágás* ('Grey Goose') and *Jónsbók*. Furthermore, there are extensive poetic texts, including the *Poetic Edda*, and the historical work *Landnámabók* ('The Book of Settlements').

3 Chapter and page references to the family sagas are based on *Íslendinga sögur og þættir* (1987), except otherwise stated. All translations from the Icelandic editions cited are ours.

References

Baxter, P.T.W. (1991), 'From anthropological texts to popular writings', *Bulletin of the John Rylands Library* 73 (3), 105–24.

Bird-David, N. (1999), '"Animism" revisited: personhood, environment, and relational epistemology', *Current Anthropology* 40 (Supplement): 67–79.

Cancian, F.M. (1986), 'The feminization of love,' *Signs* 11 (4), 692–709.

The Complete Sagas of Icelanders Including 49 Tales, Vols. I–V, (1997), Reykjavík: Leifur Eiríksson Publishing.

Descola, P. (1996), *The Spears of Twilight: Life and Death in the Amazon Jungle*, London: Harper Collins.

Durrenberger, E.P. (1992), *The Dynamics of Medieval Iceland: Political Economy and Literature*, Iowa: University of Iowa Press.

Durrenberger, E.P. and D. Durrenberger (1987), 'Translating Gunnlaug's Saga: an anthropological approach to literary style and cultural structures', *Translation Review,* 21–2, 11–20.

Earle, T. (1997), *How Chiefs Come to Power: The Political Economy in Prehistory*, Stanford: Stanford University Press.

Fried, M. (1967), *The Evolution of Political Society*, New York: Random House.

Gelsinger, B.E. (1981), *Icelandic Enterprise: Commerce and Economy in the Middle Ages,* Columbia: University of South Carolina Press.

Gledhill, J. (1988), 'Introduction: the comparative analysis of social and political transitions', in J. Gledhill, B. Bender and M.T. Larsen (eds), *State and Society: The Emergence and Development of Social Hierarchy and Political Centralization*, London: Unwin Hyman.

Gurevich, A. (1992), *Historical Anthropology of the Middle Ages*, Cambridge: Polity Press.

Hastrup, K. (1985), *Culture and History in Medieval Iceland: An Anthropological Analysis of Structure and Change*, Oxford: Oxford University Press.

Hyatte, R. (1994), *The Arts of Friendship: The Idealization of Friendship in Medieval Early Renaissance Literature*, Leiden: E.J. Brill.

Íslendinga sögur og þættir, Vols. I–III, (1987), Reykjavík: Svart á hvítu.

Lepowsky, M. (1990), 'Big men, big women, and cultural autonomy', *Ethnology* 29 (1), 35–50.

Lowenthal, D. (1985), *The Past is a Foreign Country*, Cambridge: Cambridge University Press.

Mauss, M. (1954), *The Gift: Forms and Functions of Exchange in Archaic Societies*, trans. I. Cunnison, London: Cohen and West Ltd. First published 1923–24.

McGovern, T.H., G. Bigelow, and D. Russell (1988), 'Northern islands, human error, and environmental degradation: a view of social and ecological change in the Medieval North Atlantic', *Human Ecology* 16, 225–70.

Meulengracht Sörensen, P. (1992), 'Some methodological considerations in connection with the study of the sagas', in G. Pálsson (ed.), *From Sagas to Society: Comparative Approaches to Early Iceland*, Middlesex: Hisarlik Press, 17–42.

O'Brien, J. and Roseberry, W. (eds) (1991), *Golden Ages, Dark Ages: Imagining the Past in Anthropology and History*, Berkeley: University of California Press.

Paine, R. (1969), 'In Search of Friendship: An Exploratory Analysis in "Middle-Class" Culture', *Man* 505–24.

Pálsson, G. (1995), *The Textual Life of Savants: Ethnography, Iceland and the Linguistic Turn*, Chur: Harwood Academic Publishers.

Patterson, L. (1987), *Negotiating the Past: The Historical Understanding of Medieval Literature*, Madison: University of Wisconsin Press.

Phillpotts, B.S. (1913), *Kindred and Clan in the Middle Ages and After: A Study in the Sociology of the Teutonic Races*, Cambridge: The University Press.

Piker, S. (1968), 'Friendship to the Death in Rural Thai society', *Human Organization* 27 (3), 200–4.

Pinson, A. (1979), 'Kinship and Economy in Modern Iceland: A Study in Social Continuity', *Ethnology* 18, 183–97.

Rich, G.W. (1989), 'Problems and prospects in the study of Icelandic kinship', in E.P. Durrenberger and G. Pálsson (eds), *The Anthropology of Iceland*, Iowa City: University of Iowa Press, 53–79.

Sigurðsson, J.V. (1992), 'Friendship in the Icelandic Commonwealth', in G. Pálsson (ed.), *From Sagas to Society: Comparative Approaches to Early Iceland*, Middlesex: Hisarlik Press, 205–15.

Sterk-Elifson, C. and Elifson, K.W. (1992), 'Someone to Count On: Homeless, Male Drug Users and their Friendship Relations', *Urban Anthropology* 21 (3), 235–51.

Strathern, A. (ed.) (1979), *Ongka: A Self-Account by a New Guinea Big-Man*, transl. A. Strathern, New York: St. Martin's Press.

Sturlunga saga, Vols I–III, (1988), Reykjavík: Svart á hvítu.

Todorov, T. (1990), *Genres in Discourse*, Cambridge: Cambridge University Press.

Turner, V.W. (1971), 'An Anthropological Approach to the Icelandic Saga', in T.O. Beidelman (ed.), *The Translation of Culture: Essays to E.E. Evans-Pritchard*, London: Tavistock, 349–74.

Uhl, S. (1991), 'Forbidden Friends: Cultural Veils of Female Friendship in Andalusia', *American Ethnologist* 18 (1), 90–105.

Ziolkowski, J.M. (1995), 'Twelfth-Century Understandings and Adaptations of Ancient Friendship', in A. Welkenhuysen, H. Braet, and W. Verbeka (eds), *Medieval Antiquity*, Leuwen: Leuwen University Press, 59–81.

—5—

Building Affinity through Friendship
Claudia Barcellos Rezende

The modern friendship ideal is of course far from universal, in scope and in intensity, and why this is so suggests something about the conditions that sustain it [. . .] The modern friendship requires the very impersonality of administration, contractualism and monetized exchange over against which it is culturally distinguished.

Allan Silver, 'Friendship and Trust as Moral Ideals'

One of the things that struck me most when I returned to Brazil, after living in England for four years, was the frequency with which the term 'friend' was used. In restaurants, people often called the waiter 'friend', as they did in the streets when asking someone for information. Many of my relatives spoke of their maids, a common subject of conversations, as 'friends' or 'part of the family' and vice versa. Although as a Brazilian I knew these types of behaviour did not necessarily establish 'a real friendship', they seemed incredible to me after coming back from England, where I had never heard such use of the word 'friend'. Did this mean that, in Rio de Janeiro, where I lived, something like a discourse on friendship permeated the differentiated, and often unequal, relations in the public domain? Because for the English people I studied in London, friendship was very much a relationship restricted to the private sphere, formed between people thought of as equals.

Of course, all of these were general impressions experienced by a Brazilian readjusting to her home country after having been immersed in a very different society. However, they set some important theoretical questions. How could I figure out the behaviour of Brazilian people like myself, belonging to the urban middle class, who thought of themselves as 'Westerners'? These were people who were constantly marking off circles of intimacy, oriented by an individualist outlook, in the Dumontian sense, and yet called strangers in the streets 'friends'. Moreover, in a hierarchical relationship such as that between maids and employers, how could people at times describe it as a friendship? If these could be seen as personal

I would like to thank Santiago Villaveces for reading and commenting on a earlier draft of the paper.

questions in my coming to grips again with my identity as a Brazilian, they raised a more fundamental, and to me intriguing, theoretical issue about the place of friendship in the private sphere.[1] Were personal relations like friendship to belong always to the private domain? Or was this found only in the so-called 'Western' societies? What about Brazil, where its most 'Western' social groups have a distinct view about personal relations and their presence in the public domain? Certainly, there were at least two issues here: how different societies conceptualize the division of social life into public and private spheres, and how different perceptions of friendship may locate it variously within this divide. There was a third underlying problem as well: the idea that friendship requires equality between people – more difficult to secure in the public domain – in order to flourish as a dyadic relationship.

Various authors (e.g. Allan 1989; Paine 1974; Suttles 1970) have stressed the need for symmetry or roughly equal status between friends so as to distinguish it from hierarchically structured kinship relations and from the more utilitarian patron-client relations. Underlying this argument is the idea that inequality, understood here as differences in material means and often as well in social status, will fundamentally harm a voluntary relationship built strongly on affection, loyalty, intimacy and mutual support. This idea in turn reveals two important assumptions. The first is that intimate and affective relations should be kept apart from relations guided by material interest, hence creating separate domains of relations. The second is that material interests are negatively valued because their pursuit produces differences among individuals who are essentially seen as equal. The latter reveals an anguishing contradiction in 'Western' individualism: the reconciliation of actual social differences among groups of people with the idea that by 'nature' they are all equal.[2] Thus, there is a genealogy of ideas behind the association of friendship with equality that anchors it deeply in modern 'Western' thought.

It is feasible, therefore, to inquire as Silver does 'whether equality is a condition of friendship' (1989:279). He argues that in the past some forms of friendship were built precisely on the inequality of status, so that friends could provide each other with substantively distinct resources. In the Renaissance, patrons and clients, lords and vassals, offered each other services that were not identical but equivalent in moral and practical worth. Indeed, as Silver continues, 'equality of condition might conduce to rivalry and jealousy' (281). He concludes that the concern with anti-instrumentalism is chiefly linked to a modern view of friendship as a relationship to be valued 'for its own sake', hence excluding equality as its universal condition. His main argument, therefore, meets with a relativistic perspective common to anthropology, which I certainly endorse. In our comparative studies we should be careful not to extend notions – of equality, of friendship and of the person – which have a particular historical and cultural development in our comparative studies.

I want to argue, however, that friendship is closely associated with equality broadly understood, that is, with affinity. In order to do so, I bring in two very contrasting ethnographic examples which nevertheless show how distinct discourses on friendship may stress affinity in contexts where social distinctions are at issue. The first is based on my research material on the relations between white middle-class mistresses and mostly non-white maids in Rio de Janeiro, Brazil. In the second example, I examine the particular perceptions of friendship in relation to work among a group of white English people resident in London, with whom I did fieldwork. These are certainly different research projects: the social groups are not equivalent and in each case the focus of my research was distinct. Whereas in my research in London I studied the discourse and practice of people connected as friends, in Rio I was looking at women talking about a particular work relationship they experienced. Fieldwork also differed markedly in each case. In London, I was collecting material for my doctoral thesis on friendship. For over one year, I focused on a network of seventeen people, white English men and women between twenty-five and thirty years old. Through formal interviews, conversations at the pub and at dinner parties, we mapped a host of subjects around the main theme of friendship. As a Brazilian woman in England, I was given narratives on friendship that implicitly contrasted the famous 'English reserve' with their idea of a very Latin kind of relationship – extrovert, festive and very physical. In the Brazilian study, I was in a very different position. Identifiying me as a middle-class employer, women who worked as maids were at first very respectful towards me, whereas with my young Mozambican assistant there was a closer identification with the discrimination black women suffer. Employers stressed over and again that they were good mistresses, while maids often portrayed themselves as victims. This was a feature of the interviews we were conducting with a group of ten employers and fifteen maids, but which was less pronounced when we talked informally to other women employers and maids.

Both ethnographic materials were dealt with as narratives on friendship, that is, as rhetorical forms in which cultural meanings about friendship create or dispute certain social realities. In the London as well as in the Rio studies, people constructed more than one narrative on friendship, weaving out themes and making assertions about how they saw themselves and how they related to others, especially to different others. In this sense, these narratives on friendship became implicit narratives on the process of making social distinctions. There were often contradictions between these narratives, reflecting ambiguities and distinct ways of thinking about the person in relation to others. In this essay, I examine the particular views on work relationships, based mostly on interview data, and the narratives of friendship that result from these.

Bridging Worlds through Friendship

> The ideal mistress [*patroa*] would be the one who could be my friend, because I would be sure that if I needed her, I would be sure that she would help me. They have this defect: while you're still good to wash their dishes, everything is fine. But later, if you need them, they forget you. (Lúcia)

> With a friend, you can tease, swear at, joke . . . but I don't have friends. I don't like friends, because there are some who give you bad advice, so I don't have friends, just family. Friendship with a mistress is something else. My mistress talks to me about her daughters who always misbehave, who see their boyfriends instead of going to school, she talks to me about these things, but it's not friendship. Sometimes, a mistress opens herself and talks to her maid [*empregada*] about her life, but I never had this. We have conversations but it's not the same. (Margarete)

When I first met Teresa, a prospective maid, her warmth and ease struck me forcefully, particularly her calling me 'Claudinha'. She was prone to using the diminutive, affectionate form, as when she referred to a friend of mine, her other employer, in this manner, thus distinguishing herself from many other maids who address their employers with the respectful *dona* or *senhora*. I was happy to think that ours would not be a markedly hierarchical work relationship. As I learned later, Teresa spoke of many former mistresses as special people, good friends who had helped her in many difficult moments. Our relationship also developed into a friendship, but within certain limits. I listened to her more than I talked myself, because of a feeling that she would not follow my psychoanalytical views on people. She, on the other hand, discussed with me very intimate problems but refused when I invited her to sit down at the table and have lunch with me, preferring to eat on her own at the kitchen counter.

My experience with Teresa reflected a form of thinking about maids and their employers in terms of friendship which I constantly heard in conversations and in the interviews my research group carried out.[3] Indeed, this reference to friendship appeared as well in other Brazilian studies about maids,[4] being generally interpreted as an illusion maids created for themselves or as a way of improving self-esteem. To me, these explanations were too simplistic and even ethnocentric, attributing too much importance to employers and passivity to maids. As interviewees told us, the friendship relation which could develop between maids and employers differed from other kinds developed between people of similar socio-economic situation. Many maids and mistresses did not become friends. Yet many of the values of friendship seemed to guide a hierarchical work relationship between women generally thought of as having unsurmountable differences.

What does it mean to be in this highly differentiated maid-employer relationship? Brazilians have had this hierarchical work relationship as part of their everyday lives since the period of slavery. Even today, most people hire, when financially able to do so, a domestic servant to take care of household chores. Although the present state regulations have increased the costs of having maids,[5] in practice each job is susceptible to particular negotiations between employers and domestic servants, who often do not get all the rights to which they are entitled.

Despite the greater formalization and regulation of the occupation in recent years,[6] domestic servants remain identified as a category of persons who submit to anything.[7] Even if domestic servants now have greater power to sue their employers, in practice the negotiations of what exactly should be done at work is largely left to each individual employer and servant. Very frequently, employers add to the list of tasks and servants either acquiesce or lose their jobs. According to the reasoning of middle- and upper-class employers, maids would submit to more than they wish to because of their socio-economic origins – these are poor women, mostly non-white, with few or no years of schooling, often from the northeast, where people are thought to be miserable.[8] There is as well a more implicit view that they are in many senses inferior, at times subhuman even, that makes it acceptable for them to become servants. In fact, this is the idea underlying the widespread use of the term *empregada* to refer at all times to women employed as maids, as if their lives amounted to no more than their jobs.

The reputed inferiority would appear, for instance, in the common complaint voiced by mistresses that house chores were not done properly. Maids forget to do certain things or else do not understand how to carry out a certain task, in spite of all the explanations they receive. On the whole, these problems are attributed to 'ignorance', explained partly by the little schooling maids have and, most importantly, by a supposedly innate mental incapacity to be 'logical'. Maids would often be 'simpletons' – ignorant, superstitious, naive – hence requiring mistresses' counsel. When they are not seen as such, they are promptly described as 'very clever'.

Together with 'ignorance', maids are often described as having a 'huge' appetite which is better satisfied with food that gives sustenance. They would prefer to eat the 'heavier' (and cheaper) staple meal of rice, beans and manioc flour than to have cheese, yoghurt and seafood (all more expensive items), for instance. This is the rationale for many mistresses who control what and how much their maids eat. Indeed, according to such a common view, the paragon of the good mistress (both in mistresses' and maids' views) becomes the person who allows her maid to eat anything she wants, and does not, therefore, 'create difference' between them.

These differences are expressed both in mistresses' and maids' accounts. Maids are very much aware of the opinions held by their mistresses. They stress the frequency with which they are taken to be 'demented' or 'mentally retarded'. Similarly, when an employer controls what they eat, they feel treated as if they were not a person but rather a dog. Their reaction is to invert the accusations and ridicule their mistresses. They often characterize mistresses who are overconcerned with tidiness and cleanliness as 'neurotic' and 'sick'. Mistresses can also be 'demoralized' when they shout at their maids or fire them and later regret their behaviour. 'Ignorance' is also attributed to mistresses who, despite their years of schooling and degrees, lose all 'good manners' when dealing with their maids, not treating them as human beings. Finally, mistresses are frequently said to behave as 'madams', superior because of their social and economic conditions; but the term is always employed by maids to ridicule them. Maids point out that, although these women may feel superior to others, they can in fact be very insecure. These kinds of mistresses may even feel threatened by their maids, fearing that the maids might be sexually attractive to their husbands.[9]

All these attributes which characterize maids and mistresses as different kinds of women become essentialized, or actually embodied, through the notion of colour. Colour includes more than just phenotypical characteristics of the person, such as skin colour, type of hair and facial features (particularly nose and lips). It refers, most importantly, to the relationship between the speaker and the person addressed.[10] Thus, mistresses often stress that among the requirements of a good maid is 'good appearance'. By appearance, they mean explicitly a well-groomed woman (from neat hair and clean clothes to clean nails and good teeth) and implicitly a non-black one. This is not a strict rule, since the majority of women who work as maids are non-white. Statistical reasons aside, mistresses find compensations for having black maids by saying that they are 'black but very clean', 'black but very pretty', 'black but very clever'. Cleanliness here refers not only to care of the body but also to moral correctness that includes sexual behaviour, trustworthiness (e.g. not stealing anything from employers) and religious beliefs as well.[11] Thus, the blackness of maids synthesizes many of those characteristics typically attributed to maids, particularly an 'ignorance' that would be perceived as innate and requiring improvement through behaviour.

Maids, on the other hand, subvert this dominant discourse on colour by depreciating the attributes associated with whiteness. When they talk about mistresses they dislike, they point out that they are 'white and ugly', 'white and thin', 'white and mean'. Whiteness here becomes linked to an ugliness and thinness that is both physical and moral, alluding to the disrespect and exploitation with which mistresses often treat their maids. However, unlike mistresses' constant references to the colour of their maids, maids only singled out the whiteness of mistresses they had problems with. In other words, whereas the former always remarked on a feature that they saw as essentially distinguishing themselves from maids, the latter did not emphasize such embodied differences in unproblematic relations with mistresses. They remained different in their social and economic 'conditions', conditions which, unlike essentialized ones, could be changed.

Thus, on the one hand, there were constant negotiations and accusations between maids and mistresses which stressed their differences, revealing an ongoing process of reaffirming the social distinctions between them. Following Bourdieu (1984), differences in the conditions of existence of maids and mistresses became embodied in particular *habitus* as well as reflected in specific tastes, which further operated to classify the various life styles. These distinction markers seemed particularly brought into play at a time when the great social cleavages that were once so readily naturalized in slavery became, in the last twenty years, the focus of major campaigns for equal rights to citizenship. Indeed, with all the recent changes in the labour legislation concerning domestic servants, the differences that separated maids and mistresses were no longer to be taken for granted.

On the other hand, however, there was a shared value placed on friendship for both maids and mistresses. Friendship for them meant the affection, care and consideration given to each other. For maids, consideration involved material aid (e.g. paying for medicine and children's schooling, helping to build one's house) as well as conversation in times of crisis. For mistresses, consideration invoked loyalty and trustworthiness, since maids worked in their homes and looked after their children, sharing their intimate lives. Being trustworthy meant not only that maids did not steal (one of the greatest preoccupations for mistresses) but that they respected, and did not gossip about, the family lives of their employers, therefore keeping to their place in the household. Both maids and mistresses recognized the peculiar quality of this friendship, often only idealized, and distinguished it from the relations with friends of a similar socio-economic situation.

These constant references to friendship, present in other studies on maids and mistresses in Brazil, have been interpreted as a reminiscent trace of an earlier, more paternalist pattern of relationship between mistresses and maids. Others, such as da Matta (1991) and Hollanda (1982), have discussed the Brazilian cultural tendency, whether in the past or in the present, to personalize work relations and the public sphere in general.[12] This impetus to personalize would compensate for and complement an extremely hierarchical social structure. If employers are opposed to servants on one level, they may be brought together on another level, that of moral correctness, for example. Thus, there is a complex articulation of contexts and relations which separate and, hence, accentuate hierarchical differences with those which promote integration and mixture.

The perception of a strongly hierarchical society produces in various groups – such as middle-class segments in Rio de Janeiro,[13] including the employers studied here – more or less two major narratives on friendship that deal distinctively with social differences. The first one permeates all spheres and speaks of what has been considered a basic trait of the Brazilian national character (Hollanda 1982): the ability to establish relationships and mingle with people of different ages, classes, races and religions. This is the idea which underlies the propagated, but now much questioned, discourse on national identity that takes Brazilian society to be a 'racial democracy', with people of different colours living in harmony. In this broad, all inclusive narrative, there has to be something greater than the social differences that can unite people: their common humanity (see also Pacheco 1986). Therefore, the sentiment of *amizade* (friendship) can exist in a variety of relationships between people who are equal or different in their social positions.

The second narrative, however, creates another level of relationship. Here, the values on trust and intimacy restrict friends to a very small, family-like circle that tends to be socially homogeneous but is not necessarily so. This exclusive narrative implies, moreover, that outside this narrow social circle people are not to be trusted because they may be competitive and disloyal. Equals may try to harm one another in order to get ahead, and social superiors can treat their inferiors as mere servants to their wishes, and not persons with rights. The sentiment of *amizade* is not enough for it is not a proof that in times of crisis people will support each other. Here, it is necessary that people show they are *amigos mesmo* (real friends).

Maids and employers combined in their views both narratives on friendship. In a broad sense, they wished that friendship could weigh more than their social differences. They also sought to build trust in a potentially conflictive relationship. For mistresses, friendship would ensure them that the maid, who is a stranger because of the different world (not only in the socio-cultural sense but often, as I have shown, in biological terms as well) she comes from, will not be menacing but reliable, loyal and trustworthy. For maids, friendship would mean that they would not be abused and mistreated like animals, because of their being poor and hence, a domestic servant. In both cases, friendship invoked what could bring them together, despite their different social positions: a common gender identity and, above all, their common condition as human beings.

Counteracting Pressure with Friendship

It's so hard to talk about [the English] without coming with the clichés of the English but I've actually been thinking about it lately, because of the people I'm working with. They are all English except for one girl who is half Indian, but she's very much English, her way of being and everything. I find it really frustrating sometimes, because I go towards them and they are all quite new to me, some of them more than others, and I go towards them and try to make conversation and get a friendship together or something . . . and you get such a minimal response sometimes and you think 'Argh!', putting all this effort. Am I actually putting any effort or maybe they don't regard it as an effort? It's funny because slowly it comes out. I think it's a kind of reservedness. I don't know if I can describe it better than that . . . sometimes people have said to me that they were frightened of me before they got to know me, and I don't understand why, if they were frightened of being criticized, that's some part of me that I don't really understand 'cause I feel so unconfident myself . . . Maybe I'm a bit pushy – what they consider pushy – and they hold back a bit and get a bit skeptical until they get to know me and have a few jokes with them, a few situations where things loosen up . . . Of course, it's not everybody but it is something that does come out . . . kind of you have to keep your pose, you don't want people to break in too quickly and find out too much about you. Depends if you're in a work situation. Work makes it harder to get through to people, because they're wary.

At the time of this interview, Anne had been in her job as an assistant manager in a voluntary sector organization for a couple of months. Being herself 'half-French' and talking to a Brazilian woman, she made us stand apart from 'the English' as reserved people, particularly 'wary' at the workplace. Anne was not an extrovert but she tried for months to establish some friendship relations at her job, until six months later she told me she had given up. Still, at a picnic she had on her birthday, she invited Martin, her manager with whom she had a conflictive relationship. Although very friendly towards one another at that time, they had a few months later a serious argument at work that threatened Anne's position.

Anne was perhaps one of the few English people I studied who constantly brought up the subject of friendships at the workplace. Whereas she wavered back and forth in attempting to come closer to her colleagues, most of the others had few friendships from work. These relationships were not considered close friendships, for they lacked the intimacy and personal disclosure which characterized the latter. They tended to be short-lived as well, given the frequent job changes in people's work careers. Indeed, some preferred not to categorize these relationships as friendship at all.

When I first met these people in 1991, they were in the process of establishing a work career. In their mid and late twenties, they were trying different jobs or studying for a post-graduate degree before launching their career. Those employed on a full-time basis held jobs in the service sector: as managers of voluntary sector organizations or small public sector agencies, as administrative secretaries, and as social workers. There were also artists and musicians who complemented their living with a variety of part-time jobs (e.g. teaching English to foreign students, looking after children in nurseries). Those who were studying for post-graduate degrees, all in the social sciences and humanities, supported themselves with grants and periodic jobs.

With no spouse or child to support, many people went through short periods of unemployment until they found a job which satisfied them. In the context of a growing economic recession and debates about government cuts on unemployment benefits, leaving a job because of personal likes and dislikes seemed to reaffirm the modern individualistic belief in the autonomy of the person from his/her social 'constraints'. And yet, this behaviour fitted into a wider and recent tendency in the British labour market (Savage *et al.*1988). Career progress in middle-class occupations – the growing service sector – was no longer achieved within one company but mostly by holding a succession of jobs, each one for a couple of years, often in different cities of the country. This pattern characterized a specific part of the service sector – the managerial class – closely associated with middle-class people and distinct from the clerical positions, increasingly occupied by people ascending from the working-class since the post war years (Abercrombie *et al.* 1988).[14]

Despite the variety of job situations at the time, everyone had experience, whether previous or actual, of working in a spatial setting with a formalized role structure. Thus, in one sense, work became strongly, and negatively, associated with the formality and hierarchy of workplaces. At the workplace, people were expected to behave efficiently, politely and with self-control, fulfilling their specific role. This expected pattern of behaviour conflicted with the value placed on 'being oneself' – being spontaneous, emotional, uncontrolled, another reflection of the underlying view on the autonomous person. The belief in autonomy was further questioned by the obligatory aspect of work – people needed their salaries to live. As I have pointed out, some more or less defied this injunction by going through short periods of unemployment. Moreover, despite their dependency on wages (or unemployment benefits), they were eager to stress that they cared little for money. Indeed, most people earned relatively low salaries (around £500 per month in 1991) and explicitly devalued the money element in their sociable activities with friends.

But work had another significant, and this time positive, meaning which was related to personal fulfillment. Everyone thought of their work careers as an important element in personal growth and satisfaction. University education was seen as a significant step towards finding out what one wanted as a career and most people had obtained an undergraduate degree. Their choices revolved around following a vocation, usually in the arts, or personal beliefs, such as contributing to the welfare of people in general and to the underprivileged in particular. This was the rationale for those who left unsatisfactory jobs in order to provide them-selves with skills as aromatherapists or masseuses, often being unemployed in the process.

The ambivalence towards work was reflected in people's relations to colleagues at work. Like Anne, most people tried to establish some sort of friendship with those they worked with. Drinking at the pub after work hours was thus very much valued because the consumption of alcohol was seen as producing greater spon-taneity, allowing people to reveal themselves outside of their specific roles at work. 'Having a laugh' at the pub added further to the contrast with the serious and controlled ethos of the workplace. More importantly, through the practice of buying rounds of drinks for others in the pub,[15] people devalued the extreme concern with balanced reciprocity, more akin to the work ethos, and favoured a generalized type of reciprocity (Sahlins 1972) which was typical of friendship relations. Inviting people from work to have dinner at home or to come to a picnic party, as Anne did with her manager Martin, was also common and represented another step in the process of establishing friendship relations at work.

However, if there were actual and frequent attempts to become friends with some people from work, on the discursive level, getting close to colleagues was seen as involving 'a lot of effort'. In Anne's view, it was very difficult to form friendships at work because people were 'wary' and tried to 'keep their pose'. People were concerned about being criticized by a colleague or a superior, because, at work, self-control should prevail and anything of the contrary could affect one's productivity. Here, self-control was significant not only because of the need to be efficient but also because of the hierarchical structure of workplaces. 'Keeping pose' thus meant a certain 'wariness' about colleagues' intentions in a context where competition and surveillance were always, even if in different degrees, present.

If appropriate at work, in friendship relations self-control was not an asset. Indeed, it was the very opposite which people strove to attain with friends: 'being themselves'. 'Being oneself' with friends involved communicating in an honest and sincere manner and being spontaneous above all. It referred to the revelation of all state of minds – from excitement to depression – as well as of information considered personal. It involved as well bodily intimacy – touching, talking about bodies and performing bodily functions in the presence of friends. 'Being oneself' with friends required time to establish trust in the mutual acceptance of personal disclosure.

However, this definition of friendship was often seen as an ideal set high which was hard to attain. This unreserved exposure, which revealed the 'true' side of the self as opposed to the more 'polite' sides, could potentially clash with people's much valued personal space – both in the physical and emotional sense.[16] Despite the strong belief that friends should support each other at all times, there was always the concern that, in being 'true' to oneself, people could 'impose' unwanted feelings on to others (and vice versa, of course). Thus, being polite was both wanted and unwanted because of its controlled behaviour, which respected other people's personal space. By the same token, being oneself was both desired and feared because of its uncontrolled behaviour that could lack consideration for other people.

Politeness and the correlated preoccupation with the preservation of personal space were regarded as values associated with the middle class. Working-class people were represented as being more honest and spontaneous than middle-class people. They were also less able to manage face-work in contexts such as cocktail parties which required, in the middle-class view, the art of politeness. Similarly, working-class people were thought to have less confidence in themselves, a quality which was part of the middle-class upbringing, in Celia's view:

> I think that middle class people have been brought up to think that they can have anything they want, if they wanted anything, they would have the means either through education or through contacts or whatever that would enable them to get it . . . You have a right to do anything in the world, you have a freedom of choice, whereas, I think, working class people are not brought up to have the same expectations, they are not told 'you can do any job you want, you can live in any country of the world'.

Celia, an artist, came from a middle-class family and, at the time of fieldwork, had a difficult relationship with her boyfriend, who had a working-class background but interacted mostly in middle-class circles. A very outspoken woman, she held ambivalent ideas about the importance of managing the art of politeness and appearing confident. To her, her boyfriend 'lacked the skills' to be polite and confident in parties, for instance, whereas she had the choice of acting so or not. At the same time, however, middle-class people found it difficult to sustain such confidence or to present themselves as confident people in all situations. Celia and Anne were just a few who talked about their 'confidence problem'. In the end, confidence often became an injunction to conceal insecurities and fears which could characterize the 'true' self.

The ambivalence towards politeness and confidence was thus reflected in the ambiguous feelings people had towards values associated with the middle and working classes. After the postwar changes in the general standard of life of the British working class, the material distinctions which separated them from the middle class decreased in importance, leaving it to far more subtle criteria such as taste, 'socializing skills', and the ideas about personal space that politeness entailed. Most of the people studied, who came from middle-class families, were very critical about what they saw as the overwhelming influence of class background on people's behaviour.[17] On the other hand, they were all concerned with the preservation of personal space, hence with politeness, a particular class value and a form of distinction from working-class people. Likewise, the few who came from working-class families disliked many of these middle-class values but now interacted mostly in middle-class circles. However, most of their closest friends had a similar class background and life-history as people who had distanced themselves from the class situation of their families.

Indeed, despite their belief in individual freedom of choice, the impact of class background in people's lives was much stronger than they would like to admit. The concern with personal space, acquired through upbringing,[18] was a fundamental value which guided all behaviour, including that among close friends. It was crucial that friends shared a similar notion of personal space, particularly important in the process of creating personal disclosure. In turn, this entailed that friends had a similar upbringing. In fact, in spite of the diversity of people in London, all close friends had a common class background, often coming from the same home town and with friendships dating back to school years.

In this light, establishing friendship ties at the workplace became difficult for reasons other than the ones pointed out by people themselves. The issue of exercising self-control at work was not just a requirement of an ethos that stressed efficiency and productivity. It was also a way of dealing with a diverse environment. This diversity involved a set of functions and roles structured hierarchically, itself a difficulty for people who strongly believed in the basic equality of all individuals. This hierarchy was not only functional but could reflect as well differences in the level of education and class background of employees. In this sense, being reserved was also a measure towards the preservation of personal space, and therefore of particular standards of social distinction, in a context where people might be located in different social positions, having as well distinct notions of what personal meant.

Therefore, friendship in the workplace only developed with great effort. Although most people strove to form friendship relations with some of their colleagues, hence the value placed on pub sociability after hours, they all expressed doubts as to its actual outcome. This perception and experience of difficulty was probably heightened in the initial career phase which people were going through. In their school and university years, people were more concerned with being part of a group than with the present distinction among which contexts and with whom they could 'be themselves'.

As two sets of values and expected patterns of behaviour, friendship and work were constructed as pertaining to two distinct arenas of life, one more private and the other more public. The latter referred to social heterogeneity and hierarchy, both of which required controlled presentations of the self. Whether for the sake of productivity or for protecting one's personal space, the 'true' self was concealed in favour of the polite and confident (but not so true) side of the self. Friendship, on the other hand, entailed the very opposite: the spontaneous disclosure of the self which could happen between people who had similar upbringing and, hence, a common understanding of their personal spaces. Friendship was not only defined in opposition to the work ethos. Friends actively sought to counteract, through their sociability practices, behaviour associated with work.

Equality or Affinity?

Narratives on friendship may differ from actual relations between friends, but they express or assert values and ideals which not only guide behaviour but are also under negotiation and dispute (Kondo 1990). More importantly, like discourses, they are deployed in specific contexts, to certain effect (Lutz and Abu-Lughod 1990). Thus, we can return to the relation between friendship and equality, in light of the two ethnographic examples given above, and ask, first of all, if it is a discursive feature mostly or if it is present also in the actual relationship between friends. If a narrative element only, in which social contexts is it emphasized? To what effect?

In the Brazilian study, I dealt with a work relationship first and foremost. Friendship did at times develop between maids and mistresses but was most often an element of their narratives. As such, friendship referred to the affection, care and consideration that both sets of women valued in their work relationship. It always appeared in the discussion of ideal or past relations, thus contrasting with more frequent experiences of dishonesty and mistreatment. The value placed on friendship did not obscure or reverse the perception of each other as very different women. The hierarchical distinctions between them – both the functional difference and the diverse socio-economic situations – were not questioned in themselves, but only when they hampered a mutual recognition of their common humanity.[19] In other words, if friendship referred in any way to equality, it was their equality as women and human beings, who could be different in colour, education, wealth or taste, that was being emphasized.

For the English people studied, such differences created greater difficulties for friendship. Because friendship was basically understood as a relationship in which people could 'be themselves', the process of personal disclosure required common notions of when and with whom to reveal the 'true' self, notions which were in turn acquired through upbringing. Thus, the relative social diversity found in the workplace, together with its hierarchical structure and ethos of self-control, stood in opposition to both discourse and actual relations of friendship. Even when there were attempts to develop friendship relations with some colleagues, it was important to leave behind behaviour associated with work in favour of the sociability and personal disclosure much valued in friendship.

In each situation, friendship as a narrative element achieved different effects. For the Brazilian maids and mistresses studied, friendship was believed to be a mechanism with which to establish trust among different others. Whether it was created in practice, the frequent mention of friendship pointed at a wish to connect people who belonged to distinct and hierarchical social places and whose social differences seemed embodied. For the English men and women analysed here, friendship separated different others by establishing trust among similar people. Although in practice there were attempts to come close to these different others, as in the workplace, friendship was continuously reaffirmed as a relationship of the private domain, where fundamental notions about the person were shared basically among people with a common class background.

On the other hand, both examples reveal that friendship as a relationship stresses affinities, be it of a particular kind – having a similar upbringing – or of a general sort – being human beings. In this sense, friendship contrasts with gender relations, which build on and give form to difference (Strathern 1988). Whether it appears in actual relations or in narratives, friendship is played against that which is seen to differentiate and potentially separate. Indeed, in the two cases analysed here, narratives on friendship elicited more or less explicit views on class differences and the ways in which social distinctions were created or reaffirmed, with a strong tendency in both examples to see them as essentialized and embodied. This emphasis on affinity does not imply that there are no differences between friends but, rather, that stress falls on those aspects which make friends similar. Such value may characterize a whole set of relations with respect to others, clearly separating, for example, friends from workplace colleagues, or throw into relief certain aspects, and not others, of a relationship, for example the affectionate treatment between hierarchical positions.

Thus, rather than referring to equality, which is closely linked to a modern 'Western' conception of the person as having identical rights, friendship should be seen as an idiom of affinity and togetherness. Phrased in this manner, we allow for different understandings of affinity and how it may be sought in relationships. It may be possible then to find references to, and experiences of, friendship in various social domains, thus breaking away from its close association in the modern 'West' to the private sphere. Indeed, if one of the pillars of the public-private divide rests on the separation of impersonal and contractual relations from those based on intimacy and trust, the presence of friendship in work relations, such as in the Brazilian example analysed here (see also da Matta 1991; Hollanda 1982), questions this particular conception of 'public' and 'private'.

If friendship is taken as an idiom of affinity, we can make room for other conceptions of the person different from the notion of the individual as an autonomous agent, equal by nature. It becomes possible, for example, to see how friendship promotes affinity in social groups strongly marked by hierarchy. In such groups, people are seen as naturally differentiated, occupying distinct spaces in the social world. Friendship between them does not demonstrate the autonomy of the person in the face of social barriers. On the contrary, these distinguishing social conditions are constantly reaffirmed. What friendship invokes, whether in actual relations or through discourse, is the affinity that brings these people together as parts of the same social world. It may not achieve its ideal but it demonstrates the value placed on being related.

Notes

1 See Kondo (1990) for a brilliant discussion against the division of personal experience from theory.

2 One of the attempts to solve this paradox has been the attribution of such social

differences to innate (e.g. racial) distinctions among individuals, which nevertheless does not detract from their common humanity (Dumont 1980; Stolcke
1991).

3 This research was carried out with two assistants, Denise Namburetto and Paulo
Martinho, between 1994 and 1996 and was supported the Brazilian funding
agency CNPq.

4 See, for instance, Motta (1986), Oliveira (1995) and Saffioti (1978).

5 Long after slavery was abolished, domestic service was still largely unregulated
by the state and so cheap that employers often paid their servants in kind –
with food, shelter and clothes. It was only in the 1980s that domestic servants
gained the right to form unions as well as to receive at least the minimum
wage, with paid vacation and a contribution towards retirement. In the last
few years, these rights have increased so that domestic service is no longer as
cheap and informal as it used to be.

6 Together with greater official regulation, domestic service has been changing
in character. Nowadays, the live-in servant is increasingly substituted by a daily
maid, who no longer sleeps at work but divides her working days among
different employers. Domestic servants explain this change by reference to
the fact that they now prefer, and can afford, to have their own homes to go
back to at the end of the day. Employers, on the other hand, say that live-in
maids are now more expensive and, furthermore, that with the greater availability of microwave ovens, dishwashing machines and frozen foods, they really
need only a weekly help with house cleaning. Some also add their wish to
maintain their privacy by not having a stranger living in their homes.

7 The term in its diminutive form, *empregadinha(o)*, is often a negative reference
people allude to when they want to affirm that they cannot be told to do things
which are not demanded by their jobs or by a specific relationship.

8 Since the decline in the sugar cane economy in the 1950s, together with the
greater mechanization of agriculture in the north-east of Brazil, peasants and
rural workers have been migrating to the southern cities of São Paulo and Rio
de Janeiro in search of jobs. Because of the greater poverty of the north-eastern
rural economy, as well as of drought problems that periodically afflict the area,
these migrants are seen as miserable and ignorant people, a representation that
is offensive to many of them.

9 Gilberto Freyre (1977) has, through his classic discussion of the frequent sexual
relations between white masters and their black female slaves, glorified not
only racial miscegenation but the sensual figure of the *mulata* (the racially
mixed woman).

10 This pragmatic use of colour attributes, which is far more common than an
essentialized reference to race as one's ancestral origins (regardless of
appearance), has posed huge problems to black movements in Brazil. It has

often been characterized as a form of alienating racial discrimination. People who have close relationships avoid characterizing each other by the dichotomous terms black and white, preferring one of the over one hundred terms in the colour gradient for a mixed person. *Preto* (black) carries the most depreciatory sense and is employed to mark social distance. *Branco* (white), on the other hand, becomes the valued end of the colour gradient, so that people often strive to classify themselves in lighter tones. These colour categories are used variously in different situations and, as in the case of maids and mistresses, with distinct meanings as well.

11 In the last twenty years, many middle class people began to seek these Afro-Brazilian cults, which in the earlier decades of the century were the object of persecution by the police. Still, they retain something of an image of superstition and evil doing. A more recent religious phenomenom is the rapid growth of evangelical movements, which are also more popular among the lower classes. Pentecostalist religions are more respected by mistresses but at times evangelical maids are qualified as extremists.

12 Indeed, among unionized maids, highly conscious of the rights they are entitled to by law, the ideal mistress is the one who is both a law-abiding employer and a friend (Oliveira 1995).

13 I am currently doing fieldwork with a group of middle-class people in Rio de Janeiro on the subject of friendship and social hierarchy.

14 Abercrombie et al (1988) refer to this change in the occupational structure as the growth of the middle class, which means here white collar and managerial occupations.

15 The physical layout of the pub – a main counter with few tables and stools around it, plus the fact that no waiters serve the tables – influences but does not determine this particular form of buying drinks. Whenever my Brazilian friends were at the pub, each one paid for their own drinks.

16 This is the idea of a 'wild within' which Corbey (1991) sees in Freud's theories. The stereotypical wild other – impulsive and lacking in self-control – became internalized in Freud's theories and demanded steering and regulating.

17 The much used expression 'class background' itself points at a representation of class which favours one's background – understood both as parents' economic situation and the upbringing they gave their children – instead of one's present situation. Indeed, despite strong beliefs in the autonomous person, there were doubts about the actual social mobility of people with working-class backgrounds into the middle class.

18 As Finch (1989) and my own study (1993) show, the concern with personal space is particularly acute in the relations of parents with their grown children. Even in the case of elderly parents who might need more support from their children, much care is taken not to 'impose' on them.

19 Most of the women who worked as maids would have one themselves if they became 'rich'. But they all stressed that they would treat them as equal, as part of the family.

References

Abercrombie, Nicholas, Warde, Alan, Soothill, Keith, Urry, John and Walby, Sylvia (1988), *Contemporary British Society,* Cambridge: Polity Press.

Allan, Graham (1989), *Friendship: Developing a Sociological Perspective,* Boulder and San Francisco: Westview Press.

Bourdieu, Pierre (1984), *Distinction: a Social Critique of the Judgement of Taste,* London: Routledge and Kegan Paul.

Corbey, Raymond (1991), 'Freud's Phylogenetic Narrative', in Raymond Corbey and Joep Leersen (eds), *Alterity, Identity, Image: Selves and Others in Society and Scholarship,* Amsterdam: Rodopi.

da Matta, Roberto (1991), *Carnivals, Rogues and Heroes: An Interpretation of the Brazilian Dilemma,* Notre Dame: University of Notre Dame.

Dumont, Louis (1980), *Homo Hierarchicus*, Chicago: Chicago University Press.

Finch, Janet (1989), *Family Obligations and Social Change,* Cambridge: Polity Press.

Freyre, Gilberto (1977), *Casa Grande & Senzala*, Rio de Janeiro: Nova Aguilar.

Hollanda, Sérgio Buarque de (1982), *Raízes do Brasil*, 15th edition, Rio de Janeiro: Livraria José Olympio Editora.

Kondo, Dorinne (1990), *Crafting Selves: Power, Gender and Discourses of Identity in a Japanese Workplace*, Chicago: Chicago University Press.

Lutz, Catherine and Abu-Lughod, Lila, (1990), 'Introduction: emotion, discourse, and the politics of everyday life', in Lutz and Abu-Lughod (eds), *Language and the Politics of Emotion,* Cambridge: Cambridge University Press.

Motta, Alda Britto da (1986), 'A Relação Impossível', in *Seminários Relações de Trabalho e Relações de Poder* (annals) Fortaleza: UFCE/Mestrado de Sociologia.

Oliveira, Edir Figueiredo de Oliveira (1995), *Elas Vieram para Ficar: um estudo de caso do sindicato dos trabalhadores domésticos do município do Rio de Janeiro,* master's dissertation, PPGS/IFCS/ Universidade Federal do Rio de Janeiro.

Pacheco, Moema de Poli Teixeira (1986), *Família e Identidade Racial: os limites da cor nas relações e representações de um grupo de baixa renda*, master's dissertation, Rio de Janeiro: Programa de Pós-Graduação em Antropologia Social/Museu Nacional/UFRJ.

Paine, Robert (1974), 'An Exploratory Analysis of "Middle-Class" Culture', in Elliott Leyton (ed.), *The Compact: Selected Dimensions of Friendship,* Newfoundland: Memorial University of Newfoundland.

Rezende, Claudia Barcellos (1993), *Friendship among Some Young English Men and Women Residents in London, 1991–1992*, doctoral-disseration, London: University of London.

Saffioti, Heleieth I.B. (1978), *Emprego Doméstico e Capitalismo,* Petrópolis: Vozes.

Sahlins, Marshall (1972), *Stone Age Economics,* London and New York: Routledge.

Savage, Mike, Dickens, Peter and Fielding, Tony (1988), 'Some Social and Political Implications of the Contemporary Fragmentation of the "Service Class" in Britain', *International Journal of Urban and Regional Research, 12*(3):455–76.

Silver, Allan (1989), 'Friendship and Trust as Moral Ideals: an Historical Approach', *Archives Européenes de Sociologie, XXX* (2):274–97.

Stolcke, Verena (1991), 'Sexo está para Gênero assim como Raça para Etnicidade?', *Estudos Afro-Asiáticos,* 20:101–19.

Strathern, Marilyn (1988), *The Gender of the Gift: Problems with Women and Problems with Society in Melanesia,* Berkeley and Los Angeles: University of California Press.

—— (1992), 'Parts and Wholes: Refiguring Relationships in a Post-plural World', in Adam Kuper (ed.), *Conceptualizing Society,* London and New York: Routledge.

Suttles, Gerald D. (1970), 'Friendship as a Social Institution', in George McCall, *et al* (eds), *Social Relationships*, Chicago: Aldine Publishing Company.

—6—

The 'Bones' of Friendship:
Playing Dominoes with Arthur of an
Evening in the Eagle Pub
Nigel Rapport

Arthur [*standing at the bar, finds Robbie sauntering up for a refill*]: Now, here's my mate! Game of bones, Robbie? Fancy a draw-in? June and I, and Doris, were thinking of having a draw.

Robbie: Aye, Arthur. Don't mind if I do, don't mind if I do.

Arthur: The 'bones' please, Maggie! [*Maggie hands Arthur one of the boxes of dominoes kept behind the bar*]. Nigel, Sid? What about you? Up for a game? [*Arthur turns around to face Sid and me, leaning on the bar on the other side of him. He raises his eyebrows quizzically, to which Sid nods and I grin, before walking with Robbie over to the dominoes table in the corner. June is already seated there, chatting to Doris, and Walter is perched on the end wall-seat*].

Walter: God, I'm in the dominoes' place! [*Walter looks about him in pretended shock as Arthur, Robbie, Sid and Nigel descend on him, and he realizes that June and Doris are obviously seated there by prior assignation.*]

Sid: Aye! So why don't you bugger off out of it, Walter Brownlea? This is the domino table, not the darts table. Go and sit somewhere else!

June: Draw-in if you like, Walter?

Arthur: Aye! Do you want to draw-in, Walter? You'll have to get a partner, mind, cos there are about six of us already.

Charles [*walking over from the back room*]: Can I draw-in for a game? Oh, looks like there's enough of you already. Never mind: carry on without me. I had a game of darts lined up anyway.

Arthur: Why don't you draw-in with Walter, Charles, and that makes eight?

Walter: No. Thanks, but I think I'll go over to darts . . . You've some courage, Nigel, playing dominoes with these sharks! I admire you [*he grins*].

Sid: Yeah: 'Bite y'legs off'! Nay, be off with you, Brownlea!

Doris: Sorry, I'm facing the wrong way now we're starting. I like to watch everything that's happening. Like who's chatting to who; who's twined! [*Doris laughs and pushes her way round the table.*]

I am grateful to Sandra Bell and Simon Coleman for their careful commentary on this piece.

The 'domino table' (informally designated thus, but known by all the regulars) is a large rectangular table with a slight lip, situated adjacent to the main door in the Eagle pub. On the benches and wall-seat circling it, ten people can be accommodated with ease, and the table commands a fine view of most of the rest of the pub. More often than not of an evening, Arthur and June, old friends of late middle age, can be found seated at the table chatting, whether before, during or after a game of dominoes, both by themselves and with others who have played with them or watched their game.[1]

Playing dominoes in the English village of Wanet represents a way for Arthur and June and others to be in the pub for an evening with a schedule, as it were, which punctuates whatever else (chatting, drinking) they may be doing, while also giving them a home base in the place as the evening passes and they move in and out of interaction with others. Dominoes, indeed, provides something of a foundation for sociality of a particular sort: for relations of amity and intimacy between those who are not affines or kin, neighbours or even local acquaintances.[2] Playing dominoes may be seen to give on to relations of friendship which negate and transcend the latter certain categories. Just as Burridge (1957:188) describes Tangu friendship as that which ranges far outside the boundaries of 'home' (among those of different languages and social organization), so domino-partners range beyond the workaday world amid a friendship which refuses categorization (cf. Rezende, in this volume, pp.79–97).

Thus it was that dominoes provided me with a route into relations in the Eagle, and in Wanet village more broadly, when I first arrived in the place as a stranger. Moreover, being socialized onto the domino table afforded me a broad perspective on the routine beyond:

Alf: You gotta play more for your partner, Nigel. Help him, be less self-centred in the dominoes you play. Like always get rid of double six, or five, or four at the start, play them bare, even if you haven't got more in that set. Cos that's what your partner will be expecting. That's how dominoes is played in Wanet.

Or again:

Arthur: I'll play doms with anyone – won't I June? – and let anyone join in the draw. Not like some people who'll just play with old friends and refuse to play with anyone new. No: I'll play with anyone – except on Sunday nights when a friend of mine comes down from Leyton, and it's widely known that on that night we play together on the little table over there! . . . I don't know why we do it, but we always have done, and now it's just for old times' sake. It's tradition, eh June? Yes: tradition.

Particularly resonant, perhaps, is Simmel's commentary on the ambiguous 'degrees of invasion and reserve . . . of reciprocal revelation and concealment' by which friendly relations are often characterized (1950:236).[3] For, facing Arthur, say, across the domino table, I seemed to be building a friendship as I sought to extend the line of dominoes between us, uncertain of his intentions as to his hand, needing his calculated input for the relationship to develop. Moreover, as complex patterns of dominoes were built up only to be broken at game's end, so there was a sense in which the intimacy between us was contingent upon its physical expression and was sundered (certainly in degree) once 'the bones' had been returned to their box and the table vacated.

Needless to say, the ambiguous foundation of sociality that dominoes provides (the foundation of ambiguous sociality), is so taken for granted by regular players and spectators in Wanet as to go largely unspoken. More normally, dominoes is an unremarked activity which accompanies talk of other matters. What I intend in this chapter, however, is to disinter that foundation, to make plain the language of dominoes, to describe the world of friendship it gives on to – bounded, small-scale, tranquil, unpredictable, well-mannered, cordial – as well as the perspective on the worlds around it which it secures – the opportunity to comment on and subtly rewrite what (and who) lies outside. For Arthur and co., the game of dominoes ushers in a milieu, a space, with an ethos of its own, safe from the flux, noise and entropy of other worlds, without direct consequence upon those worlds and yet with a view on them. Moreover, while often unremarked, Arthur and others did not necessarily refrain from giving a commentary on their feelings and thoughts towards the game, towards the transcendent perspective it provided, towards its friendly effects:

> Arthur: I like 'doms', Charles, because you can sit and talk and be sociable at the same time.

Or again:

> Arthur: When was that night we were playing here? with Charles and all? That was a super night! I really enjoyed myself. More than ever . . . Just a quiet night and no one in the pub . . . You know, Nigel, I thought later that was one of the best nights of my life! Really! One of the best nights of my life . . . A quiet evening of dominoes. Just great, right?

A further elaboration of this world of dominoes might be conveniently tied to a continuation of the interaction I have introduced above, in particular between: Arthur (a farmer and part-time builder, married, in his late fifties), June (a part-time cook, married, in her early sixties), Robbie (a farmer, married, in his early forties), Sid (a farm labourer, in his mid thirties, and married), Doris (a farmer, married, in her mid thirties) and Nigel (a part-time farm labourer and student of anthropology, a newcomer to Wanet, in his mid twenties and unmarried).[4] The interaction might also be conveniently divided into the sequential: Starting, During, and Ending the game.

Two caveats are called for, however. The making plain of the language of dominoes – ambiguous and ludic – is my own interpretation. What I identify is a discourse through which I made friends with Arthur and with others in Wanet. But discourses are situational and partial and contradictory, and individuals are too; a discourse may be seen as having no general consequences for the lives of individual talking partners or for their understandings. Arthur and I and others do not always or only or necessarily make friends like this, and some in Wanet never may. But, then, this should not belie the discourse's significance. Here is a shared way of talking together in Wanet by which a certain structure was given to local life, a certain order constructed; one way (among others) in which I learnt routinely to interact so as to engage in local relations. But there is no essential typicality to Wanet (no overarching 'social structure') which I might also identify, and it is of a diversity of such interactional routines or discourses, and their individual interpretations – an aggregation of 'limitless discursive perspectives', as Parkin puts it (1987:66) – of which social life in Wanet may be said to consist.

Starting the Game

With the dominoes spread out flat on the table, face down, and shuffled, Arthur, June, Doris, Robbie, Sid and Nigel each pick up one domino and count its spots. The persons with the two highest totals will form a team for the contest to come, as will the two lowest and the two middle. Arthur and June thus end up in one team, Sid and Robbie another, and Doris and Nigel a third. Because Doris and Nigel scored the least, they sit out the first round of the contest and must wait to meet the winners in the next round. As they slide up the wall seat and out of the way, Sid, Robbie, Arthur and June rearrange themselves so that team mates are not sitting next to each other and play will alternate from one team to another. Having reseated themselves, Sid, Robbie, Arthur and June each pick up six dominoes from the shuffled array which lies face down before them. This is done in a leisurely and polite fashion, since one unseen domino should be seen to be like any other. Having chosen six, they each turn over and examine their selection, while ensuring that no one else can; by placing the dominoes side by side it is possible to pick up all six in a fist, shielding them from the others while making them readily viewable as a set. There is thus a characteristic stance at the table with Sid, Robbie, Arthur and June each studying their own fist, removing or rearranging the dominoes in it with the other hand. There is also a characteristic sound at the table as the wooden dominoes make an appreciable click when they are set down on the wooden table and played. There are also clicks heard when one domino in the right hand or the whole fist of dominoes in the left hand is 'knocked' against the table top to signify that even though it is their turn, a player cannot 'go' because they have not got a domino which matches the numbers they must follow.

Arthur: Robbie and Sid together! I thought it might be: 'The Colonel' and 'The Chief'! [*he chuckles*] Now these two will be hard to shift, June.

Sid: You better believe it, Arthur. I reckon Robbie and me have got the drinks sewn up for the evening!

Arthur: Well, on second thoughts, not that hard to shift, happen! [*he laughs*]

Doris: I thought you said you'd only play dominoes if you were playing with me, June? Then we get parted, and you leave me with young Nigel here!

June: I tried, Doris, I tried!

Arthur: Don't you underestimate Nigel, Doris. He's become quite a player since I started teaching him what's what!

Robbie: Aye. I can just imagine what you been teaching him, Arthur Harvey! Don't you listen to a word he says, Nigel. And anyway, you can't chose your partner, Doris, That's the whole point of the game. It's like Peggy always complaining to me when we're out, that we end up playing dominoes apart and never know what the other's up to from the start of the evening to the end. But you don't wanna come out and play dominoes with your wife, do you?!

Sid: Nay! Be buggered.

Robbie: I mean, you see enough of each other at home, like.

Arthur: I see enough of you after half an hour, Robbie!

Sid: Nay! You can't play dominoes with y'wife, it's bad luck.

June: Aye. That's what they say. And I can't quite see why Peggy would want to neither! For myself, like! [*she laughs*].

Sid: So that's what you think about Robbie and his dominoes, eh June? Well, Robbie and me'll have to see about that, eh? So: whose drop? Us or you? Who drops?

Arthur: Well, they say 'ladies first', don't they? So, we'd have to give it to you and Robbie, by rights [*he laughs*]. Nay, June's total was the highest so it's her to drop.

Robbie: Aye. Here we go then . . .

The arranging of partners is the most significant feature in starting the game. If dominoes ushers in a new frame of interaction – a focus of pub interest, as well as a focus on the rest of the pub and the workaday world and workaday relations beyond it – then the arrangement of partners and opponents is the setting up of determinate relations in this new world. One will hope to reveal oneself as openly as possible to one's partner and close oneself off from one's opponents. As Arthur jokes about 'The Colonel' and 'The Chief', then, he marks the new characters whom Sid and Robbie have become, he demonstrates his prior knowledge of their abilities, and he rallies June to the cause of their own partnership; finally, he frames and signals the ludic nature of the interaction about to ensue.

The ludic frame is also the occasion for Sid's boast and challenge that the drink will keep flowing in his and Robbie's direction. Normally, such overt and ostentatious claiming of superiority would be avoided. Now, Sid congratulates himself and Robbie for finding each other. In the same way, Doris openly bemoans ending up with Nigel and not with June, with whom she had been in friendly conversation before the dominoes draw. This is both a recognition, then, that the draw has drawn a line under previous 'talking relations' (Rapport 1987) of that evening in the pub, and that in ordinary circumstances Doris might have taken this as a sign of disloyalty on June's part. The ludic frame, however, means that she must make a joke of her being 'left out', and that, equally, Nigel must not take umbrage at being regarded as second best.

The distinct frame of interaction which dominoes ushers in is perhaps most clearly flagged in the way that married couples are firmly separated and not allowed to act as domino team mates. Within the domino frame, relations are begun afresh; certainly there is no great continuation of 'external' relations such as the maintenance of a marriage partnership would represent. (Significantly, at the end of the end, when a pot of money is being set up for the winner of the final round, married couples who are on the table together might be expected to pay for one another's contribution: with the domino partnerships about to break up, the relations of the outside world are once again begun to be recognized.) Nor does gender really matter within the dominoes frame. At the start of the game, all enter as individuals, equal and separate, and, to some extent at least, their success in the game will depend on what sort of communicative relationship they set up with their partner – and non-communicative relationship with their opponents.

Finally, the teasing concerning Nigel's apprenticeship to Arthur's domino mastery and concerning Robbie and Sid's effeminacy are again demonstrations of the ludic nature of the interaction – open aspersions at which open umbrage may not be taken – and emphasis on the differentiation between the world of dominoes and that outside. Here, 'ladies first' does not apply; and, here, Nigel, the university man and urban 'sophisticate', is being educated by the 'unlettered' farmer.

During the Game

Play proceeds quite rapidly, with players being aware (from long practice) of the significance of the playing of certain dominoes at certain times for calculating who is likely to be holding what. The best of three games make up a round, and this takes some fifteen or twenty minutes. It is not too long, therefore, before June and Arthur beat Robbie and Sid in the first round, and Doris and Nigel take the latters' place. Doris and Nigel then beat Robbie and Sid, and so go on to play Arthur and June, who return from where they have been leaning on the bar chatting. Meanwhile, a member of the losing team buys the two members of the winning team the prize of a half pint of beer each, placing it on the domino table as a visible trophy. And so the evening proceeds.

Playing Dominoes with Arthur

Arthur: Nigel and Doris win again . . . Why did we ever teach Nigel!

Nigel: It's a rum do.

Robbie: What's that! A 'rum do'? [*he chuckles*] You picking up the local talk, Nigel! . . . Nay, [*laughing*] what a Sadducee and a Pharisee you are Nigel, for sure! A Sadducee and a Pharisee.

Sid: 'Parasite', you mean!

Arthur: 'Stupid boy', Nigel! [*grinning, he mimics a catchphrase from the TV sit-com, 'Dad's Army', suggesting affectionate contempt*]

Dave [*wandering over from the darts board*]: Don't wear Nigel out with dominoes. He's got a hard day again tomorrow on the farm!

Robbie: What? You can't get tired from dominoes; it's mental work.

Dave: Well, I certainly get tired! . . . God! Arthur and June and Robbie and Sid — that's a dominoes super league you're playing with, Nigel! Watch out!

Sid: So you'll have had a hard day today on the farm, Nigel?

Nigel: Not too bad.

Arthur: You know, Nigel isn't asked often enough to draw-in for a game. People forget too often to ask you, Nigel. But you should just come and barge in if you want a game, eh? [*Nigel grins appreciatively and nods.*]

Robbie: I'm winning nothing tonight! 'Knocking'.

June: But last night you were winning everything.

Robbie: Well: that's the way of the bones. We're certainly having no luck tonight against Nigel and Doris, eh Sid? No comment on you, of course, Sid, like. Dominoes aren't like darts when it comes to your partner being at fault, eh? It all depends on the dominoes you pick up.

Arthur: That's what they say, anyhow . . . [*he winks at Nigel*]

Sid: God, you're so slow, Robbie. It's lucky you're not a funeral director! . . . And your tie's knotted, you know: I wonder what else is?

Robbie: Well I bet I'm the only one in the pub who could knot it!

Sid: . . . I could've said something nasty there!

Arthur: Yeah, like how it must be hard to get a knotted prick to screw! [*he laughs at his joke, and the other men join in*]

June: God! You men are so coarse! [*she turns and straightens Robbie's tie*] What would you do without Peggy!

Sid: He'd probably go to work naked.

Doris: 'Pass'. Sorry, I keep saying that! I mean 'Knocking'. I must have been watching too much 'Mastermind' lately!

Sid: I see they're all in tonight [*looking across the bar-room*]. Reggie Whistle's 'secretary', and 'Milk Marketing Board' [*the others laugh at his characterizations*] . . . And Nigel's eyeballs are popping out at all these tourist women about the place. How about 'Doris Day' over there on the bar stool, Nigel. Fancy her?

June [*laughing*]: Don't lead him on, Sid.

Doris [*laughing, with mock embarrassment*]: Isn't he terrible, June!

Sid: And there's the parson's daughter, too. What about her, Nigel? She'd pray over you, for sure!

Robbie: My God! Is that the parson's daughter? Hell, but she's developed since I last saw her! Quite a beauty now. Twenty years ago and I'd have been after her myself [*the others laugh*]. Don't you fancy her, then, Nigel? My godfathers: I would!

Doris: I thought you were married, Nigel! So Wendy said.

Nigel: No. There's just me.

Sid: See: that's the advantage of Wanet. You can come here, like Nigel did, and you can say anything about yourself, and no one knows any better. No one knows about your past; nobody knows you from Adam! I s'pose it would be the same me being in Manchester . . .

Maggie [*coming over from behind the bar with a half-pint of lager*]: Just so you don't fall too far behind in your drinks tonight, Nigel [*she grins*]. This is the one Arthur put in for you from the last round.

Nigel: Cheers! [*he smiles resignedly and places the new half-pint beside the other one he has just started*]

Doris: You're backwatering, Nigel. Get drinking!

Robbie: 'Knocking'.

Charles [*following Maggie over from behind the bar*]: You do need a lot of looking after, don't you, Nigel! [*he chuckles and leans on Nigel's back, looking over his shoulder at his fist of dominoes*]

Sid: Uh, what dominoes are up? What am I meant to be following? Yan-Yan . . .

Doris: Aye! Nigel one'ed it up. Well done, Nigel.

Sid: Aye, he would. One-Yan: 'knocking'. Bugger it.

Robbie: You still not on bitter yet then, Nigel?!

June: Aren't they awful stirrers, Nigel! [*she chuckles*] Never keep their minds on their dominoes for all their talking, eh?

Sid: Joanna's always saying I should go get a job at the chapel cos of my great gob. And if I do, Nigel's gonna come and do the collection plate! Aren't you lad? [*Nigel smiles warily*]

Charles: God, you're ruining a gorgeous hand here, Nigel! [*he still looks over Nigel's shoulder*] You should never have played that double four. Terrible thing, temptation! Eh, Nigel? [*he laughs*]

Sid: You keep to your own game, Smith!

Arthur: Nigel can play as he likes.

June: Aye. And he was quite right to play that there.

Sid: Fuck off back behind the bar where you belong, why don't you, Smith!

Arthur: Remember how the Eagle used to be? When the landlords had to fetch the beer from the cellar all the time . . . [*he chuckles*] That used to keep them busy alright . . .

Robbie: And fit!

Doris: Aye. There was that hatch, there, wasn't there, before there was a bar at all.

Charles: Okay! I get the message! I'm going. Company's better over there anyway! [*the others laugh as he goes, grinning*]

Playing Dominoes with Arthur

Doris: Ooh! Look at Lynn sitting on the stool over there! That's not been known in the history of the world: her leaving her spot at the bar! . . . And look! It's all because Wendy has moved over there to chat to Molly and Mary.

June: You should've heard what Lynn was saying about Wendy before.

Doris: What?! . . . Oh tell me later. Isn't it awful, gossiping like this? [*she laughs, embarrassed*]

Robbie: Nay! All these bad habits you'll be picking up here, Nigel. Gossiping, and darts, and boozing, and practising dominoes . . . It's a rum do alright. [*he grins*]

Nigel: 'Knocking'.

Arthur: You were playing for yourself not your partner there, Doris! You three'ed it up when Nigel had no threes – and you knew it.

Doris [*laughing embarrassedly*]: Oh, sorry, Nigel. I'm hopeless sometimes . . . They've even dropped me from the Eagle doms team, you know, cos I was only ever good at playing with my dad as partner, and I'm not even that now . . . Mind you, I did come back from the dead, 0-2, to win in the knock-out at the Mitre on Sunday.

Nigel: Oh, did the Mitre win Monday's dominoes' match at Leyton?

June: Against New Inn? Second leg of the second round match?

Nigel: Yeah.

June: Yes they did. They got some good young players over the Mitre now, you know. Ben, Dennis, Harry Andrews . . .

Arthur: Remember what a good doms player Harry's dad was, Joe Andrews?

Robbie: Great! And draughts – chequers – too. I've not seen a better player at that than Joe.

Sid: Well, I don't mind telling you, I'm getting a bit distraught at all the dominoes I'm losing recently. I've tried different partners and it's no help; look at Robbie here! A real dead loss! . . . So I'm starting to think it's me!

Arthur: Nay. It's just that so much in dominoes is the luck of the hand. It's like you can't say you're really getting any better or worse, because so much in a game depends on your hand and your partner's, right?

Robbie: Nay, it's you alright, Askrig! your fault we're losing tonight.

Sid: Why don't you fuck-off, Milden. [*Robbie laughs*]

Arthur: Well, you can have too much of doms at a sitting, you know Sid . . .

Sid [*stretching his back*]: Excuse me, Doris! I'm not looking at your dominoes. I'm just trying to straighten my bad back. God! It's bad just now.

Robbie: Is that your excuse then, Askrig? . . . 'Knocking' again.

Doris: And me: 'knocking'.

Sid: Me too. That's it then. And it's not even worth a count. They've obviously won again . . . Beginner's luck, eh Nigel!

Robbie: Nay! It must be that I'm too soft-hearted for this . . . I win a few one night, and then I can't keep on concentrating and winning after that. It's the same in darts: I always end up easing up and making the scores more equal.

Doris: You! Soft-hearted, Robbie? That'll be the day.

Arthur: Soft in the head more like! [*he laughs, and Robbie pushes him away*]

Doris: Anyway, let's have a count. I'm no cheat: I don't want to win if I haven't. Eh Nigel?
Nigel: Right.

As a focus of the pub, and a means to focus on the rest of the pub, playing dominoes on the domino table often eventuates in a distillation in a 'purer' form of a number of characteristics of individuals' lives and interactions in Wanet worlds beyond. For example, talking with a 'Wanet accent' has a special place at the table, a special value. Here, players celebrate their own favourite catchphrases – 'its a rum do', 'what a Sadducee and a Pharisee', 'stupid boy' – and swear-words with more regularity and seeming pleasure than elsewhere; saying them here is more significant and can be expected to be more effective, more appreciated than elsewhere. Likewise, they celebrate the distinctive (Old Norse and Old English) aspects of the dialect of the Wanet area – 'Yan-Yan' – in a way rarely heard elsewhere (where 'One-One' would be the usual phrasing). At the table, people are most themselves, and their village heritage is most itself. Moreover, it is here that usurpation of local accenting by outsiders is most ruthlessly castigated and ridiculed; Nigel is not allowed to get away with mimicking Robbie's 'rum do' without some concerted ribbing.

The distillation of the domino table also means that behaviour here is often meant to be the best; here, norms of propriety are most expected and claimed. Hence the warning and indignation in Doris's voice when she accuses Nigel of 'backwatering', and not keeping in line with the consensual drinking rate; as well as Maggie's efforts in politely carrying over his beer to him from behind the bar. And hence, Doris' (otherwise redundant) statement on never cheating. Meanwhile, Arthur and June are particularly polite in making Nigel feel at home and wanted at the table, pointedly telling him, for example, how to 'read' the local talk aright ('Aren't they awful stirrers'); while Arthur repeatedly pooh-poohs the significance of winning and explains away Sid and Robbie's defeat as bad luck. Robbie himself assures Sid that unlike a darts partner, he does not hold Sid at all responsible for their team's fortunes.

This purity and moral propriety also feeds into the comments players make on seemingly extraneous details in the lives of those playing the game (including themselves) as well as the wider lives of those not playing. When Sid teases Robbie for his slowness, when Robbie agrees boastfully about the size of his sexual organs, when June mentions Peggy's long-suffering care for Robbie, and when Robbie admits to his own soft-heartedness, what is being demonstrated is not only a full and shared knowledge of one another and themselves, and their ease and openness in the conveyance of information between one another, but also the way that their knowledge reaches into the essential core of a person or a relationship. There is no place here for ignorance or for disguise. It is in this sense too that Sid's caricaturing of fellow locals and visitors in the pub –'Whistle's secretary', 'Milk Marketing Board' – can be understood. In the caricatures is the exaggeration of their essential features. Here is the insight which goes behind workaday formalities, and also the license to speak those insights out loud. For this reason too, interrogating Nigel, the recent and relatively unknown newcomer in Wanet, so as to ascertain information which has not been forthcoming off the domino table, is also legitimate. Thus: which women does he fancy?; what sort of a sexual threat does he represent?; and how truthful will he be, allaying local fears and rumours?

The distillation also makes for a rather particular relationship between the world of the domino table (and those partaking of it at a particular time) and the rest of the pub. The boundary is never hard and fast, for domino players are always leaving the table for the bar and the toilet, while those in the rest of the pub will frequently saunter over to chat, and comment on particular players and plays. Nevertheless, domino players are accorded a certain respect for the 'purity' of their pursuit.

Domino players are also accorded respect because they are local pub regulars who have frequented the Eagle (borne witness to its carryings-on) before many of its present drinkers were born – even before the present structure of the building was as it is. When Walter makes a joke, then, about mistakenly sitting 'in the dominoes' place', Sid rebukes him peremptorily ('So why don't you bugger off out of it?'), while Arthur and June extend their *noblesse oblige* and offer him a part in the game. For the same reason, Arthur's sitting down to play with Nigel occasions raised eyebrows from young non-players (such as Walter and Dave) and an aggrieved sense of a diluted interaction from other adult players (such as Doris and Sid).

The boundary of the domino world and the respect it should translate as means that the domino players do not appreciate Dave's reminder that Nigel has more work to do on the farm. In dominoes, talk of the overweening influence of work is out of place, is disrespectful, while to suggest the ludic genre of dominoes might in some way give on to the tiring world of work is inappropriate. For there is something of the domino table which properly partakes of the timeless: a game where fate consistently holds sway, and where (as Arthur is reminds) even such workaday characteristics as maturity and skill which develop over time have no impact. This is why talk on the domino table can bear absolute witness to the changes wrought by time on the world beyond the table. Changes in the structure of the Eagle can be charted, Doris's changing relations with her father can be recorded, and the life cycle of local generations can be celebrated: from parson to parson's daughter, from old game-playing skill in the Andrews family to new. From outside time, the dominoes table temporally fixes and frames the outside world.

Different people may be differently at home with the rarefied world of the domino table, nonetheless. For many of the young, it is a focus of light-hearted teasing and bantering, as we have heard. For some in middle generations (such as Robbie, Sid and Doris), there is the insecurity of not knowing whether they yet properly measure up, and the ambivalence of whether they yet wish to. Hence, Doris's distancing comment that even in the middle of a game she has the TV quiz show 'Mastermind' more on her mind than dominoes's proper wordage; also, admissions by Robbie and Sid that they cannot play well consistently. Even Arthur (perhaps in an attempt to relax the younger (and newer) members of the party he has invited to the table) has occasion to distance himself from the responsibility that participation at the domino table represents: so much in dominoes is luck that it is impossible to judge one's improvement or otherwise over the years.

Ending the Game

When one or more people have to leave, or there is a common feeling that they have played enough, the game will be drawn to a close. Sometimes this is after an hour, sometimes three: at eleven o'clock on a weekday evening, Arthur and June are often the last to leave the pub. Tonight, as 'last orders' is called for the first time at 10.25, and the Eagle begins to thin out, Robbie's wife Peggy comes over and reminds him that they should be getting back to the farm, and Doris says that she must go and extricate Fred from his darts match and get home too. It is agreed, then, that now is probably the time to 'put the dominoes to bed' by having a final game of 'Fives-and-Threes'. The dominoes are therefore placed face down on the table again and shuffled, and Robbie, Nigel, Doris, Arthur, June and Sid each place ten pence on the table to make a prize fund or 'pot'; (June has run out of money and has to go in search of her husband, Tom, to make up her contribution). Each then selects four dominoes and, counting up the spots, calculates which totals divide by five and which divide by three. The player whose totals divide most often wins the game, takes the pot of money – the sixty pence going in this case to Robbie – and then has the job of putting the dominoes 'to bed', back in their wooden case. Robbie and Peggy make their farewells, and Doris stands up to go, while Arthur, June and Nigel seem in less of a hurry and remain seated, sipping their beers.

Doris [*standing by the table*]: That makes us two-time conquerors, Nigel, because you and me also beat Arthur and June last time we played together, a few months back, remember? Even after their twenty years' experience! [*Nigel grins but Arthur and June say nothing*] Right, then. Good night all.

Nigel, Arthur, June: 'night.

Sid: Nay, I'm not a big dominoes player. It must be about a month ago I last played – with old Billy from Howth-le-dale. Remember when he came down here?

June: Billy Wether. Oh God! Noisy old man, wasn't he?

Arthur: Aye! [*laughing*]. He came in first a few months back and he took a pound at dominoes off Alf. And he must've liked it, somehow, cos he was back a few times after that, taking money off folks . . . I reckon it was that last time he was here, when you played him, that he took three pounds off Stewart. Old Billy was too good for him, Stewart said! I told him to watch him closely cos he could be cheating . . . But then we haven't seen Billy since.

Sid: I heard he's been banned from most pubs in Hogart.

Arthur: Well he is so noisy. And I hear he gets well riled when he's had a few. I mean he's alright in small doses. But he shouldn't spoil other folks' enjoyment by being so noisy and that.

June: Five minutes of his company is enough for me!

Sid: Aye! . . . But you like 'the bones', do you Nigel?

Nigel: Yeah, it's great. I feel like I'm getting the hang of it, working out what people might have, and how they play. Most people, anyway. Someone like Stewart I find hard to follow.

Arthur [*laughing*]: Aye lad! Stewart is hard to follow for everyone, cos there's no system to his play; like, he's got no method at all. So you can't make him out.

Sid: I last tried to play dominoes with Stewart when there were these two gorgeous women wandering about the place in white dresses! Some offcomer party or something. And I just couldn't keep on playing after a while, but Stewart couldn't see what the difficulty was [*he laughs*].

Arthur: No, well that's one thing Stewart isn't worried by!

June: Poor thing! . . . Nay, happen it's a blessing! [*she laughs*]

Sid: Least there were quite a few locals in tonight. Some nights it's full of the weirdest types, full of offcomers. Eh, Nigel? . . . So, do you see any IRA terrorists left among this lot, tonight, then Nigel? [*he walks off, leaving Arthur and June and Nigel laughing*].

Arthur: Aye! There goes 'The Chief' to sort things out. Quite a character is 'The Chief', eh Nigel? . . .

Nigel: Uh-huh.

Arthur: So did you win more than you lost tonight, Nigel?

Nigel: Just about, I think. Or I came out about even.

Arthur: I was the opposite . . . Aye, they say dominoes is a strange game. But what I love in it is its unpredictability. [*Nigel nods*] For example, on my four or five days' holiday each year, I like to go horse racing. Last time, on the way home from the races, at Catterick, me and Alf beat Robbie and Fred by a total of 13-2, in two pubs . . . The next night, here in the Eagle, we had a repeat contest and it was the opposite: 14-2 or something to them! And that, for me, is the wonder of the game. [*Nigel grins*] Like me and June are hopeless as partners, eh June? [*She nods*] Though separately, we're both experienced players. But as partners we get beaten by any young lads. Cos it all depends on how the dominoes come up.

Nigel: Not completely, though Arthur. There's still the skill of working out what's likely to have gone or to come. That's why you said Stewart was so difficult to play against.

Arthur: Well, there's no one way of playing, lad, so you can't just tell people how to do it. There's not just one way of giving advice. Like: a good singles hand —

five different suits, say – is not necessarily a good doubles hand – where you and your partner want to complement each other . . . Or, like: my son-in-law, Jonty, and me have long arguments cos he says he'd not drop double six bare, and I say I would: I'd always try to tell my partner what I had before trying to deceive an opponent . . . But anyway, I think I know what you mean. And you're right, lad. There are conventions of the game and you can beat opponents if you diverge from them. Or if you bluff them. And I was playing straight with you tonight, Nigel, cos I could see you were following my leads – proof of my strong suits, like – so I played straight. But there are lots of ways of bluffing . . . Like I remember once, Wilbur Hackett and me thought we'd take on two good players in a pub in Kendal, and, you know, we beat them hollow because we ignored all the conventions and played quite randomly.

Tom [*walking over from the back room and sitting down on the wall seat*]: I don't know! I come out to the Eagle to play dominoes, I wait for a game, and then I find I been left out of the draw. And then the wife comes over to me, finally, to pay up for her Fives-and-Threes and putting the doms to bed! Is that what you call friendly!?

Arthur: It's your own fault, Ryecroft, for wanting to play with your wife! [*they laugh*]

Tom: That's true. Nay, I had a good evening.

Nigel: Well, that's it for me. I'm off home. Thanks a lot for the game.

Arthur: Aye, well. We'll do it again soon, lad. Like I said. Just come over and ask for a draw-in when you want one.

Nigel: Thanks, I will. 'night.

As the game ends, and the world beyond the domino table is set to reassert itself, players negotiate their exits – their returns to workaday identities and relations. They make their parting, ludic comments on the worlds they are returning to, and their already nostalgic comments on a world of dominoes free from outside predictability, consequence and constraint. As Doris leaves the table, then, she reasserts herself as the competitive farmer, pleased to win, and pleased to have shown how the reins of adult responsibility and success have been wrested from the likes of Arthur and June. While, as Sid prepares to leave the table, the character of the rough, gruff 'Chief' returns, the self-appointed gatekeeper and guardian to Wanet, ready to save the dale and the day from all manner of offcomer intrusion and terrorism. Here is already a (liminal) parodying of the ludic capability granted by the domino table to see into the essential core of people and things, to turn around the serious fears of the workaday world and caricature them. Finally, Arthur seems keen to celebrate the luxury which dominoes represents of risk-taking without consequence. If unpredictability is the bane of his daily existence, trying to make a meagre living off a small farm and various piece-work cash-jobs, then the very same unpredictability is something he can celebrate and triumph over in the world of dominoes.

Furthermore, in dominoes Arthur seems to find a perfect foil to the everyday uncertainties of communication between people. Not only is Arthur able to maintain close and steady relations (such as with June) no matter the outcome of the activity in which one would appear to be primarily engaged, but also it is possible to play in such a way that, with learning and practice, one is able to discover (and more or less to convey) what fellow players have hidden in their hands. On the other hand, Arthur is also able to play with the conventions of dominoes strategy so that by bluffing, a fellow player is put off one's trail. In short, Arthur celebrates how in dominoes he gains mastery over both the effects of chance on his present and future life, and the effects of being misunderstood. It is as if dominoes offers a medium through which to overcome the uncertainties of verbal and other communication in the everyday world: there, the possibilities and parameters of exchange are so broad that it is impossible to be sure that one knows what is hidden behind someone else's words and gestures – however often one interacts with them.

At the same time as players negotiate their leaving of the world of dominoes, they also reprise notions concerning the moral milieu and community which it represent. Hence, there might be no one way of playing, Arthur admits, but there is something of a conventional, polite, Wanet way. Coming from another dale, Arthur's son-in-law, Jonty, is not fully apprised of the wisdom of this way (and would not drop double six bare – if it was the only six he possessed). While Tom can expect no sympathy if he seeks to overturn it (and play with June, his wife). It is only Stewart, the local adult who had learning difficulties as a child, whose play cannot be expected to exemplify this local accent. But Stewart's lack of method, system or consistency only serves to point up, in its absence, the conventionalism of the rest of Wanet players. Meanwhile, players from outside, such as Billy from Howth-le-dale, demonstrate the boundaries of community equally strongly in their play: they take money off their fellows without self-restraint, they are rowdy and possibly cheats. Significantly, then, when Arthur is outside the community of Wanet dominoes, such as in a pub in Kendal, he can imagine playing impolitely (randomly, unconventionally) so as to beat a pair of good outsiders. And he is proud to come home to the Eagle and own up to the incident later.

In short, for all, there is something in the domino table and the domino games which routinely take place there – something fixed and dependable, something timeless and transcendant, something pure and moral, something conventional and shared, something ludic and exciting, something liminal and inconsequential, something individual and fateful – with which many in the Eagle pub in Wanet feel at home, which makes them friends.

Conclusion

While not said explicitly, when Arthur referred, humorously and somewhat self-consciously, to dominoes as 'the bones', there was much I could read into his words besides a reference to their original ingredients. Here was, after all, the skeletal basis of relations of friendship, as well as an opportunity to see life to its foundation. For me, certainly, playing 'the bones' with Arthur provided the basis for one of the closest relationships I developed in Wanet – and an affection which I believe was at least in part reciprocated:

> You seem to like Wanet, Nigel, and I've enjoyed your company. Maybe this is a stupid speech and I'm not saying it the right way, but I think you and I share a philosophy of life . . . I think you must live lots of different lives, in some form of 'you': it's like your you continues . . . I might never meet you again, Nigel, but there's still the chance that I will. It's like we talk of infinity: two parallel lines meet at infinity, and the rest; but we don't really understand infinity at all . . . Well, I've bared my soul to you tonight, Nigel. Bared my soul.

Nor is it accidental that Arthur waxed his most lyrical and philosophical after an evening of dominoes; 'a quiet evening of dominoes' in the Eagle really did occasion some of 'the best nights of his life'.

John Berger makes a nice point when he describes the way in which we often find it easiest to express intimacies, to introspect, and to maintain friendly conversation, via proximate objects and actions (1967:93). Transferring intimacies between persons or intimate knowledge of oneself to the outward complexities of a football match, a car engine, a committee meeting, a fashionable outfit, a recipe, a piece of prose – so that intimacies become intricacies – provides a language for friendly and intimate expression; as heads metaphorically touch bending over the car engine, so individual worlds intersect.[5] Arthur could conclude that he and I 'shared a philosophy of life' and 'had the chance to meet again', because of the way we met across the domino table.

Furthermore, the external transference of friendly intimacies to domino intricacies enables the ambiguities of closeness to remain; so that the precise degrees of Simmel's 'revelation and reserve' are never enunciated. And this is the last point I should like to make. If 'friendship' represents 'a universal human phenomenon' (Du Bois 1974:14), 'an authentic field of intercourse in its own right' (Fried 1953:67), then it is one inherently bound up with the expression (enjoyment, employment, effectuation) of relational ambivalences. Much of the anthropological literature on friendship lays stress on a differentiation between friendship relations and others (kinship, class, status and role) on the basis of the (certain) ascription of the latter and the (potential) achievement of the former (cf. Wolf 1966:10).

Friendship is 'remarkable', Paine tells us (1974:124), for the way individuals can express and effect interest, confidentiality and intimacy independently of the cluster of institutional statuses otherwise attached to them; friendship involves a voluntary-preferential dimension, Du Bois concludes (1974:16–18), distinct from corporate relations, which provides a special gratuitousness and spontaneity. And yet, such differentiation from the institutional and the corporate is itself prone to institutionalize: in the literature, friendship comes essentialistically to embody the non- or anti-institutional.[6] What I would emphasize, instead, is the conscious playing with ambiguity, uncertainty and ambivalence which friendship affords, whereby a distinct perspective on the world and its relations (not institutional or anti- or non-) is entered into. Simmel spoke of the poignancy of friendship's mutability and mortality, its contingency and particularity (1950:124); what I would stress is the thrill of its potentiality.

Finally, then, for friendship, playing dominoes in Wanet would appear the perfect foil: a gratuitous act in ludic genre. With no mutual access to one another's hands and no definite knowledge of how each is playing them, with no complete knowledge concerning what permutations of dominoes each regards as orderly, and with no agreement concerning what fit between dominoes in the hand and on the table is to be aimed at, the nature of relations between individual players is indeterminate, to say the least. But if part of the social world that playing dominoes in Wanet gives on to concerns a lack of knowledge, part also concerns the possibility of perfect friendly relations between people to which the skilful deployment of one's 'bones' can give rise.

Notes

1 'Dominoes': a game of chance played with twenty-eight variously numbered counters, the aim being to align number with number, on different counters, and so relieve oneself of one's 'hand' of randomly selected counters before one's opponent(s).

2 Cf. Rapport (forthcoming) for a corresponding analysis of darts-playing.

3 Etymologically, too, there seem to be tantalizing ambiguities surrounding the English word 'friend' and its synonyms (not to mention many other languages [Schwimmer 1974:49; Hastrup 1987:94]). In Old English and contemporary Scots, 'friend' denotes a kinsman or near relative, and derives from the Old Teutonic 'to love'. 'Pal', meanwhile, of Gypsy derivation, might mean a brother or partner as well as a chum or friend. 'Chum' itself, a probable corruption of

'chamber-mate', could mean both a close friend and an associate with whom one shared a room; while 'mate', from Middle Dutch, can be a partner in marriage as well as an habitual companion, an equal, a friend. The American 'buddy', finally, denotes a brother as well as a most constant companion or friend.

4 The interaction is reconstructed from fieldnotes, which themselves took the form of as precise a memorization as possible of the proxemics and verbalizations of individuals in exchange (cf. Rapport 1993:55–82).

5 Berger: 'When friends recall another friend who is dead or absent, they recall how he always maintained that a front-wheel drive was safer; and in their memory this now acquires the value of an intimacy' (1967:93).

6 Hence, friendship is essentialized as: a publicly ratified socializing force, as social as it is emotional (Driberg 1935:101–2); an anti-institutional cross-cutting of kinship groups, an informally structured countervailing force which offers emotional catharsis to strains in closed groups while instrumentally opens up the possibility of new ones (Cohen 1961:375); and an institutionalization of 'mutual ministry' (Mandelbaum 1936:206).

References

Berger, J. (1967), *A Fortunate Man*, London: Penguin.

Burridge, K. (1957), 'Friendship in Tangu', *Oceania,* 27:177–89.

Cohen, Y. (1961), 'Patterns of Friendship', in Y. Cohen (ed.), *Social Structure and Personality*, New York: Holt-Rinehart-Winston.

Driberg, H. (1935), 'The "Best Friend" among the Didanga', *Man*, 35:101–02.

Du Bois, C. (1974), 'The Gratuitous Act: An Introduction to the Comparative Study of Friendship Patterns', in E. Leyton (ed.), *The Compact*, St. John's: ISER.

Fried, M. (1953), *Fabric of Chinese Society*, New York: Praeger.

Hastrup, K. (1987), 'Fieldwork among Friends: Ethnographic Exchange within the Northern Civilization', in A. Jackson (ed.), *Anthropology at Home,* London: Routledge.

Mandelbaum, D. (1936), 'Friendship in North America', *Man*, 36:205–6.

Parkin, D. (1987), 'Comparison as a search for continuity', in L. Holy (ed.), *Comparative Anthropology*, Oxford: Blackwell.

Paine, R. (1974), 'An Exploratory Analysis in 'Middle-Class' Culture', in E. Leyton (ed.), *The Compact*, St. John's: ISER.

Rapport, N.J. (1987), *Talking Violence. An anthropological interpretation of conversation in the city*, St. John's: ISER, Memorial University of Newfoundland.

—— (1993), *Diverse World-Views in an English Village*, Edinburgh: Edinburgh University Press.

—— (forthcoming), 'Problem-solving and Contradiction: Playing Darts and Becoming Human', *Self, Agency and Society*, 3.

Schwimmer, E. (1974), 'Friendship and Kinship: An Attempt to Relate Two Anthropological Concepts', in E. Leyton (ed.), *The Compact*, St. John's: ISER.

Simmel, G. (1950), *The Sociology of Georg Simmel,* Glencoe: Free.

Wolf, E. (1966), 'Kinship, Friendship and Patron-Client Relations in Complex Societies', in M. Banton (ed.), *The Social Anthropology of Complex Societies*, London: Tavistock.

Expressions of Interest: Friendship and *guanxi* in Chinese Societies

Alan Smart

In a comparison of networks[1] Ruan (1993:95) found that in Tianjian (People's Republic of China) on average 6.6 per cent of the people named were described as friends, compared with 67.8 per cent in the United States. Does this mean that friendship is relatively unimportant in China? Or are the differences the result of variations in how personal relationships are perceived and talked about? The same study found that Tianjian respondents described 37.1 per cent of their named relationships as co-workers, 7.1 per cent as subordinates or leaders, and 6.9 per cent as former classmates, compared with 19.9 per cent, nil and nil respectively for the US. Clearly there are differences in social organization that might account for these differences, particularly the all-encompassing nature of the Chinese enterprise (*danwei*) (Walder 1986), and the low rates of mobility. However, it is also likely that US respondents preferentially describe a co-worker as a friend when possible, while the Chinese respondents referred to people they worked with as co-workers, even when the relationship was close and intimate. This chapter explores these differences in ways of talking about connected others, and the implications for cross-cultural understanding of friendship.

One difficulty involved in this topic involves the status of the concept of 'friendship'. Is it an analyst's concept or a member's concept? If it is based on first-order use by members, specifically English-speakers, we must ask how useful it is for grounding a comparative project. If, on the other hand, we wish to develop the concept into something genuinely universal, we will have to be careful about dragging Western prejudices on board without careful scrutiny.

Carrier (in this volume, pp.21–38) argues that certain societies do not have friendship in any strict sense. For him, friendship is a kind of relationship based 'primarily, if not exclusively, on spontaneous and unconstrained sentiment or affection of some sort'. For him, to refer to friendship between co-workers 'is to speak of something construed as different from the relationship defined by their respective locations in the organisation that employs them'. But how do we deal with this if people do not speak about an affective relationship with a co-worker as a friendship but continue to refer to them as co-worker? Kipnis (1997:26) notes that in the North China village he studied 'a friend from within the village was usually categorized as a fellow villager'. Do we exclude such relationships from the anthropology of friendship? Or do we need to develop a concept that can encompass all friendship-like interactions?

Durrenburger and Pálsson (in this volume, pp.59–78) take an approach very different from Carrier. In their analysis of medieval Icelandic sagas, they see friendships being strategically cultivated, even bought, in order to adapt to 'the necessity of surviving in a context of shifting alliances and chaotic political manoeuvres'. In relationships between big man and follower, sometimes secured by political marriages or payments, terms of friendship are used by participants for patron-client relations that don't seem to represent 'spontaneous and unconstrained sentiment'. How can we resolve these two positions, both of which seem convincing in different ways. Do we restrict friendship to situations comparable to Euro-American 'true friendship'? Or do we expand the category to include any relationship between people which is tinged by affection or sentiment (Kiong and Kee 1998:79).

In this article, I concentrate on friendship as an idiom of interaction: a way of talking about relationships, rather than a set of criteria which can define them. In Chinese societies, friendship must be seen in the context of other idioms of interaction.

One difficulty is the low degree of academic attention to friendship in Chinese societies. Fardon (1990) has suggested that each field of regional ethnography has one set of dominant concepts on which discussions tend to centre, to the extent that regions 'become exemplars of type features and problems' (26). In Melanesianist anthropology, this dominant concept is the gift, while in Africanist anthropology it has been lineage. While family and kinship have clearly been dominant focuses for the anthropology of China, the priority of Africanists in this field (Fardon 1990:26) has marginalized studies of lineage and kinship in China. Students of Chinese societies have recently managed to increase the attention paid to it by outsiders as a result of popular and academic interest in how Overseas Chinese and China have managed to produce remarkable rates of economic growth. The concept that has been most successful in integrating the new Chinese regional ethnography is an emic one: *guanxi*, which means relationships of social connections built primarily upon shared identities such as native place, kinship or attending the same school. *Guanxi* is seen as ubiquitous in 'getting things done' in China, and among Overseas Chinese. It has been suggested that *guanxi* capitalism, based on networks rather than vertical integration or arms-length market dealings, represents a new form of organization that offers advantages in a world economy that increasingly emphasizes flexible and rapid response (Thrift and Olds 1996; Smart 1998).

Guanxi occupies some of the same conceptual ground as friendship. As a result, even though ascriptive statuses and relationships are of diminishing importance in contemporary Chinese contexts, there still has been little attention paid to friendship as such. To deal adequately with friendship in Chinese societies, we need to begin with examining the parallels, differences and relationships with the member's concept. Prior to doing so, I review discussions of friendship in Chinese societies. In the following section, I compare the concepts of friendship and *guanxi*. Finally, I explore conflict between instrumental and expressive dimensions of sociability.

Friendship in the Anthropology of China

While there are almost no studies that focus specifically on friendship in China, there is a reasonable amount of relevant information incorporated into historical and ethnographic accounts. Since at least the fifth century B.C., five important relationships by which human life should be ordered have been listed and ranked. In the classic volume *Doctrine of the Mean* is written that: 'There are five universally applicable principles . . . that of the relationship between ruler and minister, that of father and son, of husband and wife, of elder and younger brother, and of friend and friend' (Baker 1979:10). These five human relationships (*wu lun*) were 'arranged in order of priority, and with the exception of the last one were all superior/inferior relationships' (11). Unlike most other kinship terminologies, sibling relationships in Chinese kinship are ranked by age. This has even had an impact on secret societies which emphasize brotherhood among members: hierarchy persists since brothers are not all alike, and sworn brotherhood manages to simultaneously signal equality and hierarchy. Only the relational idioms of friendship remove ranking from the relationship.

That friendship was in practice often more important than in the classic ranking is indicated by Morton Fried's ethnography *Fabric of Chinese Society* (1969), which was unusual for the time in its close attention to non-kin relationships. Friendship, defined as 'a relationship between two or more persons based on mutual affectation and sympathy and devoid of the object of exploitation', Fried (1969:226) found 'clearly exists on all levels of Chu'uhsien society'. He noted, for example, the tendency for the mother to act as a 'prime mover in organizing' her son's marriage had been reduced and her place taken by 'friends who are not related by blood' (59). He described a case where a Mr Chang was in financial difficulties, and where 'Not only did nearby friends respond to his needs with more alacrity than distant relatives, but they outdid nearby relatives as well' (91). Overall, Fried asserts that 'ties of friendship are of paramount importance in facilitating the normal flow of social relationships in emergency' (208).

Fried strongly distinguished between friendship and *ganqing*, a term that literally translates as feelings of closeness. He argued that in relationships between unequals, there were often attempts to cultivate closer relations. For Fried, *ganqing* 'differs from friendship in that it presumes a much more specific common interest, much less warmth and more formality of contract, and includes a recognized degree of exploitation' (226). It was, for him, 'the primary institutionalized technique by which class differences are reduced between non-related persons'. Friendship, by contrast, 'makes a tacit assumption of equality' (103). In current times, a similar contrast is often made between friendship and *guanxi*[2] and I suggest below that the distinction between relations based on instrumental versus affective goals is less clear that it may sometimes appear.

Fried stresses the importance of friendships based on having been classmates (*tongxue*). The age-class groupings in school facilitated the formation of friendships and cliques. Rather than being transient, the importance of these friendships becomes greater over time. After graduating, the student often is still 'tied to a few or many of his classmates by strong emotional and common interest bonds'. Some of these ties weaken but few die away completely. Fried notes that: 'After many years the mention of common participation in a class [. . .] will serve to erect a bridge between strangers. Many boys go on with the friendships made in school until they even challenge the kinship structure for loyalty' (185). In Hong Kong and Taiwan, ties with classmates are extremely important as well, and are often more useful than kinship ties, since *tongxue* are more likely to have skills or information that are relevant to the situation.

Although Margery Wolf doesn't explore the concept of friendship itself in detail, she is one of the few ethnographers who have emphasized its importance within rural Chinese society. This may be because of her innovative emphasis on women's communities, informal networks that are given no formal place in the patriarchal official society.

As she notes: 'Few women in China experience the continuity that is typical of the lives of the menfolk' (1972:32). Instead, women had to subvert official structures to create systems of support. The dominant focus on men in regard to the Chinese family has missed the complexities of the system: 'With a female focus, however, we see the Chinese family not as a continuous line stretching between the vague horizons of past and future, but as a contemporary group that comes into existence out of one woman's need and is held together insofar as she has the strength to do so' (37). Women have few formal resources, and their defences are based largely in loose and unofficial networks of friends and neighbours (52).[3] For young brides, friendships outside their husband's relatives are critical because by the end of the first year of marriage 'a young women should have enough friends in the village to at least make her side of any conflict public' (147).

Friendship and its variants have received more attention among migrant communities. In discussing newcomers in Southeast Asia, Chan and Chiang (1994:210) comment that: 'Instrumental friendship is contracted for the purpose of attaining access to resources whereas expressive (emotional) friendship stresses the satisfaction of emotional needs individuals have for one another. In most cases, both types of friendship were likely to exist simultaneously, rendering the patron-client relationship an ambiguous yet dependent one.' Newcomers were helped, but 'the support given by one party was manipulated in exchange for instrumental gains. Helping was thus a double-edged social behaviour, a contested negotiation between impulses of altruism on the one hand and egoism grounded in economic calculus on the part of both parties on the other' (210). The cultivation of interpersonal relations 'was essential for orchestrating the success of a business endeavour'. The interpersonal relationships the entrepreneur was engaged in 'could not approximate the close, intimate, "expressive" ties exemplified in family relations, nor were they strictly "instrumental" ones as some affective sentiments were also involved' (223–4). Even towards workers, there was often an ideology of cultivating friendship, and not just paternalism (113).

Redding (1990:36) argues that horizontal networks are 'fundamental to an understanding of Overseas Chinese social and economic life'. Their networks are built of 'very specific personal relationships, many of which may have been initiated for their practical usefulness and then maintained to a point where genuine friendship has cemented them. The important point is that cooperation outside such linkages cannot be taken for granted' (36). Redding does not see instrumentality and expressivity as opposed, but as potentially interrelated phases in the cultivation of a relationship.

More generally, there are many accounts of the ways in which *tongxiang* (native place) associations help to smooth the adjustment of migrants to the new context. Strand (1995:406) says that urbanization was accomplished in a 'socially organized fashion by sojourners who found in their common locality ties a powerful remedy for their vulnerable status as strangers'. He argues that of the varieties of shared (*tong*) identities native place 'was among the most important and supple'. The construction of *tongxiang*-based connections is 'one of the most persistent and effective social strategies employed by urban Chinese' (Strand 1995:406). Rather than just supporting narrow regionalisms, 'In many cases, grouping by locality was the first step to cross-locality alliances among merchants, politicians, and students' (406). At present, the high rates of labour mobility from the interior of China and the countryside to the new economic opportunities on the coasts and cities is bound up with strong reliance on *tongxiang* ties to provide information about available jobs and to adapt to new conditions.

Voluntary associations are another context in which reference to friends is common in ethnographies of Chinese societies. Pasternak (1972:107) suggests that cross-kin associations are organized on the basis of friendship. In an account of the 1989 student movements in China, Wasserstrom and Liu (1995:389) note that 'informants stress that personal friendships and other ties established and cemented in private settings played a crucial part in the mobilization process'.

It is common in accounts of fieldwork experiences for comparisons with patterns of friendship in the anthropologist's home society to be made. Gates (1987:6), for example, states that:

> Etiquette exists in part to smooth and order human relations, to create a framework within which friendship is possible. The meaning of friendship itself differs from the American version, however. Chinese make few casual, short-term acquaintanceships as Americans learn to do so readily in school, at work, or while out amusing themselves. Once made, however, Chinese friendships are expected to last and to give each party very strong claims on the other's resources, time, and loyalty.

Gift exchanges, she notes, are important in Chinese society, where friendship is 'expected to express itself tangibly as well as symbolically'. Giving gifts helped incorporate her into 'the fabric of a Chinese relationship by showing informants that I understood important Chinese cultural rules and standards, thus making me familiar and trustworthy despite my alien appearance and origin. Mutual usefulness framed by etiquette that demonstrates for each other's dignity comes close to being a definition of Chinese friendship' (15).

Beaver (1995) discusses her discomfort at the expectations in friendships that she made among academics in China. She notes that their collaboration with her research 'was, above all, to cultivate me as a Sinologist, who could then facilitate their participation in the intellectual world outside China. It was to facilitate their departure from China. Their investment of social capital in me was a way of achieving greater options for their professional lives' (34). Sponsorship for emigration was a common goal in cultivating a relationship and she notes that friendship with a 'Westerner is an avenue out of China [. . .] Not many friendships turn into sponsorships, but for Chinese, it's worth a try; friendship is a profitable investment' (34).

This analysis builds on an implicit contrast between friendship in China and in the United States, where Chinese make strategic investments in friendships. She does not discuss analogous relationships among academics in North America, yet my experience is that many relationships are along similar lines, and we don't necessarily have negative feelings about that. For example, when senior academics offer their juniors opportunities to publish or simply offer them encouragement or constructive criticism of their research, both sides can benefit. This, essentially, is the basis of graduate supervision, which is hardly incompatible with friendship.

It may not be appropriate to view all of the efforts to cultivate Beaver as 'friendships', even in the Chinese idiom, since the instrumental aim would have been foremost in a number of cases. Instrumental and expressive facets of friendship are certainly not incompatible in either Chinese or Euro-American contexts. The difference is that the Euro-American cultural definition focuses more on the expressive dimension, leading to instability in friendships that revolve around mutual (instrumental) gains more than close intimate expressive relations.

This contrast between Western and Chinese friendship is even clearer in this account by a Western journalist, who writes that, '[W]e soon began to sense that friendship to the Wangs, and to other Chinese, carries obligations that it doesn't to a Westerner' (Butterfield 1982:47), i.e. high levels of reciprocity, and expectations of assistance. His wife and himself

> [. . .] felt we were being subjected to a pressure that wouldn't have existed in the West. Barbara described it as claustrophobia. But I thought it was something more. Friendship in China offered assurances and an intimacy that we have abandoned in America; it gave the Chinese psychic as well as material rewards, that we have lost. We ourselves did feel close to the Wangs, but as Westerners the constant gift-giving and obligations left us uneasy' (47).

These accounts of experiences of Americans with Chinese gift exchange and friendship suggest that the boundary between expressive and instrumental relations are different in the two contexts, a theme that will be returned to later.

In perhaps the most substantial early account of friendship in China, Vogel (1965) suggested that there had been a change in personal relations in China after the 1949 victory of the Communist Party, involving a decline in friendship and the rise of comradeship. This shift resulted from uncertainty about whether conversations would remain private or whether they might be brought to the attention of authorities. Betrayal of friends was a constant theme of the time, since 'refusal to supply information about a friend is rare because it would cause the authorities to take a more serious view of the problem'. For most citizens, the question 'is not whether to supply information, but how and how much to supply to minimise the consequences for one's self and one's friends' (47). Disclosure to authorities did not necessarily lead to broken friendships, but the risk of trust (and the risk to the receiver of the information) undermined friendship more generally.

By contrast, comradeship is based on an ethic of universalism (Vogel 1965), in which personalism and direct relationship is to be replaced by fundamental equality in which relationships are mediated through the Party-State. It should be noted that the Chinese term usually translated as comrade is *tongzhi* (shared convictions), and thus represents an addition to the variety of *tong* shared identities that have been discussed (Kipnis 1997:159). Vogel states that as an ethic comradeship is similar to 'the moral ethic governing work relationships in the West. One is expected to be friendly but not to form such deep friendships that they interfere with doing the work' (1965:59). Gold (1985) is skeptical about how far comradeship actually penetrated.

Another variety of friendship-like relationship is the colleague or co-worker (*tongshi*). Yan (1996) suggests that villagers don't refer to other villagers as *tongshi,* even when they work in the same agricultural collectives, unless they have a non-agricultural career. Colleague as a relational idiom is primarily a feature of urbaniza-tion and commercialization. It is a relatively important sociable tie in Hong Kong, although not as all-encompassing as in Japan, but the distinctive development of the urban economy in the People's Republic has dramatically heightened its salience in everyday life (Walder 1986). Ruan concludes that people working in organiza-tions which provide high levels of benefits have many common activities and interests:

> [. . .] and their social circles are likely to be overlapping. Take as an example two Chinese employees who work for the same factory: they may live in the same neighbourhood, since housing is provided by the factory; they are likely to belong to the same leisure club, which is organized by the factory too; and their children may go to the same school attached to the factory. In short, they belong together to multiple social circles. Now take two Americans who work together. Except on the job, they have much fewer opportunities to meet than the two Chinese co-workers (1993:104–5).

There are, then, a variety of friendship-like relationships[4] which are talked about in terms of shared identity and have received more explicit attention than has friendship. The implications are discussed below.

Friendship and *guanxi*

Perhaps the main problem in developing an account of the nature of friendship in Chinese societies is that the concept of *guanxi* has absorbed much of the attention that might be devoted to it (*guanxi* has often been suggested as a key to under-standing Chinese societies, whereas the same has never been said for friendship). This, combined with the existence of a variety of alternative relational idioms that occupy much of the discursive terrain, means that reference to friendship in the literature is peripheral to the main issues of contention. Clarifying the relationship between friendship and the other relational idioms is essential for any attempt to fit Chinese experiences into a comparative understanding of friendship.

Yang (1994) sets up a strong contrast between *guanxi* and friendship, although acknowledging their close interrelationship in practice. She suggests that friend-ships serve 'as bases or potential sites for *guanxi* practice'. It is understood in popular discourse as being 'more disinterested, less instrumental, and ethically purer than *guanxi* relationships' (111). While friendship is frequently appropriated by *guanxi*, '[I]t is also friendship that is most often set up in contrast to guanxi in popular discourse. Notions of friendship are expressed in the different categories of "heart-to-heart friends" (zhixin pengyou) and friends who use each other (huxiang liyong), a contrast that follows the distinction between expressive or emotional friendship and instrumental friendship' (117).

'Heart-to-heart friends' are 'real friends'. They cannot be used 'as an instrument to acquire resources, because in real friendship, one gives without thinking of a return' (117). Such friends are rare and people have 'more "ordinary friends" (yiban pengyou) than "heart-to-heart friends"' (117). Ordinary friends are more like what Allan (1989) describes as mates: people with whom one can have a good time, but without sharing much intimacy.

Yang's analysis opposes friends and *guanxi* partners, affection and instrumental goals, and is consistent with Western ideas of how friends are distinguished from other kinds of relationships: voluntary, non-exploitative, and non-hierarchical. Is this adequate or is there more similarity between *guanxi* and friendship than this account would suggest?

Ambrose King (1991) sees Chinese societies as *guanxi*-based rather than individual-based, as in Western societies, or group-based, as in Japan. The self is seen in Confucian philosophy as actively constructed by the individual 'who is capable of defining roles for himself and others, and is always at the centre' (113). One result is that the boundary between self and group is 'relative and elastic' and this elasticity of the boundary of the group: 'Gives the individual enough social and psychological space to construct his kuan-hsi [*guanxi*] with an unlimited number of other individuals on kinship or fictive kinship bases' (113).

Whereas Yang (1994) tends to present *guanxi* as opposed to true friendship, King is less inclined to see the two as necessarily in conflict. He suggests that inculcation of a universalistic ethic in the People's Republic[5] has produced a more negative attitude towards *guanxi* than is found among Overseas Chinese. *Guanxi* may serve as a base for resistance to Party-State control (Yang 1994), but it has also always been the Party cadres who have the best *guanxi* and it thus may also operate to increase inequality of access to scarce resources (Oi 1989). Among Overseas Chinese, *guanxi* is usually perceived more positively. Indeed it is often seen as a central part of an Asian way of doing business and organizing societies that is both more moral than the hedonistic individualism of the West and more effective (Smart 1997). There are ways to incorporate *guanxi* and personalistic obligations without undermining organizational rationality (King 1991).

Yan (1996:224) found that the North China villagers he studied recognized different parts of their *guanxi* networks, which he terms the personal core, the reliable zone, and the effective zone, defined on the basis of the 'degree of reliability in interpersonal relations'. While the personal core consists of family members, the reliable zone includes good friends, and the distinctions between the two are not clear, because 'close friends may be regarded as closer than relatives' (100). In the effective zone, there is greater emphasis on short-term reciprocity and balance. In the wider society, outside the effective zone, connections are unavailable, and in order to receive favours 'short-term, instrumental gift-giving' (bribes) are necessary (100).

In creating *guanxi* relations, what Yang (1989:39–40) calls transformation changes strangers into links in each other's *guanxi* networks by establishing a basis of 'familiarity' between the two parties, generally by appealing to shared identities. A shared identity can usually be found, sometimes by severely stretching boundaries. In cases where 'discovering' a shared identity is not possible, second-order familiarity can still be constructed on the basis of shared identities through a third party. A foreigner may have gone to the same university as his counterpart's uncle.

These shared identities reveal their significance in the term *tong* (together or united) that is a part of the main types of *guanxi* bases: *tongxiang* (shared native place), *tongshi* (colleagues), *tongxue* (classmates) and so on. In the Chinese patrilineal kinship system, even cousins are classified as either *tong* or *wai* (outside). This point returns us to the findings of the survey of discussion partners in China and the US by Ruan, and the question of whether the greater reference to co-workers in China was more a product of different social organizations, or of differences in the use of idioms. Clearly, the encompassing nature of the *danwai* in China means that co-workers are more likely to be associated with outside working hours, but there is also a discursive factor, which is related to varying conceptions of the self and relationships.

Introducing someone as a 'friend' doesn't provide any information about the background between that party and yourself, only about the quality of the relation-ship. It doesn't identify whether the initial linkage between you was through school, work, a shared leisure activity, or shared locality. Such information can, of course, be elicited, but its secondary status signals that what is important is the expressive character of the relationship, rather than the context in which it developed. If we assume, though, that a friend of a friend is a possible expansion to one's *guanxi* network, then background information is necessary to engage in transformation, since it provides clues about what kinds of identities might be shared.

Referring to a relationship under the rubric of one of the *tongs* emphasizes shared membership in a group or category, unlike the term friend which highlights the relationship alone. To identify someone as a colleague rather than a friend is to emphasize the practical connections at the expense of the expressive dimension. If King (1991) is right, and the Chinese version of the self is formed and reformed through fluid construction of relationships and positioning itself within them, then information about these relational webs is critical for all parties. Selves and relationships are more explicitly contextual and situational than is common in Western styles of interaction.

In Chinese, networks are called *guanxiwang*, literally nets of relationships (Yang 1994:64), and are first-order concepts (used by participants) rather than simply second-order concepts (analyst's concepts). Many of the difficulties of daily life in socialist China, both before and after the economic reforms, are coped with through reliance on networks. The networks are grounded in the dyadic relationships of which they are composed, and are created and maintained through exchanges of favours, gifts, information, and support. *Guanxi* exchanges combine instrumentality with solidarity, gift with commodity, and, as I have argued elsewhere, serve to combine capitalism with socialism. When networks cross boundaries as loaded and fraught with difference, separation and conflict as that between capitalist Hong Kong and socialist China (Smart and Smart 1991, 1998), these ambivalences, contradictions and accomplished resolutions (usually *ad hoc* and temporary) contained within these exchanges are fundamental to the nature of the connections, linkages and practices that result.[6] These ambivalences make it necessary that much that is central to these exchanges and to the *guanxi* networks must be excluded from the performance, kept from becoming explicit.

What does all this mean for friendship? As mentioned before, friendship fits within a discursive terrain largely occupied by the concept of *guanxi* and its allied relational idioms.[7] Friendship is simultaneously a base on which *guanxi* ties can be built, and a cultural resource for criticism of (certain kinds of) *guanxi* practice. In this discursive terrain tensions between affective and instrumental dimensions of social ties are powerful but ambivalent. One resolution is consistent with Western accounts of friendship that emphasize the non-instrumental nature of friendship practices, i.e. the art of *guanxi* exploits and manipulates 'real friendship'. Another resolution questions the separability of affective and instrumental social action, and accepts the instrumental use of friendship as long as this is done in suitable ways, in accordance with *li* (etiquette or ritual). I will examine this issue in the next section through a discussion of the boundaries between gifts and bribes, friends and connections.

Friends and Connections, Gifts and Bribes

As discussed above, Yang (1994:111) found that in popular discourse friendship is seen as 'more disinterested, less instrumental, and ethically purer than guanxi relationships'. I argue in contrast that by its very character, *guanxi* straddles the affective/instrumental divide, and amongs its strengths is precisely the way in which it does this. *Guanxi* without the affective dimension of solidarity and trust would not be as effective in providing the instrumental advantages that it does. Rather than seeing personal relations as premodern social patterns which have been diminished to a greater or lesser extent by modernity and urban industrialization, the liberal theorists of the Scottish Enlightenment argued that commercial society purified friendship 'by clearly distinguishing friendship from interest and founding friendship on sympathy and affection' (Silver 1990:1487). The development of the market was thought to make possible disinterested relations in domains falling outside the market itself and 'therefore newly distinguishable from the interplay of interest' (1484). In contexts where: 'Vital resources are not created and distributed impersonally by markets and bureaucracies, one has no choice but to be, in Ferguson's disapproving phrase, "interested and sordid" in all interactions, because in such settings vital resources are obtained largely through what modern culture and theory see as personal relations' (1484). The relevance to *guanxi* and China should be clear: movement toward 'market socialism' has not produced impersonal distribution of critical resources and application of rules. Instead, *guanxi* is critical to negotiating the murky waters of getting things done. So is the fusion of affective and instrumental dimensions of personal relations found in *guanxi* simply a result of it being a premodern, premarket, form of social organization where the conditions of separating out a disinterested form of friendship are not easily available? The dangers of an ethnocentric evolutionism in such a view should be clear. The Asian critique of Western capitalism is founded on the rejection of such assumptions of the need for strictly separated domains of economy, polity and society (domains which are, of course, only imperfectly separated in the Western nations).

In considering the alleged opposition of interest and sentiment, we must consider questions of social exchange. This is particularly true for *guanxi* and friendship, since *guanxi* is commonly regarded as founded on a gift economy and Chinese friendships seem to be more involved with high levels of gift exchange compared with American friendship. Yan (1996:14) concludes that gift giving plays a 'leading role in maintaining, reproducing and modifying personal relations', partly as a result of the way in which social structure in China 'rests largely on fluid, person-centered social networks, rather than on fixed social institutions'. Gift exchange helps to form *guanxi*, and sometimes to build such relations into intimate friendships. But connections can also be exploited and misused, and prior to the Chinese economic reforms, *guanxi* operated in part as a 'second economy', as a substitute for the missing market mechanisms (Gold 1985). The boundaries between interested but legitimate economic relations, affective and solidary social relations, and illegitimate interested relations of corruption, then, all come into contact in the realm of *guanxi*.

Clearly *guanxi* can be used for instrumental purposes, and this usage is recognized by members. However, it is referred to as the art of *guanxi*, because the style of exchange is critical to its effectiveness. Although a relationship may be cultivated with instrumental goals foremost in mind, the forms must be followed if the goals are to be achieved. The relationship must be presented as primary and the exchanges, useful though they may be, treated as secondary.[8] If, instead, it becomes apparent that the relationship involves only material interest and is characterized by direct and immediate payment, the exchange is classified instead as one of bribery (Yang 1989:48).

Personal influence is important in Chinese business interactions, but it can only go so far before it is considered to be bribery. Solinger (1984:57) found a tendency to equate bribery with money: 'In socialist China, after decades of indoctrination in anticapitalist morality, people bribe with gifts more often than with cash. "There was nothing wrong: no money changed hands."'

Giving cash for a favour is more transparently bribery within the social etiquette of gift exchange in China because of its general connotation of buying something, in this case the favour or service, but it isn't the only practice that can be interpreted as bribery.

Cultivating *guanxi* is not just the usage of customary forms to disguise what might otherwise be recognized as corrupt exchange. Instead, the exchanges are used to cultivate and strengthen relationships which are expected to continue (Pieke 1995:501). In the process, not only advantages and obligations are achieved, but also some degree of trust. It is the strengthening of trustworthy social relationships which is the main legitimate objective of the use of *guanxi* by Hong Kong investors in China (Smart 1993), and this seems to be a common expectation. Many exchanges that take the form of gifts are conceived of simply as bribes, but reliance on them is an inadequate foundation for secure investment. A more reliable strategy is to rely on social connections, activating and strengthening them rather than relying on bribing unconnected officials.

There are both legal and informal aspects to the concept of the bribe. Lewis (1976:197) suggests that 'the difference between acceptable "gifts" and improper "bribes" depends upon arbitrarily and delicately poised cultural conventions which, moreover, vary according to context'. Taken out of its legal context the conception of bribes as 'improper inducements' seems to be an adequate gloss. Impropriety may consist in breaking the law, or in explicitly subordinating the relationship to instrumental aims.

As gift exchange is used in foreign investment in China, it is clearly undertaken extensively for instrumental purposes. However, if we conclude that gift exchange and *guanxi* is nothing but a manipulative tactic used to gain profits and other desired goals, we fail to understand the basis of its effectiveness. Instrumental purposes should be presented as subordinated to the greater aim of developing relationships. Where an exchange is not intended to create such relationships, but simply to achieve some immediate objective for which the relationship would be a useful means, then though the form of the gift may appear to be followed, its content is different, a deal or a bribe rather than a gift exchange. Where this manipulative intent becomes apparent to the receiver, the gift may be refused or devalued, so that the manipulation, through its very transparency, may fail to achieve its instrumental intent. Exploitative use of gift-exchange is only made possible by the existence of forms of gift-exchange which attach priority to the relationship rather than to immediate instrumental objectives. The distinctive feature of *guanxi* is that it incorporates both genuine sentiment or *ganqing* and a series of techniques for getting things done. To emphasize one dimension at the expense of the other is to miss the critical point about *guanxi*, both practically and academically, which is its ambiguous fusion of the two dimensions. The ambiguity of *guanxi* allows it to adapt to dramatically different types of situation, changing its features and practices, but without ever losing its importance.

Conclusion

It is not surprising that guanxi has received more theoretical attention than friendship in Chinese studies. By fusing interest and sentiment, and by acting as a nexus where political, economic and social relations come into a tight and often contentious interface, the practice and discourse of guanxi occupy strategic terrain for any discussion of Chinese political economies, and people's responses to the dramatic social changes that have been a continual feature of the last century or more of Chinese history.[9]

Friendship, by contrast, occupies a place of much less contention, representing the secure support of close personal relations, becoming an issue of concern only when the security of such relations are threatened, for example by the imposition of an ethic of comradeship. It is when such relations are extended farther, and when they become tightly intertwined with instrumental ends, in other words *guanxi*, that the concerns of political regimes and popular discourse becomes more intense. But it is clear that there are no sharp and uncontested boundaries between friendship and *guanxi*, and that the practices and expectations of the two realms of social interaction are connected rather than discontinuous. Friendship is a claim that is made about certain types of *guanxi*, but that does not negate the position of that friend within a *guanxi* network.

How does this conclusion relate to the earlier description of the varieties of friendship-like relationships based on shared identities? The close connections between *guanxi* practices and solidary personal relationships means that in most cases friendships are formed by the continuation and intensification of the same sets of activities that are used in what Yan (1996) calls the 'extended zone' of *guanxi* networks. Whether or not we accept the argument that friendships in precapitalist societies could not separate out the domains of interest and affiliation, it is clear that the boundaries between them are less clear-cut in Chinese than Western societies. Furthermore, for the most part, Chinese people are more comfortable with the recognition that friends may receive instrumental utility as well as emotional satisfaction from their relationship, as long as the principles of reciprocity and the non-subordination of the relationship to the utilities are maintained. The existence of close linkages and common practices between *guanxi* networks and affective friendships provides a variety of reasons why the contextual source of a relationship (colleague, classmate, shared native place) would be of greater salience than in Western idioms of interaction. Furthermore, the formation of friendships and of *guanxi* more generally also share the interactional practices of asserting shared identities as an important early step. All of these practices are consistent with arguments that Chinese societies are structured on the basis of fluid, person-centred networks rather than on corporate groups or rugged individualism. Throughout Chinese culture, even in favoured gambling games like mah-johng, there is a consistent emphasis on the contexts within which things occur, and providing information about such contexts is what relational idioms like classmate do more effectively than dyadic terminology like 'friend'.

Notes

1 The specific question asked was 'Looking back over the last six months – who are the people with whom you discussed matters important to you?' (Ruan 1993:91). The data are drawn from the American General Social Survey and a survey of 1,011 urban Tianjin residents over eighteen years of age.

2 Interestingly, Yang (1994:122) suggests that the 'tactical and instrumental dimension of *guanxixue* does not exist in ganqing', in strong contrast to Fried's interpretation that *ganqing* is an idiom opposed to friendship. In the contemporary period, *ganqing* seems to be applicable as a measure of the intimacy of all relationships while the contrast with friendship is more likely to be made by reference to *guanxi*.

3 Yan (1996:108) discusses the term *tunqin,* literally translating as village kin, although they are not real kin. They are fellow villagers with whom one has social intimacy and exchange relations – not all villagers are *tunqin*. Thus, they are village friends, but again it is a form of reference that emphasizes the shared locality as well as the intimacy. Yan (108) found that most participants in celebrations were *tunqin*, not kin, and argues that 'voluntarily constructed friendship and the *tunqin* relationship play a decisive role as important as the preordained kinship'.

4 Nor are the relations discussed above the only ones that could be treated as friendship-like. The extremely common use of fictive kinship (see Kipnis 1997:32), for example, could also be fruitfully examined if space permitted.

5 It is undeniable that there is, and has been for a long time, a strong streak of cynicism towards these universalistic ethics of comradeship. However, this cynicism does not preclude acceptance of the ideals of sacrifice for the common good and the desirability of a more equal and just society.

6 Here I am drawing on Cohen's (1986) insistence on the *ambiguities* of symbols and cultural resources. The ability to present a situation or action in completely different ways has been critical to daily life in China, particularly during the post-1978 reform era where practices have often been in advance of what is officially permitted.

7 Space does not permit an adequate discussion of all the relational idioms that should be addressed here. *Ganqing, renqing, mianzi* (face), and *yiqi* (loyalty) are all terms that evaluate relationships which should be incorporated into this analysis.

8 The following section draws substantially on the analysis in Smart (1993), but the argument is abbreviated. The point that in *guanxi* transactions are expressions 'of a longer-term commitment that transcends the specifics of one particular event' is also made by Pieke (1995:501).

9 The uncertainty of politics in China, particularly during the Cultural Revolution, provides an analogue to the insecurity and threatening situation that formed the context for instrumentally significant friendships in the account of medieval Iceland presented in this volume by Durrenberger and Pálsson.

References

Allan, Graham (1989), *Friendship: Developing a Sociological Perspective*. Boulder: Westview Press.

Baker, Hugh D.R. (1979), *Chinese Family and Kinship*, London: Macmillan Press.

Beaver, Patricia D. (1995), 'The Chinese Construction of an American Anthropologist', in Bruce Grindal and Frank Salamone (eds), *Bridges to Humanity*, Prospect Heights: Waveland Press, 23–36.

Butterfield, Fox (1982), *China: Alive in the Bitter Sea*, Toronto: Bantam Books.

Chan, Kwok Bun and Chiang, Claire (1994), *Stepping Out: The Making of Chinese Entrepreneurs*, New York: Prentice-Hall.

Cohen, Anthony (1986) *Symbolising Boundaries: Identity and Diversity in British Culture*, Manchester: University of Manchester Press.

Fardon, Richard (1990), 'Localizing strategies: The Regionalization of Ethnographic Accounts', in R. Fardon (ed.), *Localizing Strategies*, Edinburgh: Scottish Academic Press, 1–36.

Fried, Morton (1969), *Fabric of Chinese Society*, New York: Octagon Books. First published in 1953.

Gates, Hill (1987), *Chinese Working-class Lives*, Ithaca: Cornell University Press.

Gold, Thomas (1985), 'After comradeship: Personal Relations in China Since the Cultural Revolution', *China Quarterly*, 104:657–75.

King, Ambrose Y. (1991), 'Kuan-hsi and Network Building: A Sociological Interpretation', in Tu Wei-ming (ed.), *The Living Tree: The Changing Meaning of Being Chinese Today,* Stanford: Stanford University Press, 109–26.

Kiong, Tong Chee and Kee, Yong Pit (1998), 'Guanxi Bases, Xinyong and Chinese Business Networks', *British Journal of Sociology*, 49:75–96.

Kipnis, Andrew B. (1997), *Producing Guanxi: Sentiment, Self, and Subculture in a North China Village*, Durham: Duke University Press.

Lewis, I.M. (1976), *Social Anthropology in Perspective*, Harmondsworth: Penguin.

Oi, Jean (1989), *State and Peasant in Contemporary China*, Berkeley: University of California Press.

Pasternak, Burton (1972), *Kinship and Community in Two Chinese Villages*, Stanford: Stanford University Press.

Pieke, Frank (1995), 'Bureaucracy, Friends and Money: The Growth of Capital Socialism in China', *Comparative Studies in Society and History* 37 (3):494–518.

Redding, S. Gordon (1990), *The Spirit of Chinese Capitalism*, Berlin: De Gruyter.

Ruan, Danching (1993), 'Interpersonal Networks and Workplace Controls in Urban China', *Australian Journal of Chinese Affairs,* 29:89–105.

Silver, Allan (1990), 'Friendship in Commercial Society: Eighteenth-century Social Theory and Modern Sociology', *American Journal of Sociology*, 95 (6):1474–504.

Smart, Alan (1993), 'Gifts, Bribes and guanxi: A Reconsideration of Bourdieu's Social Capital', *Cultural Anthropology*, 8 (3):388–408.

—— (1997), 'Oriental Despotism and Sugar-coated Bullets: Representations of the Market in China', in James Carrier (ed.), *Meanings of the Market*, Oxford: Berg, 159–94.

—— (1998), 'Economic Transformation and Property Regimes in China', in John Pickles and Adrian Smith (eds), *Theorizing Transition in Eastern Europe*, London: Routledge.

Smart, Josephine and Smart, Alan (1991), 'Personal Relations and Divergent Economies: A Case Study of Hong Kong Investment in China', *International Journal of Urban and Regional Research*, 15 (2):216–33.

—— (1998), 'Transnational Social Networks and Negotiated Identities in Interactions Between Hong Kong and China', in Michael P. Smith and Luis Guarnizo (eds) *Transnationalism From Below*, New Brunswick: Transaction Publishers, 103–29.

Solinger, Dorothy S. (1984), *Chinese Business Under Socialism*, Berkeley: University of California Press.

Strand, David (1995), 'Conclusion: Historical Perspectives', in Deborah Davis *et al.* (eds), *Urban Spaces in Contemporary China,* Cambridge: Cambridge University Press, 362–94.

Thrift, Nigel and Olds, Kris (1996), 'Refiguring the Economic in Economic Geography', *Progress in Human Geography* 20 (3):311–37.

Vogel, Ezra (1965), 'From Friendship to Comradeship: the Change in Personal Relations in Communist China', *China Quarterly,* 21:46–60.

Walder, Andrew (1986), *Communist Neo-traditionalism: Work and Authority in China*, Berkeley: University of California Press.

Wasserstrom, Jeffrey N. and Liu, Xinyong (1995), 'Student Associations and Mass Movements', in Deborah Davis *et al.* (eds), *Urban Spaces in Contemporary China*, Cambridge: Cambridge University Press, 362–94.

Wolf, Margery (1972), *Women and the Family in Rural Taiwan*, Stanford: Stanford University Press.

Yan, Yunxiang (1996), *The Flow of Gifts: Reciprocity and Social Networks in a Chinese Village*, Stanford: Stanford University Press.

Yang, Mayfair M. (1989), 'The Gift Economy and State Power in China', *Comparative Studies in Society and History* 31:25–54.

—— (1994), *Gifts, Favors and Banquets: The Art of Social Relationships in China*, Ithaca: Cornell University Press.

—8—

Friendship, Kinship and the
Life Course in Rural Auvergne
Deborah Reed-Danahay

Whether social maturity is defined by marriage, parenthood, or the assumption of occupational responsibilities, the period from nascent sexual maturation to the assumption of adult social roles appears everywhere to be the time during which non-familial gregariousness, particularly friendship, acquires greatest emotional urgency for the individual.

Cora Du Bois, 'The Gratuitous Act'.

Now as before, when their work was completed, youth enjoyed a special privilege: that of having a good time.

Françoise Zonabend, *La Memoire Longue.*

That there is a vast literature on friendship in Europe and North America which approaches it in terms of emotional or psychological processes, rather than in more social terms, suggests that middle-class notions of friendship as private, personal and pertaining to individual choice (Lamont 1992; Moffatt 1989; Paine 1969; Varenne 1986) have affected research in this field. The social meaning of friendship requires further attention by anthropologists, particularly in Euro-American contexts where friendships are culturally understood in middle-class terms to involve dyadic, intimate relationships of a deeply personal nature. Several ethnographic observers of both kinship and friendship relations in rural parts of Europe have described the ways in which friendship and sociability outside of the household vary over the life course, with significant differences for men and women (Gilmore 1975; Kennedy 1986; Leyton 1974; Ott 1981; Uhl 1991; Weinburg 1975; Wylie 1974; Zonabend 1980). Friendship is generally reported in this literature to be heightened during the period of youth, and to decline after marriage – especially for women. In proposing explanations for the differences in friendship patterns among men and women, and between youth and adults, most observers have adopted a compensatory view of friendship. This is illustrated in the quote at the beginning of this chapter by Françoise Zonabend, based upon her research in a French village in Burgundy. Youthful sociability, with its emotional rewards, is contrasted with the more gruelling demands of adult life and its accompanying obligations and restrictions of kin ties. Similar arguments have been made for adult friendship: friendship compensates the individual for the stresses or failings of kinship.

My ethnographic research in the Monts Dore region of central France and, more specifically, in the dairy farming community of Lavialle, shows that friendship among youth is, as in other rural European contexts, heightened. In this chapter, I suggest that while these friendships may have significant emotional meanings for individuals, they have important social meanings with consequences for adults as well as for youth. Youthful sociability in Lavialle plays an active role in courtship, in peer socialization, and in the formation of social bonds that persist throughout adulthood, cutting across household ties. Moreover, the strength of peer friendships is connected to the adaptation of the community to social change, in that age-mates provide forms of social support for new adaptations and changes.

Friendship, Gender, and the Life Course: Ethnographic and Historical Approaches

There has been little detailed study of friendship among children and youth (Bukowski *et al* 1996). The exceptional nature of youth friendships has long been noted (Eisenstadt 1956) but there have been few attempts by anthropologists systematically to study youth sociability outside of the context of institutionalized (and kin-based) forms of age-grading or initiation. There have also been few attempts to place youthful friendships within the context of the overall life course. An early attempt to situate youthful friendship in the context of the life course was that of Cora Du Bois, who adopted a psychological approach which held that friendship plays a role in ensuring that personality is not entirely flattened by the requirements of ascribed roles (1974:32). Du Bois relied upon psychological theories of individual personality development, and assumed a universal human need for certain levels of 'intimacy' and 'creativity'. The overall message about friendship in her ideas is that it is somehow ancillary to the social field of kinship. Either it helps prepare people for relationships of intimacy in marriage or it operates as a foil to the burdens or emotional shortcomings of kin and family roles. Du Bois viewed friendship as a potentially creative force that plays a compensatory emotional role for the individual, and drew from Henry Stack Sullivan's theories suggesting that same-sex (chum) relationships in youth are pivotal in the development of the capacity for adult intimacy and concepts of self-worth in the individual. Du Bois further posited that the degree of intimacy in marriage would vary inversely with endurance after marriage of friendships formed in adolescence. In societies where a high degree of husband-wife intimacy is valued, she suggested, there would be few culturally sanctioned opportunities for same-sex friendships after marriage. Conversely, where there is less emphasis on husband-wife intimacy, there would be more opportunities for extra-familial friendships that persist throughout adulthood. I have reviewed Du Bois' ideas here in some detail because they outline an approach that is typical in much of the literature on friendship in rural Europe.

European ethnographies of friendship by and large adopt the position that friendship plays a compensatory role for the individual. David Gilmore has described patterns of friendship in the Andalusian town of Fuenmayor as working to counteract individual alienation in a classically atomistic community characterized by a lack of alternative dyads such as patronage and fictive kinship (1975:311). For males, friendship flourishes in adolescence through the *pandilla* bands of youth in which sociability also becomes an instrument for courtship. After marriage, these friendship bonds formed in childhood and youth deepen. Ties of adult male friendship are highly valued, and, Gilmore writes, seen as the ultimate social good in a basically untrustworthy world (321). In his focus on adult males, Gilmore does not address the patterns of friendship among children or females. He does, however, suggest that women rarely retain close female friendships formed in youth after they are married, and form close bonds only with mothers and daughters. Leyton (1974), basing his claims on an Irish study that also places emphasis on male friendships, similarly dismisses adult female friendships as rare, suggesting that women, who are permitted to have social intimacy only with mothers and sisters, suffer from psychological stress without these compensatory friendship ties.

The observations of Leyton and Gilmore about the decline of female friendships after marriage are countered by the studies of Sarah Uhl in Andalusia (1991) and Robinette Kennedy in Crete (1986) which focus more closely on women. Uhl and Kennedy point to the 'hidden' or 'veiled' nature of female friendships. However, the compensatory model of friendship is also present in their approaches. These studies of friendship in rural southern Europe confirm Du Bois' suggestion that in societies where husband-wife intimacy is less valued, there will be more emphasis on friendships after marriage. Southern Europe is generally characterized as a society in which male and female spheres are traditionally kept quite separate, and in which what has been termed the public domain is dominated by male sociability and friendships (Gilmore 1975; Herzfeld 1985; Driessen 1983). Women in such societies, as Uhl and Kennedy show, also cultivate and value same-sex friendships, although these are less evident to outside observers and often remain hidden from males. Kennedy argues that, in the Cretan village she studied, animosity between men and women is characterized by paranoid distrust (1986:122). Female friendships after marriage remain hidden and secret from public view, and, according to Kennedy, intimacy between women balances (or compensates for) the animosity in their marriages. Similarly, Uhl argues that women in Andulasia have the same emotional needs as do men for a release from the tensions of family life (1991:93).

The compensatory view of youth friendships in regard to kin and family roles is particularly evident in Laurence Wylie's (1975) description of adolescence in the southern French town of Peyrane. For the people of Peyrane, the harsh realities of adult life must be softened with a carefree period during youth. Wylie explains that 'the five or ten years between school and marriage are relatively free, free of the harsh discipline of school which the young people have left behind them, free of the family responsibilities they will eventually have thrust upon them. This is the period of life which the people of Peyrane call the happiest years of one's existence' (99). It is, moreover, considered the duty of the young person to have a good time (103). There is a sharp contrast between the carefree adolescent and the serious adult, and the transition from one to the other is expected to occur by the age of eighteen or nineteen, when marriages generally occur. There are two social reasons for youthful excess, according to Wylie and his informants. First, it is considered important to experience excess in order to understand the importance of sobriety and adult seriousness. Second, the sexual and social freedom to form friendships and acquaintances among a wide social network is important to courtship and the exogamous (outside of Peyrane) unions typical in this village. In Wylie's analysis, youth are compensated for the hardships of adult life through their relative freedom while at the same time contributing to the reproduction of exogamous kin networks.

Two studies in other regions of Europe report this same phenomenon of youthful friendships declining in adulthood. Sandra Ott, based on her research in the Basque region, observes that friendship is an important basis of association only for children and young, unmarried people; only they, and not their elders will classify someone as *akiskide* or friend (1981:78). Elliot Leyton (1974), in a study of friendship and kinship in Northern Ireland, points to the importance of friendship and intimacy as compensatory in adolescence, particularly among males. Unlike Wylie, Leyton nuances the study of friendship with a consideration of social class. Leyton suggests that among the lower-class men in the fishing village he studied, kin and family demands are very strong and many people considered to be friends are often agnatic kin. While friendships formed during adolescence do persist, especially among males, new friendships are rarely developed in adulthood. Moreover, Leyton writes that intimacy and intensity occur only in adolescence (96). Such adolescent friendships provide relief for lower-class male youth from the social structural and psychological stresses of family demands. They permit an arena for open discussions of sexuality, mediate generational conflict, and enable the circulation of gossip. Adolescent friendships produce structural tensions, however, threatening kinship groups because family secrets are in continual danger of being leaked (99). The upper-class men in the village continue to form new extra-familial friendships in adult life because they have less need of family economic ties.

The view of friendship apparent in the above studies is one based upon an

individualist model. Krappman (1996: 21) summarizes this viewpoint in his statement that 'friendship can counteract problems that result from social disorientation.
To put it in a more positive light: friends try to realize the values, aims and desires
that individuals in a given society are striving for.'

Historical studies of youth in groups in early modern Europe expand our
understanding of the role of adolescent friendship bonds beyond the emphasis on
compensation for the emotional failings of kinship ties that colours much of the
ethnographic literature. Michael Mitterauer (1993), in his comprehensive historical
overview of youth in Europe, shows that youth sociability in traditional societies
contributed to courtship, peer socialization, and to social censure by its upholding
of the moral order through such rituals as the French *charivari*. Hans Medick
describes spinning bees (*Spinnstube*) in early Modern Europe, particularly in
Germany, whose typical supporters were the age and friendship group of the youth
and the neighbourhood (1984:317). These were linked to courtship customs and
to the sexual culture of youth at the time, for it was at such spinning bees that
youth met potential marriage partners and experimented with sexual behaviours.
Medick shows that, despite attempts to suppress them as socially disruptive, gossip
and other forms of social and moral control had always been central to the spinning
bees so that 'sensuality, boisterousness, and serenity in popular cultural life always
went together with a rigorous and violent social-moral control' (336). Natalie
Zemon Davis has also shown the important role that youth traditionally played in
the enforcement of moral authority in early modern France. Through *charivari*,
youth publicly chastised couples who had entered into inappropriate marriages.
Davis concludes that the carnival form adopted by youth groups not only reinforced
order but also worked to suggest alternatives to the existing order (1975:123).
These historical approaches see youth, in their gregariousness, as active social
agents who are involved in cultural production, social control and some limited
forms of disruption of the social order. This approach to the social meaning of
youthful sociability is in stark contrast to the ethnographic perspectives reviewed
above that stress the meaning of youthful sociability to the individual.

In the following analysis of friendship in Lavialle, I focus on the cultural and
social-structural aspects of friendship over the life course. I do not intend to dismiss
psychological approaches as irrelevant to studies of friendship; rather, I want to
contribute to a more actor-oriented approach that examines the role of sociability
and friendship in forms of cultural production. I have been influenced in my
approach by recent writings in the field of youth studies (Amit-Talai and Wulff
1995; Mauger 1994); feminist approaches to friendship (Griffiths 1995; Hay 1997);
and theories of social agency (Bourdieu 1980; Giddens 1991; Willis 1981).

Deborah Reed-Danahay

The Case of Lavialle

The Monts Dore region of Auvergne, in the French department of Puy-de-Dôme, is a farming region that has always supported some limited tourism, especially in the spa towns of le Mont Dore and la Bourboule. More recently, hiking and cross-country skiing bring tourists at various seasons to the region. However, many of the small farming communities in the region, isolated by the rugged and mountainous terrain, have remained isolated and culturally insular. The commune of Lavialle is one such community. The most striking thing about Lavialle is its rural, much off the beaten track, nature. It is too far from the closest city, Clermont-Ferrand, to be within commuting distance or to become part of the suburban fringe. The economy of Lavialle is based on family-run and owned dairy farms, with some diversification in beef, veal, and sheep raising. The seventeen or so villages scattered throughout the commune now have a population of about 370 year-round residents. Most of the inhabitants of Lavialle depend upon farming for their livelihood or are the adult children or siblings of farmers. Those inhabitants who do not farm are of two types. Most are either natives of Lavialle who are related to members of farm families, but who make a living in artisanal trades or some other local industry (such as at the dairy or sawmill). A much smaller group is composed of newcomers who have bought or rent houses in the community but are not related through kin ties to other Lavialle families. Such newcomers are extremely rare in Lavialle. This is due to the fact that many farms are still viable and there has not been much selling of property to non-kin, as has happened in other regions of France, and to the existence of more desirable locations for relocation in France. While some summer homes bring outsiders not connected through kin ties to Lavialle families, most vacationers inherited their homes and are members of native Lavialle families in the minds of current inhabitants.

Lavialle has a largely kin-based social structure connected to the families that own and operate the dairy farms. The household structure is closest to the stem model, with a nuclear family of husband, wife, and children comprising the basic unit. Lavialle does not exhibit the same extreme public/private dichotomy in sex roles found in rural settings in Mediterranean Europe, as described above in the work of Gilmore (1975), Kennedy (1986) and Uhl (1991). Husband and wife intimacy is highly valued in Lavialle, and the couple work together closely in managing the farm. Inheritance tends to favour eldest males, but there are many farms that stay in the female line with males marrying in. There are also cases where grandchildren inherit their grandparents' farms, when a parent has not done so. And there are cases where unmarried siblings have stayed on together on a farm. When a child assumes control of the farm, he or she goes into debt in order to pay off the monetary shares of the estate due to their siblings, and daughters inherit equally with sons in these arrangements.

One of the main dilemmas for farm families in Lavialle is to ensure an heir to the farm. The social and cultural reproduction of the family and farm is of paramount concern to these families, and socialization strategies are aimed at this goal, as I have shown in much detail elsewhere (Reed-Danahay 1996a). Several factors have always threatened this process of cultural reproduction: education, economic hardships, and the allure of urban life. Despite the vagaries of French agricultural policy and changes associated with the European Union, farmers in Lavialle have received sufficient state support through subsidies and other forms of protection to keep their small farms afloat. Lavialle's families have been relatively successful in making sure that at least one child will stay on the farm. Among the cohort of school-age farm children whom I studied during my initial fieldwork in Lavialle in the early 1980s, each child who had an opportunity to become a farmer has now done so. Either by marrying into another farm household or assuming the role of heir on their own farm, boys and girls in Lavialle are continuing to farm. Moreover, their siblings and cousins who have not entered farming have remained in the community or at least in the region. A salient feature of Lavialle social life is the strength of youth sociability and friendships, and there are both informal and institutionalized forms of youth sociability. These friendships endure into adulthood.

I often find that I must explain to outsiders why children in Lavialle would want to continue farming, and in order to pursue my arguments about friendship, it may be necessary to add a word about this now. When I was interviewed in the summer of 1997 by a reporter from the main newspaper of the Auvergne, *La Montagne*, about my book *Education and Identity in Rural France* (1996a), the young woman reporter, herself a native of the suburbs of Clermont-Ferrand, expressed amazement that the youth of Lavialle do not all want to leave. She spoke of her own cousins, who lived in small villages in the plains region outside of Clermont-Ferrand and who had told her that as soon as they could, they would escape what they viewed as the dead-end life of their village. This is a very typical reaction that I get from urban or suburban French when I discuss my research with them. I have become increasingly convinced that the strength of youth friendships and ritualized forms of youth sociability in Lavialle play as large a role as the family itself in encouraging local youth to remain in the community and to continue their social and familial ties into adulthood. Friendship and kinship are mutually reinforcing in Lavialle, and the strong peer bonds that are encouraged during youth provide incentives to maintain local social attachments that go beyond obligations to family or the desire to farm. Youth friendships play an active role in the social life of the commune. They do not simply constitute a prelude to adulthood or marriage, or a compensation for the hardships to come, but set up enduring social ties that encourage young people to stay in the local region.

Strangers, Friends, Neighbours, and Kin

In anthropology, it is common to think in terms of a kinship vs. friendship binary because of our disciplinary preoccupation with kinship. However, the stranger vs. friend binary is equally important to consider. Particularly among cultural groups for whom the presence of strangers is a marked event, rather than an everyday occurrence, the meaning of friendship can be elucidated through investigations into the social forms for dealing with strangers. In Lavialle, most friends are chosen among distant kin or kin of other natives of Lavialle or among age-mates who are natives of Lavialle. It is rare for a stranger to become a friend. Both kin and friend are placed in opposition to the category of outsider, who is by definition neither kin nor friend. People who are considered to be strangers or outsiders in Lavialle are called *forains*, a catchall term that includes tourists, newcomers, and unknown passers-by. Strangers (*des forains*), that is people who are not connected through kin ties, are handled with a great deal of caution and wariness by the Laviallois, as I was when I arrived there for the first time.

Two retired English couples have recently bought houses in Lavialle, at opposite ends of the commune. I have not yet had the opportunity to meet them, but my native informants in Lavialle regard these newcomers with trepidation and complain that, since they do not speak French, there is no basis for communication. They keep to themselves, I have been told by neighbours of one of the couples, and they do not mingle much with the locals. Other outsiders include a French college professor at the regional university and his family, who have been living in Lavialle for several decades, and who are neither connected to Lavialle families through kin ties nor from the local region. The traditional outsiders in Lavialle have been the teachers and the priest. Now, however, there is no resident priest and the current teachers in the local primary school do not live in Lavialle. Two teachers from the nearby middle school rent an apartment located in the town hall building (*le mairie*), but they do not participate in local social life to any significant degree. In general, social life in Lavialle is focused around members of local families with roots in farming. To be a *forain* is to have a marked status in Lavialle.

I remember one of the first realizations that my presence had come to be seen as commonplace during my fieldwork in Lavialle, and that I had ceased to be a *forain*. I was at the communal fountain one afternoon in front of one of the cafes washing my clothes. Two of my neighbours were standing outside with me chatting when a car drove up and circled around the parking area of the cafe. It was closely scrutinized by each of us, since we did not recognize the person behind the wheel. One of the women then asked, rhetorically, 'Who is this stranger driving by here?' The person eventually drove off, so we never found out. But the meaning of the incident for me was that I had become one of 'us' in relation to 'them' (outsiders and strangers). The incident also shows the rarity of the presence of unfamiliar people in this still mostly face-to-face community.

Several years have passed since that incident, and the presence of outsiders in Lavialle has increased since then. I was initially a rarity not only for being an outsider but a true 'foreigner' (not only non-Auvergnat, but non-French). Lavialle has experienced an increase in tourism and travel during the past decade that makes the presence of *forains* a bit less unusual, but still relatively rare. There are more summer visitors who pass through, although their numbers are still not significant. Nevertheless, the inhabitants of Lavialle scour the countryside for clues about change or newcomers and can still keep track of these. When I returned there for a brief visit in the summer of 1998, a male acquaintance of many years who is my age told me when we ran into each other that he thought I might be in Lavialle because he had noticed an unfamiliar car parked in the hamlet which had the license number of a rental car. The gossip networks of Lavialle work to keep track of any unfamiliar people or sightings (cf. also Mohl 1997).

Friendship and Sociability

In order to approach the topic of friendship in Lavialle, concepts of selfhood and of displays (or, more accurately, non-displays) of social intimacy must first be established. Friendship in Lavialle is embedded within a social world of face-to-face relationships and widely encompassing kin networks. Privacy and secrecy are also factors in the cultural constellation of friendship ties in Lavialle. Unlike the value for openness described by Gilmore (1975) in his informants in Andalusia, most people in Lavialle would more highly value a person who keeps their own counsel and is not open to others. *Pudeur* (literally, reserve) is the word used by my informants to describe a stance of caution in revelations about the self to others. The Laviallois, most of whom are members of dairy-farming families, do not share the same bourgeois preoccupations with formalities of *politesse* as do Michèle Lamont's upper-middle-class informants in nearby Clermont-Ferrand (1992; cf. also Le Wita 1988). In Lavialle, the valued social person is simple and modest (never putting on airs), but at the same time maintains a wary and defensive posture (*se defendre*) toward strangers and casual acquaintances. Situational contexts determine various degrees of social intimacy, but mistrust of all but the closest of intimates is the norm.

Linguistic expressions of friendship are another consideration. Sharon Kettering (1992) indicates that *cousin* often meant friend in early modern France and that friend often has an erotic connotation in modern French. The term *ami/amie* (French for friend) is not heard often among members of farm families in the mountainous region of les Monts Dore in which Lavialle is located. There are several explanations that can be offered for this. First of all, the word *ami/e* is most often used to refer to amorous intentions or ties. Second, in the mostly face-to-face communities in which people in this region live, where others are often aware of what type of relationship people have with one another, people are referred to by name without need to mark the relationship explicitly in any other way. Third, other labels are used more often – such as neighbour, age-mate, cousin. For instance, a woman who has a friendly relationship with another woman in her hamlet might say in speaking to her husband that *la voisine* (our neighbour) came for a visit today, or simply – La Maria came over. A fourth explanation is that two other words, used mostly by adolescents, are the common terms for friend – *copain* (for male friend) and *copine* (for female friend). While these terms have sexual connotations in mixed-sex contexts, they are the terms most often used for same-sex friendships among adolescents. Another term for social intimate, particularly among males, is that of *camarade*. Adults however rarely refer to friends in these ways, preferring not to mark a relationship that is probably clearly known to most people anyway as close. It would be a mistake to say that adults do not have friends because they do not use the vocabulary of friendship. Leyton (1974) shows that in Northern Ireland, 'friend' can refer to a kinsmen who is also a friend or to a non-kinsmen. It is the opposite in Lavialle, where an idiom of kinship or neighbour-ness is most often used for friendship among adults.

Pierre Bourdieu (1972) has identified a salient feature of kinship and friendship in rural France in his discussions of the term *cousiner* (cf. also Mohl 1997). The act of *cousiner* means to pick and choose among cousins in identifying which members of one's kindred will be acknowledged as kin. Although Bourdieu does not refer to bonds of friendship *per se* in this context, he is indicating that from the total universe of kin some ties will be cultivated more than others. This social manipulation can enhance one's social capital: 'Poor people are poor in kin; rich people are rich in kin' (1972:1109; my translation). The phenomenon of relationship of cousin to friend has also been noted by others (Paine 1969; Rich 1980; Weinberg 1975). The act of *cousiner* means to activate social support and aid from among one's kindred, as Bourdieu describes it, and implies an instrumental view of social ties. In Lavialle, where so many families have lived for generations and local endogamy is high, the potential kin links between residents are numerous. A kinship idiom is used to express friendships in the case of *cousiner*. Affinal links and shared hamlet residence (neighbourliness, which often overlaps with cousinship) also constitute idioms for expressing close dyadic bonds in adulthood.

Colette and Yolande have been friends for many years and are now both married, in their forties, and mothers. They both live a middle-class life in the metropolitan area of Clermont-Ferrand, but are originally from farming families. Colette is from Lavialle and Yolande from a nearby commune. Their friendship is underpinned by affinal ties. Both of these women have siblings who married into the same third farming family, and the three communes involved have a high degree of intermarriage. Relationships formed during youth, when adolescents attend dances in nearby communes, reinforce ties connected to marriage. Yolande and Colette are explicit that they are friends (*copines* – a term that they use with some irony now that they are no longer youths), but never hesitate to mention as well that they are related through marriage. Another case of kin and friendship involves Marie-Paule, daughter of a farming family in Lavialle who married a farmer from another commune and now lives there with her husband and two children. One of Marie-Paule's closest friends is a distant cousin from a third commune that is right next to Lavialle. She refers to this woman as her cousin, not her friend, but they socialize and visit each other often and clearly have a relationship that would be considered one of friendship; Marie-Paule and her cousin practise what Bourdieu called *cousinage*. Two men who are close friends, Jean-Jacques and Marc, are related through their mothers. Although they are of approximately the same age, they are literally in a relationship of uncle to nephew. Many adults in Lavialle, as these cases show, develop intimate same-sex relationships through ties shaped in the context of kinship.

Friendship and the Life Course in Lavialle

Individuals in Lavialle are deeply embedded within kin networks and are closely associated with their families and farms. The main social unit is the household (*la maison*), which is both an economic and a kin unit. Households can be composed of two nuclear families (*ménages*), usually headed by a son and his father. The wider kindred (*le nôtres*) provide a bases for social and economic support and are active in life cycle rituals. Households in Lavialle are clustered into small hamlets scattered throughout the territory of the commune. Typically, there are no more than ten households in any one hamlet. Lavialle is a political unit, with a mayor and town council. It also has its own primary school that serves all children in the commune up to the age of eleven, when they begin to attend a nearby middle school. There are several voluntary associations in Lavialle, such as the fishing club, the hunting club, the youth club and the old-age club.

Lavialle social divisions are numerous. Besides those among households, there are important geographical divisions – whereby the commune has three main 'neighbourhoods' perceived as quite distinct in the minds of the inhabitants. There are also, of course, gender and age distinctions. One of the major social divisions in Lavialle is political. The commune is divided almost in half by a left/centre-right political split. These political affiliations are connected to kinship ties, but there is a great deal of intermarriage between the two groups. Most of the time, however, children are associated with the political affiliation of their father. These political divisions are not as closely tied to religious behaviour as one finds in other regions of France, and most inhabitants of Lavialle consider themselves to be Catholic –

albeit with much variation in church attendance. In general, those to the right politically are more apt to send their children to Catholic secondary schools (located outside of the commune) but this is not a clear-cut division.

It is the active adults in Lavialle who perpetuate these social divisions through their selective participation in various types of social interaction. Adulthood as a time of heightened social divisions and restrictions works to reinforce social organization, political rivalries, and economic competition. Adulthood in Lavialle is a time to reinforce differences among families, not solidarity. People are busy making their farms profitable, raising children and keeping up the prestige of their family. To become an adult in Lavialle is defined primarily through marriage and the birth of a child, as well as with assuming the farm for a farm couple. A married farm couple in Lavialle is expected to behave differently from unmarried youth. This is particularly the case for women. Adulthood in Lavialle is a time of heightened gender and sex role divisions – divisions that are less evident at other stages of life. This has implications for differences in adult friendship patterns for males and females, although not on the scale described for southern Europe (Kennedy 1986; Uhl 1991). Work on Lavialle farms involves a sexual division of labour whereby men attend primarily to the milking of the cows, the care of adult animals, the buying and selling of animals and work in the fields. Women have domestic duties of child care, cooking and shopping, but also participate significantly in farm labour. They tend to young animals, garden and help with cleaning up after the milking. They also help in field labour during hay-making and at other times. On farms in Lavialle, husband and wife work closely together in managing the farm and making decisions about it. There is a spatial segregation of males and females in some 'public' contexts, in that women rarely enter the cafes except in the company of their husbands for special occasions and men rarely enter the shops in Lavialle and neighbouring towns. In other public contexts, however, such as parent meetings at the school or communal dances and meals, adult men and women socialize together in mixed-sex groups. Given the nature of the sexual division of farm labour in Lavialle, men tend to be more spatially mobile throughout the course of a typical day and have more opportunities to socialize with age-mates and neighbours. While there are some men who frequent the cafe (and are known as being less serious than others because they do so), many men do not, and Lavialle does not have the same male cafe culture that has been described in other European contexts (Driessen 1983; Gilmore 1975; Herzfeld 1985). Women tend to spend larger portions of the day at home tending to children and household chores, which leads to more social isolation for them. Women are more restricted than men and have fewer opportunities to socialize with other women once they establish their own households. Women in Lavialle see other women after church on Sunday or Saturday night, at shops, on market days and through limited social visits. Neither men nor women, however, are expected to spend a great deal of time 'socializing' during the week, since there is a strong value for appearing to be hardworking in Lavialle.

Adult friendships in Lavialle are based upon the ties formed during adolescence. People who went to school together and are the same age refer to themselves as *classards* (cf. also Weinberg 1975 and Ott 1981), and they meet on a regular basis for ceremonial meals to mark important birthdays. Middle-aged people in Lavialle are conscious of the *bandes* (cliques) that they socialized with and in which they dated as youths, and continue to retain informal and warm social ties with these peers. Communal dinners and dances at the community centre sponsored by the various voluntary associations in Lavialle provide opportunities for these former youths to socialize. Cousins, affines, and closer kin constitute a network for mutual visits and weekend outings. Despite the fact that political divisions, which surface in particular during elections, work against ties outside of the family, friendships formed during youth persist and work to counteract this trend. Although my own observations of Lavialle social life are not as rosy as this, many people in Lavialle retain the perception that '*on s'entend bien ici*' (we get along well here; we understand each other).

The lives of young children are focused around the family (including grand-parents, aunts, uncles, and cousins) and household. Children in Lavialle tend to play together in mixed-sex groups at social occasions during which their families socialize with other families. Called *les gamins* or *les gosses*, children will form small play bands when they accompany their parents to gatherings such as meetings, dances, or festive meals. Children tend to be friendly with children whose parents are the friends of their parents. Living in isolated hamlets, children cannot count on having playmates their own age living nearby, apart from siblings. When they do play with children at home, it is mostly cousins who come to visit, rather than non-kin. Although peer socialization is important at school, there is little out of school visiting among classmates.

It is the youth (*les jeunes*) and aged (*les vieux*) who have the most autonomy to form social attachments in Lavialle. A voluntary association for retired inhabitants of Lavialle has become increasingly active during the past two decades. Called the *Club du Troisième Age* (literally, The Third Age Club) this group is currently headed by a man who spent his childhood in Lavialle as the son of the local baker, but who lived all of his active adult life in Clermont-Ferrand working as a house painter. When he retired, he returned to Lavialle. His daughter, raised in the city, preceded him in returning when she married a Lavialle farmer about five years before her father's retirement. The club president maintained his ties of kinship and friendship with other Laviallois during the many years that he lived in the city, visiting often. An important vehicle for this were the periodic meals that age-mates hold in Lavialle to celebrate significant birthdays. This club is a focal point for socializing in a mixed gender group for older residents of Lavialle. Political rivalries and other points of tension that become important for adults in their active years are minimized in this group, which has returned to the group camaraderie of the youth. Meals are organized twice a month – with one held at the cafe mostly associated with the political left in Lavialle and the other with the centre/right. This is not only to give business equally to the two groups, but it is also a symbolic recognition of political divisions alongside a group cohesiveness based on ties of kinship and friendship that overcomes such divisions.

It is especially during adolescence that youth in Lavialle are encouraged to form close personal ties to friends (social intimates). Youth in Lavialle (*les jeunes*) have three contexts outside of school to form social ties and to meet other youth: the youth club, *les conscrits*, and informal cliques or *bandes*. The least formal and most far-reaching of these are the cliques of youth from different local communities that socialize together, going to dances in the region and having small parties at each other's homes. In these contexts, friendships are formed with same-sex youth from different communes, or from different hamlets within Lavialle. They often involve youth from communes which also exchange marriage partners. Girls from Lavialle, for instance, will form friendships with girls from other communes in which these Lavialle girls are also dating boys. Marriage often result from dating in these groups, although there is also a high degree of male-female camaraderie and friendship that is not based exclusively upon sex and dating. Girls are permitted as much freedom as boys to go out at night and drink and have a good time during their teen years.

These mixed-sex *bandes* play an important role in marriage ritual in Lavialle (Reed-Danahay 1996b), helping to mark the changing status of the newly-weds from those who can participate in youthful sociability to those who must become more settled and *serieux*. In a late-night, highly irreverant ceremony, *la rôtie*, the youth of the community who are *copains* with the bride and groom burst in upon the couple in their bed and provide a youthful comment on the positive and negative aspects of marriage. This event, which involves drinking and both sexual and scatological jokes, marks the last time that the new couple may socialize in such a highly 'scandalous' way with their friends.

The other two contexts for youth sociability are focused more closely on the commune of Lavialle as a socio-political unit. The Youth Club (*L'Association des Jeunes*) is a voluntary association whose members include teenagers from Lavialle as well as young married people who are not yet parents. This group organizes trips, fund-raisers, and dances. Youth who are attending school away from Lavialle or young people who have moved to work in the city return on the weekends to take part in the club's activities along with their peers who are at home. This group cuts across political, kin, and other divisions in the commune. Both males and females are active in the leadership of the club, and its members often go on to hold local political office. The current mayor of Lavialle is, for instance, a former head of the Youth Club.

Midway between the formality of the Youth Club and the informality of the *bandes* of youth who socialize together is the age group of *les conscrits*. Both males and females in Lavialle participate in this group during their late teens for two years. The *conscrits* organize the annual summer festival in Lavialle and hold events to raise funds for this throughout the year. I have described the workings of this group and the ritual of the festival elsewhere (Reed-Danahay 1997). The *conscrits* form a highly ritualized group and adopt their own theme song, wear a special hat, decorate a special truck which they drive through the commune at the time of the festival and work closely together in organizing the festival. They are permitted a great deal of autonomy throughout this period, and develop extremely close bonds with each other. Dating among this group is not as important as it is in the *bandes*, and the *conscrits* develop a spirit of camaraderie among both girls and boys. Participation in the *conscrits* group is limited to people with kin ties in Lavialle. Therefore, while cousins who live in the outskirts of Clermont-Ferrand and visit their grandparents or aunts/uncles often may participate, 'outsiders' or summer vacationers who reside in the commune, may not. The close bonds of age-mates that develop through this group persist into adulthood and form important cross-cutting ties across households in Lavialle. Young people in Lavialle are eager to be old enough to participate in this group, and the vitality of this ritual in Lavialle marks it as particular in this region.

Two factors in the lives of youth of Lavialle that may have promoted friendships and social ties outside the local region and its kin networks in the past have, paradoxically, recently diminished in importance. Mandatory military service, which traditionally took Lavialle males away from home at age eighteen (unless their families could get a dispensation in terms of economic needs on the farm), is in the process of being gradually phased out over the next few years. Secondly, while most of Lavialle's youth have attended middle school as boarders for the past few decades, recent changes in transportation have resulted in the elimination of this practice. Those who go on to a *lycée* in the city will still attend as boarders during the week from age fifteen or so, but younger adolescents are spending even more time in the community than they did when I first arrived in Lavialle in the early 1980s. And many farm youth attend an agricultural high school that is close enough to Lavialle for them to live at home during this time. These changes will most likely work to reinforce the continued social ties among local youth who are also linked through kin networks.

Conclusions

In this essay, I have suggested that friendship patterns vary over the life course in Lavialle. During adolescent years, young people in the rural French community of Lavialle play an active role in the persistence of social life and the cultural adaptation of Lavialle families to social change. Heightened sociability during adolescence in Lavialle is associated with interconnections between family and friendship, and the tension between family ties and friendship ties is a productive one. In Lavialle, friendship is not discretely separate from kinship. Through the process of *cousinage* (Bourdieu 1972), the institutionalization of local youth rituals and the role of youth sociability in courtship, local kindreds (*les nôtres*) work to perpetuate kin networks. However, friendship must not be viewed merely as the handmaiden to the kinship system. Young people in Lavialle form friendships that persist in adulthood and that help form cross-cutting ties that promote concepts of local attachment that go beyond that of the family and farm.

While studies of friendship that focus on individual emotional needs, viewing friendship as a compensatory form of social relationship, provide a valuable perspective on the meaning of friendship, there are important social meanings as well. My intention here was to shed light on the ways in which friendship and sociability in groups enable youth to play an active role in forms of cultural production. The case of Lavialle suggests that further studies are needed on such issues as the extent to which friendship persists after marriage; variations in male and female friendships; and the relative importance of youth sociability. It also suggests that anthropologists look further at the relationships between friends, strangers, and kin.

Furthermore, this research shows that kinship and friendship may be highly overlapping, rather than occupy different, realms of relationship. Although my research is from rural France, where one might expect kinship to play a strong role in friendship (or vice versa), this situation is not dissimilar from what I have observed among my neighbours and students who live in the suburbs of Dallas and Forth Worth. While, as I discussed above, the Laviallois use a kinship idiom to express friendship, in this region of Texas friendship is used to express a relationship of kinship. It is not at all uncommon for 'locals' to label a father, mother, sister, or brother as a 'best friend'. I cannot adequately address this phenomenon here, but it does suggest that assumptions about the distinctions between kinship and friendship in Euro-American contexts require some rethinking.

References

Amit-Talai, Vered and Wulff, Helen (1995), *Youth Cultures: A Cross-Cultural Perspective*, London and New York: Routledge.

Bourdieu, Pierre (1972), 'Les Stratégies Matrimoniales dans le Système de Repro-duction', *Annales*, 4–5:1105–25.

—— (1980), *Le Sens Pratique*, Paris: Les editions de Minuit.

Bokowski, William M., Newcomb, Andrew and Hartrup, Willard (1996), *The Company They Keep: Friendship in Childhood and Adolescence*, Cambridge and New York: Cambridge University Press.

Davis, Natalie Zemon (1975), 'The Reasons of Misrule', in *Society and Culture in Early Modern France*, Stanford: Stanford University Press.

Driessen, Henk (1983), 'Male Sociability and Rituals of Masculinity in Rural Andalusia', *Anthropological Quarterly*, 56 (3):125–33.

Du Bois, Cora (1974), 'The Gratuitious Act: an Introduction to the Comparative Study of Friendship Patterns', in E. Leyton (ed.), *The Compact: Selected Dimensions of Friendship*, Newfoundland Social and Economic Papers No.3, Toronto: University of Toronto Press.

Eisenstadt, S.N. (1956), *From Generation to Generation: Age Groups and Social Structure*, London: The Free Press of Glencoe.

Giddens, Anthony (1991), *Modernity and Self-Identity: Self and Society in the Late Modern Age*, Stanford: Stanford University Press.

Gilmore, David (1975), 'Friendship in Fuenmayor: Patterns of Integration in an Atomistic Society', *Ethnology*, 14 (4):311–24.

Griffiths, Vivienne (1995), *Adolescent Girls and Their Friends: A Feminist Ethnography,* Aldershot and Brookfield : Avebury.

Hay, V. (1997), *The Company She Keeps: An Ethnography of Girls' Friendships*, Buckingham: Open University Press.

Herzfeld, Michael (1985), *The Poetics of Manhood: Contest and Identity in a Cretan Mountain Village*, Princeton: Princeton University Press.

Kennedy, Robinette (1986), 'Women's Friendships on Crete: A Psychological Perspective', in J. Dubisch (ed.), *Gender and Power in Rural Greece*, Princeton: Princeton University Press.

Kettering, Sharon (1992), 'Friendship and Clientage in Early Modern France', *French History*, 6 (2):139–58.

Krappman, Lothar (1996), 'Amicitia, Drubjba, Shin-ya, Philia, Freundschaft, Friendship: On the Cultural Diversity of a Human Relationship', in Bukowski *et al*, 1996, 19-40.

Lamont, Michèle (1992), *Money, Morals and Manners: The Culture of the French and American Upper-Middle Class*, Chicago and London: The University of Chicago Press.

Le Wita, Béatrix (1988), *Ni Vue Ni Connue: Approches Ethnographique de la Culture Bourgeoisie*, Paris: La Maison des Sciences de l'Homme.

Leyton, Elliott (1974), 'Irish Friends and Friends: the Nexus of Friendship, Kinship, and Class in Aughnaboy', in E. Leyton (ed.), *The Compact: Selected Dimensions of Friendship*, Newfoundland Social and Economic Papers No.3, Toronto: University of Toronto Press.

Mauger, Gerard (1994), *Jeunesse et Societés: Perspectives de la Recherche en France et en Allemagne*, Paris: Armand Colin.

Medick, Hans (1984), 'Village Spinning Bees: Sexual Culture and Free Time Among Rural Youth in Early Modern Germany', in H. Medick and D.W. Sabean (eds), *Interest and Emotion: Essays on the Study of Family and Kinship*, Cambridge: Cambridge University Press.

Mitterauer, Michael (1992), *A History of Youth*, trans.Graeme Dunphy, Oxford and Cambridge: Blackwell.

Moffatt, Michael (1989), *Coming of Age in New Jersey: College and American Culture*, New Brunswick: Rutgers University Press.

Mohl, Perle (1997), *Village Voices: Coexistence and Communication in a Rural Community in Central France*, Copenhagen: Museum Tuculanum Press, University of Copenhagen.

Ott, Sandra (1981), *The Circle of Mountains: A Basque Shepherding Community*, Oxford and New York: Oxford University Press.

Paine, Robert (1969), 'In Search of Friendship: An Exploratory Analysis in "Middle Class" Culture', *Man* 5: 505–24. Reprinted in Leyton (1974).

Reed-Danahay, Deborah (1996a), *Education and Identity in Rural France: The Politics of Schooling*, Cambridge, Cambridge University Press.

—— (1996b), 'Champagne and Chocolate: Taste and Inversion in a French Wedding Ritual', *American Anthropologist* 98 (4):750–61.

—— (1997), 'Persistence et Adaptation d'un Rite de Passage: La Fête Communale et les Conscrits dans une Commune du Puy-de-Dôme', *Revue d'Auvergne*, 539 (2):130–6.

Rich, George W. (1980), 'Kinship and Friendship in Iceland', *Ethnology*, 19 (4):475–93.

Uhl, Sarah (1991), 'Forbidden Friends: Cultural Veils of Female Friendships in Andalusia', *American Ethnologist*, 18 (1):90–105.

Varenne, H. (1986), Creating America, in H. Varenne (ed.), *Symbolizing America*, Lincoln and London: University of Nebraska Press.

Weinberg, Daniela (1975), *Peasant Wisdom: Cultural Adaptation in a Swiss Village*, Berkeley: University of California Press.

Willis, Paul (1981), 'Cultural Production is Different from Cultural Reproduction is Different from Social Reproduction is Different from Reproduction', *Interchange*, 12 (2 and 3):48–67.

Wylie, Laurence (1974), *Village in the Vaucluse*, third edition, Cambridge: Harvard University Press.

Zonabend, Françoise (1980), *La Memoire Longue: Temps et Histoires au Village*, Paris: Presses Universitaires de France.

Friends and Networks as Survival Strategies in North-East Europe

Ray Abrahams

I use the term 'friends' here in a broad and relatively loose sense to refer to participants in a range of significant, positive, and ideally longer-term personal connections. This is in contrast to more narrow usage which distinguishes a friend sharply from a mere 'acquaintance' as two poles of a continuum of intensity and mutual commitment. These connections are typically not based, at least directly, upon family and kinship ties or on sexual relations, though some degree of overlap is possible. In contrast with kinship and family links, they are achieved rather than simply ascribed, and the often proclaimed 'We are just good friends' clearly expresses the contrast with 'lovers'.

A broad approach to the term is in keeping with important aspects of reality. Proverbial references to 'friends in need', and qualifiers such as 'close' or 'really good', suggest that 'true' friendship is an ideal less often achieved than some might hope. There is also commonly an element of rhetoric in the word's use, ranging from the formality of 'my learned' or 'my Honourable' friend to the everyday embellishment of casual relationships with its aura of significant attachment. Such variation in intensity and mutuality of personal commitment in different individual cases of 'friendship' may make it difficult to pin down, but it is nonetheless intrinsic to its 'achieved', and therefore developmental, quality and its combination of moral and organizational characteristics.

As with other terms, too tight a definition can run into further difficulties when we come to deal with other cultural settings, even though closely comparable forms of tie occur in a wide range of societies. A cursory review of work on African 'blood-brotherhood' reveals serious differences within that category, let alone between it and our European concepts; and not all European usage is the same. Finns, for example, do not mark off kinship and friendship quite as sharply as we tend to do in Britain. For many, their 'friends' (*ystävät*, singular *ystävä*) may include siblings and cousins as well as unrelated persons.[1] At the same time, the term is used quite sparingly for a narrow range of close attachments, while another word, *tuttava*, which literally means 'acquaintance', seems to be less 'cold' and casual than its English counterpart, and can be used colloquially in many situations where an English speaker might use 'friend'. My impression is that the related Estonian term *tutvus* has a comparable more salient quality. The Estonian version of a once popular Soviet joke suggests this. The joke, which is highly relevant to the subject matter of this paper, tells how a new and harsher penalty for serious crimes was to replace capital punishment. The perpetrators were to be sentenced to fifteen years without connections (literally 'acquaintances'). A literal translation would, however, fall rather flat on English ears, and 'friends' would be a better term if one had to choose. Coupled with this, Estonians do at times, of course, distinguish between 'friends' proper (*sõbrad*, singular *sõber*) and 'acquaintances'.

Friendship is commonly compared and contrasted with patron-client links. The chief contrast turns on the asymmetry and inequality which mark the latter ties, as opposed to the ideally egalitarian nature of friendship. At least ideally also, friendship links are often thought to be less overtly instrumental than those between a patron and a client. In the present context, some similarities between the two are probably more interesting. Here I have in mind the fact that patron-client ties appear to serve as valuable resources for their participants in a wide range of structural settings. The early interest which anthropologists expressed in them in the 1960s was largely focused on the way they seemed to provide a sort of escape, especially for the politically ambitious, from the stranglehold of kinship ties. As such they were seen as a move towards more 'modern' forms. Later work, however, such as that of Gellner and Waterbury (1977), contrasted them with the impersonal struc-tures of 'modernity' and saw them as a harking back to kinship-like forms. Both viewpoints are, of course, defensible, since typologically such ties lie somewhere in between the polar opposites of kinship and bureaucracy. The same is broadly true of friendship, which similarly can serve readily as a resource in situations where the mainstream structures of society fail to satisfy the needs of its members. Such situations arise in many different settings, including those of both state socialism and free-market capitalism, and the patterns of bureaucracy accompany-ing these. It allows individuals to establish links to mainstream institutions and at times to by-pass them, and it helps to provide access to both material and less tangible, emotional comforts in a world which otherwise appears all too impersonal, intransigent and cold.

Estonia in the Early 1990s

The joke I quoted earlier relates to well-known features of Soviet society. Goods were often scarce, and choice was commonly more limited than many wished. Bureaucratic rules and the attempts of state-socialist planning to force the varying circumstances and needs of localities into a single 'command' framework auto-matically created problems which they could not solve. Individuals acting on their own behalf, and often on behalf of local collectives, were constantly tempted to seek ways of circumventing the difficulties they encountered in gaining access to goods and services, and the development of useful friendship ties and networks was an important survival device in such circumstances.

The situation I encountered in Estonia, in both the city and the countryside, when I began research there in the early 1990s combined such difficulties with those of the political and economic transformations which accompanied the 1980s policies of *glasnost* and *perestroika*. More goods and a wider range of opportunities were now on offer, but money – or at least the hard currency needed for their purchase and exploitation – was scarce, and sometimes the bureaucratic machinery was not readily adapted to the changes taking place. As a Western European social scientist – and the first to work over a length of time in rural communities there – I rapidly found myself instructively involved in some such situations.

Thus, a brief preliminary visit to the island of Saaremaa was mediated for me through the kindness of a well-known television journalist (the wife of an academic with whom I was planning to collaborate) who circumvented ferry queues, arranged accommodation at a Party 'dacha', and managed to get food served at a restaurant which was, like many others, closed because it could not get adequate supplies to remain open to the general public. The following year, when I began research proper, I needed to obtain a multiple re-entry visa. Persistent attempts of a London visa agency to get one for me through the Soviet authorities in Britain failed, and I went to Tallinn hoping to obtain one there. The division of the Estonian Academy to which I was linked had an 'international relations' officer who managed, against the odds, to get one for me through personal intervention with relevant officials. She explained that while it was technically possible to issue such visas, the immigration offices were not sure how to do so, and they had to be persuaded to embark into what was as yet relatively unknown territory to them. On another occasion, the daughter of another academic I was working with was trying to get a visa to go to Finland immediately following her forthcoming marriage. Her father had managed to get help from a colleague to arrange an appointment for her at the Finnish Embassy, and I accompanied her there. There were queues of people outside the closed doors, all anxious to get visas, and it seemed impossible to let anyone inside know that one had come for an agreed appointment. Eventually, my own request in English to a diplomat who briefly showed his face was surprising enough to achieve entry and, subsequently, the granting of the visa.

I quote these few personal examples because they fit well with general patterns which prevailed at the time, and as such form a genuine part of data gained through 'participant observation' in Estonian society. I should also stress, not for my own sake, but in order to portray the true flavour of the situation, that all these and other comparable transactions took place in the context, and contributed to the development, of longer-term personal connections rather than through the payment of any monetary 'sweeteners' or fees. They formed part of patterns of more general reciprocity which were, as I have suggested, a vital and well understood resource for individual and family 'survival'.

This is not to say that, especially in the city, more direct payment for 'favours' of one sort or another did not also exist. Tales were also circulating at the time of 'cash for visas' paid to local agents, and of sexual favours given in return for home repairs and decoration. Also, forms of sex tourism, especially by Finnish males, seem to have been a significant source of income for some urban women who were keen to get hard currency and the access it provided at that time to such 'luxuries' as bananas, Finnish coffee and chocolate, and various electrical appliances. But this existed over and aside from the patterns I describe, and also separately from other sorts of 'payment', such as the ubiquitous half-litre of vodka which I will discuss later.

The Rural Scene

I turn now to data from the countryside. The period of my research was essentially one of experiment and hoped for transformations in the rural areas. The Soviet system of collective and state farms, imposed on Estonia in the late 1940s, was already under threat in 1989, two years before the country became independent. As in several other contexts, Gorbachev had shown himself willing to envisage changes in this area, and the Estonian Soviet Socialist Republic passed a new Farm Law in December of that year. The law explicitly encouraged the restoration of former family farms and the creation of new ones, alongside and on an equal footing with collective and state farms. This was followed, in 1991–93, by a variety of more radical legislation on property, land, and agricultural reform. Many individuals and their families were at least initially excited by the new possibilities which such reforms appeared to offer them, and a considerable number began to try to make a living through family farming. Others meanwhile resisted such developments – some had vested interests in the Soviet system while others, who supported other forms of large-scale farming, were not convinced that such a move 'back to the future' was a viable option for agricultural development. The need for help through friends and acquaintances appears to have been important in all sectors of rural society at that time, but the forms it took and the network patterns involved varied in significant ways.

A key feature of such variation was the role of certain individuals as particularly active 'networkers', building up a wide range of connections for themselves and also serving as central points of juncture for links between others who were less well connected. Such individuals, unlike most though not all of their neighbours, had developed highly valuable connections which stretched well beyond their own local community, and in many cases beyond Estonia itself. The fact that Estonia is a relatively small country (c. 45,000 sq. km.), within reasonably easy reach of

rich countries such as Finland and Sweden, facilitated the development and maintenance of such relations, though fuel shortages and poor telephone connections
were a frustrating feature of the situation there during the first period of my research
(there was significant improvement later).

The choice of my first fieldwork location in 1991 stemmed from meeting such
a 'networked' individual. I was in Tallinn, and my chief collaborator at the Estonian
Academy told me that he had arranged for us to meet a leading official in the
Estonian Farmers' Union along with another Union officer who was also reputedly
Estonia's first new family farmer. It turned out that this second man spoke Finnish
and some English, and when he heard about my interests in the new developments,
he immediately offered to help me and invited me to stay on his farm in the
South-East of the country.

This man, M.S., as I shall call him, was in his forties. He had a remarkable
array of connections, and his invitation to me formed part of a broader pattern of
acquiring and developing potentially useful links whenever opportunity arose in
the course of his rather varied career. A former sailor, he had started to learn English
when he fell overboard off the coast of Scotland and was briefly hospitalized there.
He had attended courses at Leningrad University, and had later worked as a cultural
officer in his original home region of Paide in central Estonia. He was originally
married to a Lithuanian, by whom he had two daughters, but this marriage broke
up and he married his present wife who came from the Antsla area of Võru region
where he now lived. They moved to their present home, an old farm house which
he bought in 1983, when his wife's relatives told them that the place was for sale,
and he got a job at the local *Kolhoos* (collective farm) in charge of stores and with
some responsibility for buildings. The job, and his earlier work, provided him
with opportunities to acquire friends and other contacts in many different places.
These included a Finnish businessman for whom he organized coach trips and
accommodation for Finns who wanted to take advantage of the opening up of the
country for wild boar and other hunting. More important for his farming, however,
was the link he forged with a Swedish farmer through his own and the Swedish
Farmer's Union. This man was helping him to plan his farm as part of an aid
program, so that it might serve as a model for his neighbours. His Swedish
connections had also enabled M.S. to acquire a variety of vitally important, used
farm equipment both for himself and for a number of his neighbours. In addition
he had dabbled for a time in politics, and had stood unsuccessfully as a candidate
in the first free elections. While he did not completely preclude further such
involvement in the future, he was concentrating at the time I met him upon making
a good living out of farming.

Men like M.S. are relatively rare, though there are enough of them both in
Estonia and elsewhere, including eastern Africa, for me to have encountered several
of them in the course of my research. They tend to occupy the central areas of

local network stars, and their connections beyond these link them to other, often comparable individuals in other parts of the country. M.S. was connected in this way to several men in neighbouring and more distant areas. Such men tended to share his energy and entrepreneurial talent, and were willing to liaise with him in a variety of one-off or longer term ventures in addition to exchanging information and ideas. Access to machinery, to fuel, or to a vital spare part for a car could be importantly facilitated in these ways, and beyond this such contacts helped such men to keep up to date with new developments.

In August 1992 I accompanied M.S. on a visit to one of them in the neighbouring Valgamaa region. This man also had a 'school farm' and his own Swedish farmer connection associated with it. M.S. went to see him concerning a grain-drying system which he had learnt about from him some weeks earlier, but had only now found time to explore further. A Finnish company – apparently in some difficulty in its home market – was selling the system cheaply to Estonian farmers with the help of a Finnish government aid subsidy and an American-financed Estonian government loan. M.S. had, it turned out, missed the boat for that year and would have to wait to see what was on offer elsewhere. The Valgamaa man had taken the system onto his own farm for himself and for three neighbours who were sharing the Estonian loan and its repayment with him.

While we were there, a young man who was also visiting the place told M.S. that he was trying to obtain a plough for his tractor and could offer a 3,000-litre water tank in exchange. M.S. immediately agreed to this swap. The plough was needed for the following spring and he had a spare one in his former area which he could get hold of in due course. The tank would meanwhile be delivered to him in a couple of weeks time. It would be very useful to him because it was a dry summer and it would help to provide water for his cattle in the fields.

Later that month, M.S. also took advantage of a trip to Tallinn to call in on another farmer friend in central Estonia. This man had managed to obtain a large quantity of sugar from a government agency in return for a consignment of potatoes. Because of shortages, the sugar was now very valuable, and M.S. contrasted it with the money which the man had received for his grain crop. The man was now willing to let M.S. have some sugar, though he did not generally sell it on but preferred to use it to make vodka which produced a further added value. M.S. at this time also managed to obtain some sugar from a trading trip his brother-in-law had made to Poland.

In trying to understand a man like M.S., a number of factors have to be taken into account. His career history clearly helped to place him structurally in a good position to make connections and acquire friends with whom he could engage in a variety of reciprocal relations. At the same time, this history, and still more the benefits he managed to reap from it, turned to a considerable extent upon his personal qualities. These included a valuable combination of openness both to new people and to new ideas, a sharp intelligence, and enormous energy which he poured into any undertaking, whether it was the hard drudgery of dairy farming, or driving long distances, or looking after a demanding visitor such as myself. The first of my several visits to his farm lasted two weeks. He collected me from Tallinn, at the other end of the country, and he drove me back there afterwards. He arranged for me to visit as many other new farmers as I could, and accompanied me on visits to them, serving as my first interpreter and field assistant. He also tried to make sure that I encountered as wide a spectrum of political opinion as possible, including visits to collective and state farms whose managers were not enthusiastic about new developments. He also devoted as much time as he could, between these and his farming activities, to answering questions and discussing the changing situation. During this visit he refused steadfastly to discuss the question of payment for his work, and for board and lodgings. At the end he agreed somewhat reluctantly to take what I could sensibly offer him from my funds, and he made it clear, in a way more reminiscent for me of 'traditional' African than 'modern' European stereotypes, that ties to people were more valuable than cash.[2]

Not all such well-connected individuals had enjoyed M.S.'s varied career, and had made their own significant connections by other routes. Some, for example, were graduates of one sort or another – many were trained at the Agricultural University in Tartu or at a variety of technical institutions – and had been posted under the Soviet system to workplaces all over the country. This again was an important source of later contacts both within the agricultural field and beyond into the world of business and bureaucracy. Summer student work camps appear to have been an important place for forging friendships. I was told that in the evenings after work, when groups of them would get together for a song and for a drink, individuals gradually found others with whom they could safely voice their political ideas and doubts, and that such lasting ties could later be reactivated if a need arose. Access to information and to each other's expertise was commonly sought and provided through such contacts. In these and other contexts, I might add, the improvement of telephone services during the early 1990s was important for communication both at local and, increasingly, at national and international level.

Before moving on to some other aspects of Estonian 'connections', three further points should briefly be discussed concerning the material so far presented. The first is that the key rural figures I have pointed to as links within and between local networks appear to be mainly if not always men. The urban situation is somewhat less clear-cut, and this probably reflects the fact that many ambitious and well-educated women leave the rural areas for work in towns. I encountered relatively few women who were farming in their own right rather than as part of a husband-wife team, and the majority of these were on the island of Saaremaa which has a stronger tradition than mainland Estonia of male labour migration and fishing and, relatedly, of relatively independent female involvement in agriculture. Of course, most of the men in question were themselves married, and here other factors clearly come into play – and especially the greater mobility of men outside the domestic sphere which is partly though by no means wholly linked to child-rearing.

At the same time, as I have discussed elsewhere (1994; Abrahams and Kahk 1994:141–3), it would be wrong to present a general impression of Estonian rural women as domestic drudges under the control of their husbands and irrelevant to networks of connections both within and between local areas. There are, for example, a few women in positions of authority, and with some farming interests, in local government, and such women are extremely well connected. Many farm wives are also active and respected partners in a joint farm enterprise, and their greater domestic involvement in child-rearing and in cooking is better understood as part of an accepted division of labour rather than as evidence of male domination. Again, many such women are important links in the development of chains of connection by their entrepreneurial husbands. I have already noted how M.S.'s move to Võru arose through information he received from his wife's family. In addition, he received a wide variety of help from both his sisters and his wife's brother, including important further links to others through the latter. Similarly, one of his fellow central figures in another area had valuable connections through his wife who is computer-literate, with many years of work experience in the local urban statistical office, and has Finnish and Swedish family links through her father.

The second point is that, in the main, such men have tended to keep on relatively equal terms with their neighbours, rather than to take on a more obviously 'patronly' role towards them. An interesting exception was the head of a state farm in south Estonia, who was presiding over the transformation of his farm, and whose access on his own and others' behalf to connections to the outside world was still closely tied up with his position of authority within the farm. This conjunction seemed to allow the man considerable scope, at least at this juncture, to present himself as a patriarchal figure benignly looking after the interests of the members of his state farm focused community.

At the same time it is no accident that such men were popularly spoken of as 'red barons' during the Soviet period, an epithet which neatly combined reference both to their socialist pretensions and their similarity in many ways to the feudal lords of the manor in the system of serfdom which preceded the beginnings of a free peasantry in the nineteenth century. Indeed it seems to have been a harking back to the ideals if not the rather mixed reality of such a free peasantry that largely lay behind a powerful ethic of egalitarian individualism in the rural areas. In general, lording it over others was not a ready option for contemporary individuals whether they aspired to it or not, whatever the pattern of their connections within and outside their localities.

Another way in which this showed itself is that wealthier, more active farmers seem to have found it difficult to attract paid labour to their farms for any length of time. M.S. had tried to do this after his sister's brother gave up as a resident helper on his farm, but he found it hard to get good workers. He explained this in terms of old attitudes encapsulated in the Estonian concept of *sulane*. This term for a farm labourer carries evocations of both feudal days and harsh conditions working for some of the richer farmers who emerged after the feudal period. The term acquired a generally pejorative flavour, mainly in contrast to being one's own master, and no doubt also for some in contrast to the ideals of socialist egalitarianism, which were however badly tainted for most people by the connection with Soviet imperialism. M.S. argued, somewhat grumpily, that anyone who worked regularly as a labourer on another's farm would soon start to be known as 'x's *sulane*', and that would be a strong deterrent for them.

Lastly, it is important to make explicit that individuals have also found it useful to belong to more formal organizations, such as the Farmers' Union. These have tended generally to work as complements to the kinds of connections I have been discussing, as can be seen from the fact that men like M.S. and his friends have made some of their most important personal connections through membership of such groups. In addition, such associations clearly provide an important mechanism for coordinating and jointly representing farmers' or others' interests in ways that individual connections cannot do. As well as the Farmers' Union there were associations representing the interests of those who supported the retention of what seemed to them the better features of the *kolhoos* system. Also, M.S. himself with some of his associates eventually tried to start an organization of 'production farmers' as an alternative to the Farmers' Union. He felt that the old Union was letting down more active farmers like himself in favour of a wide variety of small-holders and 'hobby farmers' whom he did not consider to be serious producers.

The 'Spirit' of the Gift

As elsewhere in the former Soviet Union and Eastern Europe, the giving of vodka in return for services has been very common in Estonia. Myriam Hivon (1994) has published an interesting account of this phenomenon in the northern Russian countryside, and I deal with it only briefly here. It merits some discussion in the present context as a pattern of behaviour which occupies a possibly enlightening border area between direct reciprocity between 'friends' and commercial payment for work. Also, like other forms of reciprocity, including many cases of friendship itself, the giving of vodka is flavoured by a mixture of uncertainty and ambiguity, and perhaps a dash of mutual wishful thinking.

Vodka-giving in Estonia follows well-worn Eastern European tracks. At least at the time of my research, vodka was a common form of offering in both town and country in return for a variety of services rendered by the recipient. A common example in the countryside was when a collective or state farm tractor driver gave help to a villager whose small private plot required turning over. In most cases, as in this one, the recipient of such specialized services was not in a position to reciprocate directly with comparable help of their own, and payment of one sort or another in some form of general 'currency' made good sense. The key point here, of course, is that people in such circumstances often preferred both to give and to receive the spirit rather than cash, and many tried to make sure that they had a stock of bottles for use when such need arose.

A number of different factors were involved here, and it seems likely that their influence has varied regionally, historically, and perhaps even from one individual case to another. One which was salient at the end of the Soviet period was that, unlike money, vodka was inflation proof and as such a more attractive proposition than cash. This factor, however, seems to have been only one part of a longer and more complex story in which vodka symbolized a non-commercial quality in the transactions in question. In part such a quality seems likely to have stemmed from vodka's power to evoke the many sociable contexts, including weddings, birthdays and the like, in which the spirit was an essential traditional component. This warm social quality, and indeed the mere fact that the drink could be enjoyably consumed directly without further conversion, marked a contrast to the cold impersonality and inedibility of cash, and had a softening effect on the transactions in question. Receiving money for the private use of collective and state farm equipment smacked clearly of the criminally commercial. Helping out someone in need and receiving a small bottle of vodka in response for the help was arguably more a matter of kindness and gratitude than illegality. It implied a relationship of mutual concern between the parties which preceded and persisted well beyond the immediate transaction. In short it was a friendly gesture, and it fitted well with the perceptions I have emphasized above that, at least in the prevailing conditions, useful ties to people were more valuable than cash resources.

It remains to add in this context, however, that even monetary transactions may be handled in a comparable way. My account above of difficulties in trying to pay for my accommodation is but one example of a widespread pattern. Thus on one occasion I accompanied M.S. to a farmhouse in a neighbouring village where a young man had some welding equipment. M.S. had a tractor attachment which needed repairing, and the man did this while we waited. When the job was done, M.S. took some cash and simply thrust it into the man's hand. On the way home he explained that such situations were quite delicate. The man did not have fixed prices. If he had asked him how much he wanted, the man would say he did not know. If you gave too little, he would be less helpful next time, and tell you that he was too busy at the moment.

Conclusion

The role of connections between friends and other well-disposed acquaintances which I have discussed in this paper clearly fits well within a social and economic system marked by a variety of scarcities which cannot satisfactorily be handled through the medium of cash and the market. While I accept that such conditions of scarcity – of goods, services, and information – were relatively harsh in Estonia at the time in question, it would seem naive to assume that impersonal transactions simply based upon a combination of bureaucracy and the shifting market equilibrium of supply and demand can at any time provide an adequate solution to the problems faced by individuals as they try to organize their lives. Evidence ranging from the longer term mutual trust of stockbrokers in major European capitals to that of rural villagers operating under better conditions of supply than those obtaining in early 1990s Estonia appear to make this clear.[3]

I have discussed some such material in my earlier work on rural Finland (1991), and it may be useful here to give two or three examples from that work. Thus I have described how one farmer was asked to do some work for a retired neighbour, and how the neighbour insisted upon paying well above a going rate for casual labour and made sure that the helper was extremely generously fed and watered. The same neighbour also insisted on paying generously for petrol when he was given a lift by the same farmer. The latter wanted to refuse the money and the neighbour eventually banged the notes down on the table in mock anger and departed. In another case, two farmers who found it uneconomical to own individual combine harvesters, purchased one jointly. When I asked if they had a written contract between them setting out conditions of joint use, I was told that if such a contract were needed the arrangement would not work. Long-term acquaintance and mutual trust were the key ingredients.

These are but a few of many similar examples of longer term collaboration between individuals in the much 'softer' economic conditions of modern rural Finland. At the same time there is evidence, both from my own experience and from some other sources, to suggest an interesting difference between the patterns prevailing in the two countries. Whereas the central position of a few particularly active, well-connected individuals emerged as a major feature of the Estonian scene, this did not appear to mark the situation I observed in Finland where the pattern was much more one of a 'collection' of mutually valued dyads between co-operating individuals. It is true that some individuals were actively involved in more such links than others, but this did not imply, as in the Estonian case, that they formed an organizational point of focus for others within their neighbourhood and, with this, that they had more ties than others to comparable persons outside it.

A recent article by Lonkila (1997) lends some support to this contrast, albeit in a Russian-Finnish urban context. It is based on a short comparative survey of informal exchange behaviour, with regard to favours, goods, and information, of school teachers in St Petersburg and Helsinki. The Russian teachers engaged in more numerous and more diverse exchanges, both among themselves and with others, than their Finnish counterparts. They also made considerable use of so-called *blat* exchanges in which access to a variety of resources, often of a kind 'ideally' accessed via formal institutions, was obtained through informal links to well connected 'brokers', and in general their exchange relations were more often mediated through third persons. Comparable relations among Finns 'were of a more dyadic nature'. It is especially this point which appears significant in the present context, though the implied willingness and ability of Finns to satisfy more of their needs through more formal channels is also, of course, important.

This said, it seems clear that there, as in Estonia, the fostering of good relations between individuals makes good practical sense in a variety of contexts. At the same time, it would not seem sensible to yield to the temptation to treat such ties as simply evidence of calculating economic rationality, though this is no doubt true in some cases. Ledeneva (1997a:53) interestingly discusses this point. She suggests the idea of a 'calculative ethic' as an alternative way of handling the attitudes involved. Russians, she suggests, believe that one should help others, and that this will lead in due course, perhaps in indirect and unexpected ways, to receiving help from others oneself. Lonkila (1997) describes such attitudes in post-Soviet Russia patterns as 'inherited' from Soviet days and based on a continued lack of trust of official institutions, and this suggests a partially emotional attachment to them as part of a longer term cultural repertoire as well as a recognition of their persistent value.[4] More generally, as with a language one speaks fluently, people anywhere who participate in these kinds of personalized relations are liable to get caught up in them to some degree. Indeed they arguably have to do so in order successfully to generate the necessary patterns of behaviour with a suitable degree of spontaneity. Such relations involve an expectation of at least some trust and mutual commitment which, while no doubt tempered by convenience, are commonly real enough. It is this quality, or at least its symbolic assertion, which ultimately marks the spectrum of relations between the deepest forms of friendship at one end and border cases of vodka-giving, *blat*, and 'over the odds' payments at the other. It is also, I consider, arguable that, notwithstanding a considerable degree of cultural and historical variation, we are dealing here with a quite fundamental element in the toolkit of survival with which human nature is endowed.

Notes

1 In a study of friendship in an English-speaking village in Northern Ireland, Leyton (1974) notes a sharper contrast with standard English patterns. There the word 'friend' is locally used especially to refer to close kin, while 'mates' or 'chums' are more common terms for non-kin friends.
2 The traditional patterns I refer to, in which the maintenance of good relations between persons is a high priority, are well documented both for African and other so-called 'simpler' societies. For discussions of different aspects of this in Africa cf. Abrahams (1965), Beattie (1963, Chapter 6), and Wilson (1951).
3 Cf. Cohen (1974:98–102) for a discussion of informal co-operation and mutual trust among stockbrokers and others in the City of London.
4 For further discussion of this phenomenon see also Ledeneva (1997b and 1998).

References

Abrahams, R. (1965), 'Neighbourhood Organization; A Major Sub-system among the Northern Nyamwezi', *Africa*, XXXV, 168–86.
—— (1991), *A Place of their Own: Family Farming in Eastern Finland*, Cambridge: Cambridge University Press.
—— (1994), 'Women and Rural Development in Contemporary Estonia', *Rural History*, 5, 2: 217–26.
Abrahams, R. and Kahk, J. (1994), *Barons and Farmers: Continuity and Transformation in Rural Estonia (1816–1994)*, ed. R. Abrahams, Gothenburg: Inter-European Research Program, University of Gothenburg.
Beattie, J. (1963), *Bunyoro*, New York: Holt, Rinehart, Winston.
Cohen, A. (1974), *Two Dimensional Man*, London: Routledge and Kegan Paul.
Evans-Pritchard, E.E. (1933), 'Zande Blood Brotherhood', *Africa*, VI, 4, 369–401.
Gellner, E. and Waterbury, J. (eds) (1977), *Patrons and Clients*, London: Duckworth.
Hivon, M. (1994), 'Vodka, the "Spirit of Exchange"', *Cambridge Anthropology*, 17, 3, 1–18.
Jaakkola, M. and Karisto, A. (1976), 'Friendship Networks in the Scandinavian Countries', *Research Reports*, No.11, Helsinki: Research Group for Comparative Sociology, University of Helsinki.
Ledeneva, A. (1997a), 'Between Gift and Commodity: the Phenomenon of Blat', *Cambridge Anthropology*, 19, 3, 43–66.

—— (1997b), 'Practices of Exchange and Networking in Russia', *Soziale Welt*, 1997, 2, 152–70.

—— (1998), *Russia's Economy of Favours: Blat, Networking and Informal Exchange*, Cambridge: Cambridge University Press.

Leyton, E. (1974), 'Irish Friends and 'Friends': The Nexus of Friendship, Kinship and Class in Aughnadoy', in E. Leyton, (ed.), *The Compact: Selected Dimensions of Friendship*, Newfoundland Social and Economic Papers, No. 3, Toronto: University of Toronto Press.

Lonkila, M. (1997), 'Informal Exchange relations in Post-Soviet Russia: A Comparative Perspective', *Sociological Research Online*.

Wilson, M. (1951), *Good Company*, London: International African Institute and Oxford University Press.

-10-

Localized Kin and Globalized Friends: Religious Modernity and the 'Educated Self' in East Africa

Mario I. Aguilar

Kinship relations have been over stressed in the anthropology of Africa. To judge from the bulk of the data available on African societies, it would be possible to suggest that friendship as such has never 'existed' within organized or segmentary social organizations. The reasons for such research paradigms are clear. Anthropologists have traditionally based their writings on periods of fieldwork, during which they have tried to understand societal organization. To that effect, kinship relations have in many cases given clues to the analysis of societies, based on our participant observation, as African individuals themselves have represented their lives through the idiom of kinship rather than friendship.

One of the exceptions found within the anthropological literature is that of the Nyakyusa (Tanzania). For them, and within the extraordinary setting of age-villages, *ukwangala* (the enjoyment of good company) becomes a central cultural value that is extended to 'the mutual aid and sympathy which spring from personal friendship' (Wilson 1951:66). Such personal friendship is also described by Gulliver, who describes at length the co-operation between two second cousins amongst the Ndendeuli (Tanzania). Potential competition between Ali and Konga was minimized by their somewhat distant kinship relations, and over the years they maintained a continuous relationship based on close friendship (Gulliver 1971:116–17). Gulliver was prompted to investigate further cases of friendship, finally to realize that friendship was indeed difficult to study, because it was hard to define the distinction between 'friend' and 'visitor' (301).

Through a review of the literature, one could argue that relations of friendship have been present in the expressive parameters of anthropologists and their informants, and within their daily relationships with their close field-assistants.

My thanks and gratitude to Paul Baxter, who during one of my visits to his home in May 1998 pointed me to the possible meanings of friendship within Boorana. Subsequently, and with his usual enthusiasm, he copied for me entries from his unique collection of Boorana (Oromo) dictionaries to aid my research and understanding of pastoral societies. Paul, *nagaat!*

Yet authors of African monographs have concerned themselves more with orderly, established social relations expressed through kinship than with social relations expressed through friendship. A whole realm of cultural and social representation has in that sense not been explored, and sometimes, one could argue, distorted.

The same general omission of friendship as an analytical tool can be detected in studies of African pastoralism. Arguments put forward within those monographs on pastoral societies have dwelt considerably more on kinship relations expressed through the sharing of resources and the management of herds than on any social conditions of relatedness of a non-structured manner. However, there and elsewhere, and as suggested by Holy (1996) in the context of the study of kinship within anthropology, there are other relations outside those comprised by kinship. Such relations, particularly friendship, are crucial for our understanding of African societies and pastoralism in particular. Kinship, understood by Holy as 'a culturally specific notion of relatedness deriving from shared bodily and/or spiritual substance and its transmission' (171) remains central to anthropological concerns; however, it needs to be complemented by other social and individual relations, including friendships within a particular society.

Thus, in this chapter I am concerned with friendship as a cultural and specific notion, within the geographical context of East Africa, and particularly within the cultural context of pastoral societies. I argue that while pastoral notions of friendship do exist, they are nevertheless mediated by different experiences of friendship present within a constant encounter between pastoral memories (traditions), pastoral diversification (modernity) and pastoral continuity (education). Therefore, such symbolic mediation can only be understood by suggesting that kinship, friendship, and cultural diversification are complementary notions within the ideological construction of contemporary pastoralism.

Using the ethnography of the Boorana, three areas will be explored in this chapter in order to argue for a multi-vocal perception of friendship; the localized realm of household animal husbandry; the communication between pastoral friends outside grazing areas; and the friendship acquired with other non-pastoralists through participation in the social life of communities attached to churches and mosques. These three spheres of friendship relations express the constant interaction between pastoralists within and beyond their geographical areas of residence, between a centralized cultural system and a state that contains it, and between the localized and the globalized systems of symbolic classification and social experience that contain them.

I argue that friendship as a social and human process is culturally and contextually constructed, and cannot be equated with relations of self-conscious individualism, mostly predominant in Western societies, such as Western Europe and the United States. Therefore, in assessing 'friendship' within pastoral societies, I follow the methodological assumption that suggests that friendship as any other social phenomenon is culturally constructed, and that while on the surface of the initial encounter it could be termed a human universal, its manifestations are influenced by localized ways of being human and of being social. I also argue that the social importance of friendship within societies and groups of individuals varies, and does not necessarily conform to a liberal model of commodity value.

Universal and Particular Categories of Friendship

There is no doubt that friendship is perceived as important within Western society. Thus, individuals are described as those who have friends, those who have lots of them, and those who have none. Social interaction known as friendship has therefore become a commodity that, when acquired, enhances the personal value of a person and has direct implications for the creation of European and American personhood. Therefore, while ethnographic accounts of friendship within society are not common, indications of the close relationships between anthropologists and their friends are more common.

It is an ethnographic reality that, given the important relation between friendship and personhood, issues related to friendship and our 'friends' in the field have remained an important component of our monographs' acknowledgements, emphasized by our current climate of personalized and self-indulgent writing. From the point of view of the anthropologist, those who are not field informants, or field assistants, but who have been useful to the anthropological project, have been labelled friends. For example, in a recent work on pastoralism, Elliot Fratkin (correctly) makes the distinction between 'field assistants in Kenya', 'friends and family in Ariaal [northern Kenya]', and some others. He thanks those others 'for their friendship and advice in the United States', as well as his 'ongoing collaborators' based in the US (Fratkin 1998:xv). Thus, companionship and collaboration as different from friendship is acknowledged by Fratkin as well as by Paul Spencer, who acknowledges the support of the Chamus elders (Spencer 1998:viii).

It seems that anthropologists have found friends and companions, not only among the people they study but also among field assistants. However, kinship terminology finally takes precedence over conviviality, as shown in the case of one Sudanese and Norwegian research team among the Hadendowa of the Sudan that was 'virtually adopted' by the people themselves (Manger *et al.* 1996:17). Friendship and adoption by the 'Other' is certainly understood as a valuable asset that gives authority to the researcher. If fieldwork and the researcher's attachment to the field is a sign of promising scholarship, friendship and localized acceptance convey ethnographic authority.

Those parameters of adoption reiterate anthropological conceptions of otherness, and I would wish to disassociate myself from them. Friendship among pastoralists cannot be understood from the parameters of Western ethnocentricity, in which friendship is understood from the point of view of all powerful, self-centred individuals. I have continually been asked: 'Did you have many friends when you lived with the Boorana?' My answer has been: 'Not really. I lived there, I was part of their daily life, and I liked their way of life; however my friends lived in Nairobi.' I was, as a fieldworker, located within an orderly and localized segment of Boorana society where I had rights and obligations within fictitious conceptions of kinship, within symbolic constructions of ritual membership and within semi-colonial relations of power whereby I was white and presumed to have some spheres of influence outside Garba Tulla District.

It is clear that the whole area related to anthropologists and their (pastoral) friends could be explored. That is not my task in this chapter; however, I needed to make clear that social relatedness does not equal friendship and that friendship, as a human experience and as a practice, is not universally understood in the same way. I am aware that most of the Boorana I know would only talk about friends in the context of outsiders, and particularly when using other media of communication, such as Swahili or English (see letters in this chapter).

I will focus primarily on the ways that people within pastoral societies construct and develop social relations of friendship. I contest any parameter of complete opposition between kin and friends, and instead I explore their complementarity within the ethnographic context of East African pastoralism.[1] However, I will also assume that while kinship and friendship constitute complementary social categories, they are nevertheless culturally distinct. Thus, in my opinion, while monothetic categories can create problems of later redefinition and possibly misperceptions, any idea of a 'polythetic definition' with a certain number of possible features or characteristics pertaining to such phenomena (Barnard and Good 1994; cf. Holy 1996:169) can create confusion from the start, and are not terribly helpful in the understanding of fluid social relations within a qualitative model of social interpretation.

After exploring some culturally localized conceptions of friendship, I will explore the expansion of the pastoralist world into other landscapes, such as urban and educational centres, and the symbolic and classificatory systems of other globalized traditions. From such an expansionist perspective, it can be argued that two particular phenomena have provided elements of rapid change in relation to the pastoralist conception of kin and friends: (a) the conversion or exposure to Christianity or Islam; and (b) the wider involvement of children from that world of pastoralism in a contemporary Western system of education. Thus, pastoralists have provided continuity through memorials and the symbolic imagination (Aguilar 1999) but have also diversified in economic terms (Hogg 1981).

Such diversification of their way of life has opened avenues for more fluid social categorizations, a departure from the pre-colonial dichotomy between kin and strangers. Conversion to Christianity or Islam has also provided other kin and other friends, while the schooling of children away from their kin and their localities of origin has also created other categories of friends. Within those landscapes of school communities or within the communication system of the post office and of the literary world, very different social parameters of pastoral friendship have been explored, very different indeed than those culturally bounded social expressions associated with pastoral societies within the colonial period.

Colonialism, Pastoralism, and the Bounded Imagination

By the end of the First World War, most of East Africa had already been explored and colonized by Britain. Political and geographical boundaries were created and peoples understood as bounded tribes were 'invented'. Pastoralists presented administrative problems owing to their constant movement, their ignorance of 'proper' boundaries and their sporadic if not endemic ethnic warfare (for example, see Fukui and Turton 1979). Thus, colonial officers faced nightmarish moments in their residency within East Africa, trying to control the movement of people along with their herds. One clear example of such colonial ordering was the creation of the Northern Frontier District (NFD) in Kenya, a bounded colonial territory, with people and animals within, that could not leave the territory without administrative permission. Pastoralists were perceived as unfriendly, tough, and always attacking each other. They were different from other peoples within the British territories because they kept moving their herds within dry territories in search of water and grazing.

It is clear that pastoralists provided, and still do, a distinctive kind of societal organization, because their whole life, their systems of symbolic classification and their daily social organization are all organized in relation to the centrality of their herds (cattle, camels, sheep, goats), so that 'the relationship of pastoralists to their livestock herds is a complex one and determines much of the character of their society' (Fratkin 1998:88). During the colonial period such societies were stratified by age (Baxter and Almagor 1978), and within some of them, systems of age-sets were central in order to organize quick responses to societal co-operation and political organization, for instance among the Boorana.

In such a context of colonial ordering, anthropologists focused on the functioning of institutions and the actual social organization of localized pastoral groups by studying their conceptions of kinship and marriage as well as their use and allocation of resources and cattle (Evans-Pritchard 1940). Symbolic classificatory systems provided emic explanations for such social systems, and became part of studies of pastoralism (Evans-Pritchard 1956). Relations of friendship were therefore secondary to the primary affiliations provided by kinship and the ritual obligations that brought clans or age-sets together in order to secure the continuity of the pastoralist way of life.

However, within those ethnographic studies, and the larger Ethnographic Survey of Africa,[2] anthropologists such as P.H. Gulliver noticed that there were other social ties, not directly linked to those of kin. In the case of Jie and Turkana, bond-friends (*lopai* [Jie], *lopei* [Turkana]) represented stock-associates, not related by kinship, but capable of conferring reciprocal stock rights with an element of 'pseudo-kinship'. Those bond-friends existed as a result of mutual convenience and trust, allowing links of reciprocity, outside kin relations and obligations (Gulliver 1955:209–10).

It is in connection to social reciprocity that relations of friendship within pastoralism need to be widely understood. In these very localized contexts all social relations are publicly expressed by economic or ritual exchange; however, conviviality and sociability create situations where individuals and groups prefer the companionship of some rather than others, within the limited flexibility of kin relations and social expectations. Thus, I once again stress the fact that Western parameters of friendship do not necessarily fit the cultural sense of pastoral societies. A person needs to be kin, or be in some kind of specified social relation, otherwise he will be considered a stranger and therefore a potential enemy. Categories of kin and friend in such localized pastoral worlds are inter-related because friendship as a way of ritual or economic relatedness creates an extension of the biological or classificatory relations portrayed through social structures of kinship.

In the case of the semi-nomadic pastoralist Boorana of Kenya and Ethiopia, the importance of affines (*soda*) has been an important parameter of social classi-fication. As part of a larger ethnic group (the Oromo) the Boorana ideological foundation of 'sameness' arises out of the centrality of *gada*, a ritual and political age-system that, in the past, organized and indeed made publicly clear and orderly all social relations. However, and as suggested by Paul Baxter, 'many, probably most, Oromo have no personal experience of *gada*, but every Oromo child will have attended many marriages and is constantly made aware, by the respect that affines must be accorded during their constant comings and goings, that it has a large group of classificatory affines' (1996:179).

In Boorana, friends are known as *jaala, hariya, fira*. However, as in the case of *fira*, friendship implies a relationship of mutual assistance, whereby 'you help me . . . I help you' (Leus 1995:298). Within those larger and habitual cultural para-meters of social classification, friendship is a term allotted to people of the same sex, who cannot be covered by the language of kin relations and kin allocation. Therefore, males do not talk about female friends, because the word for a female friend would be *jaalto*, a term used to signify a lover or a mistress (Leus 1995:471).

Within the Boorana Gutu (the Boorana 'proper') there are ways of identifying social and kin relations. After initial greetings, Boorana request moiety identifica-tion. There are two possible responses as there are only two moieties: Ghona and

Sabbo. All those who ascribe themselves to a given moiety are considered brothers and sisters, and share self-ascribed kin relations. Thus, an immediate confusion can arise when using the Swahili or the English languages in daily conversation. My male field assistant kept referring to my female field assistant as his sister when using the English language, while I kept using the expression 'after all she is your friend' when other Europeans were present at my house. Knowing that they had different sets of biological parents could not explain why they were brother and sister. The fact that both belonged to the same moiety and therefore could not marry each other meant that, when conversing in Boorana, I could not refer to them as being 'friends' since this term would imply an incestuous relationship.

Even so, friendship is culturally expressed by the fact that men of the same age and social rank, or women of the same age and social rank, enjoy each others' company, and therefore consider themselves friends. In such a pastoralist setting it would be impossible to understand or portray friendship as expressed by two or three people who spend time together, to the exclusion of others. Within the world of pastoralism it is impossible and inconceivable to create any kind of social exclusion, as numbers of people are relatively small, and all are socially dependent within the daily demands of managing herds and of communally managed economic and natural resources.

There are ways however, for friendship to be consolidated outside kin relations, and those ways are certainly fundamental to the life of herders beyond settlements where their families and kin reside. In Boorana, for example, shepherds develop a particular relationship through their life together, looking after the animals, eating and sleeping in rough places while moving their herds from one ecological niche to another. A relationship of closeness does develop when unmarried shepherds spend days and nights away in isolation from their villages and kin, or in the case of Maasai, when unmarried *moran* live outside their kin villages, and express their togetherness as a separation and social independence (Spencer 1988:86–94).

We also need to consider the pastoralist world as existing beyond local boundaries, within a climate of post-coloniality and as part of an ongoing social creation of communities living within a globalized reality of mixed temporalities. In other words, because pastoralism implies a cultural ideology and an imaginative process of boundary construction (Aguilar 1999), the geographical boundaries are always reconstituted by pastoralists, who can live and work somewhere else, but who send their extra cash and their resources 'home', where other relatives look after the cattle or the goats they have bought.

The Post-Colonial Expansion of Friendship

The children of pastoral societies constitute a new cultural phenomenon, because some of them, particularly those attending secondary schools, need to leave their parent's places of residence in order to attend boarding schools somewhere else. While secondary schools do exist within pastoralist areas, the educational policy of the government of Kenya ensures that secondary school students attend school outside their immediate locality. Sponsorship for school fees is much sought after and those pastoralists who have access to some cash invest, with great sacrifice, in education for their children. They do so knowing that in the future they and their children will have better opportunities for jobs, and particularly for developing networks and relations of exchange within the post-colonial market economies of East Africa.

While youngsters pursue education outside their rural areas, they remain influenced by a pastoralist ideology that allows them to perceive themselves as pastoralists within other geographical areas. They miss weddings and funerals, births and naming ceremonies; however, they avidly keep themselves up to date on the expansion of their kin relations. They keep in touch by post and when pastoralists know that a vehicle is leaving their area of residence literally hundreds of letters are prepared and commended to drivers and passengers. Letters as vehicles of communication also constitute vehicles of cultural signification, as the absence of them is perceived as severing ties, and becoming part of some other community. In the case of those young pastoralists attending schools outside their parents' places, letters become the only vehicle of constant communication with friends, that is with youngsters of other Kenyan ethnic groups whom they encounter within their places of education.

Letters are written by an individual but they usually convey news and thoughts that relate to several people, for example a family or a household. In a locality such as Garba Tulla where only a minority of the population can write fluently, secondary school students are encouraged to write what others, particularly their extended family, tell them. The following letters were produced by a female Boorana, who at the time of writing was a secondary school student at Igoji, near Meru. Boorana letters do not carry the same degree of privacy and confidentiality that we assume in Europe. They were part of public knowledge and some of them were read by most youngsters in the area.[3]

The letters were written by Fatuma to particular people; however, they had been read by several people after their arrival, either at the school, or at different locations in Garba Tulla. They constitute ethnographic data regarding perceptions, old and new, on kin and friends within a pastoral context.

Letter to a US Sponsor

Igoji High School
P.O. Box Igoji (Meru)
3 March 1988

Dear Sponsor,

May God bless you with lots of happiness, inspiration and success! We are fine, I hope you are fine too. Life goes on and my studies are hard, I study lots, day and night. The school is fine, the other students are fine, and my friends are fine too.

Back home things are not too good. The rain has not come, and people have gone hungry . . . however through your help my family has had something extra, and some new goats that will make things happen in the future. My mother eats posho, and my small brothers are well. Since we lost my father, life has been hard, however, life is never easy for Boorana. We work, we have animals, then the shifta [bandits] come and take it away, then we quarrel with the Somali, and then we are happy again. I hope that one day you will come and see where we live, and see our animals.

I would like to meet other people from your country, and particularly write to other girls like myself, so as to become friends. I have many friends from other parts of Kenya in my school, while back home I have my family, but not friends. However, some of my companions from the manyatta have also gone to other schools, and I miss them!

May Allah bless you and your family.

Your loving daughter,

Fatuma Hassan

Letter to a School Mate, Who Later Died, and Was Also Sponsored from the US

Garba Tulla Development Office
P.O. Box 12
Garba Tulla (via Isiolo)
11 April 1988

Dear Hadija,

I hope that God has kept you well and happy in your school, so far away, and so cold. You are not only a sister, but a friend. We are all sisters, even when Boorana or Sakuye, because we have shared the hardships of school outside. It is hard to go to school, and very hard to think of leaving home.

We are all fine here! I came home in a lorry, and we stopped in Kinna and had some tea with relatives. There were lots of people, however I was very happy when I saw Milimani [the hills of Garba Tulla town) at a distance. My mother, father and brothers are fine. I came to the Mission this morning to see the Sisters, and to see if there was anything from my sponsors in America.

My sister is getting married and it will be a big wedding in the manyatta [Boorana settlement]. We will help build her own manyatta and we will sing love songs. I wish I were married and settled with my own, rather than going to school. I have had lots of milk, delicious (dansa gudo!!!), rather than the maize and beans of the school.

My rafiki, I miss you!, but we will see you soon. Bring things from Nairobi, bring goats, and books, and ornaments.

God bless you always, and give you a good husband in the future!

Fatuma

Letter to Her Younger Sister

Igoji High School
P.O. Box Igoji (Meru)
21 October 1987

Dear Sista,

I hope you are well, and enjoying your schooling! Father ordered me to write to you, as I just came back to school.

I spent two weeks in Garba, as we were all sent home for having rioted, according to the Headmaster. It was dry, and animals were suffering. However, no shifta in sight. Mother is well, however has had some malaria recently. She is well, and just worried about us. She feels that it would be good for us to marry and to be able to settle down. However, as you know education is important, and Boorana friends at the school are like brothers and sisters, they speak the same language, and they know the same traditions.

I hope you have many friends at your school. I feel that I miss my brothers and sisters from Garba, but at the same time I have other friends, Kenyans like myself. I would like to visit their homes some day, and see how other peoples live. My mother seems to think that the world is made of kin [sodda],[4] while I would like to have many, many friends in this world.

Write back soon! Till we meet in Garba again, love from all of us.

Fatuma

This sample of relevant letters expresses a changing spatial and cultural reality. Not all pastoralists live within arid areas but their pastoral heritage and their pastoral ideology remain central for their own construction of the world around them. Thus, letters written in the English language provide particular means of communication rather than an alteration of cultural parameters. It is through those letters that Boorana remain in touch with their own world, geographically isolated, and at the same time they expand their world of relations and of friends, by being in touch with other non-Boorana youngsters. Two related but different sets of social clues are used for the spoken and for the written. In conversation Boorana perceptions of kinship and friendship are used, while in written letters English parameters of social interaction, and even Swahili words such as *rafiki,* are also used.[5] While the spoken reflects a spatial delimitation of culture, the written relates them to other locations in Kenya, in Europe, or even in the United States.

The experience of schooling itself provides contact with other youngsters who are not related by cultural constructions of kinship or classificatory issues of moiety construction, and therefore can be labelled as friends. Moreover, because those 'friends' have related themselves with Boorana youngsters via a lingua franca such as Swahili or English, communication with them remains within the use and practice of that cultural mediation associated with those inter-ethnic languages. However, those young people seeking education outside their areas constitute a minority within the Boorana communities of Eastern Kenya, and they represent the diversification of pastoralist strategies (Aguilar 1998a). For them, enemies as such do not exist. Not having experienced warfare with neighbours, they classify their own world as between Boorana kin and Kenyan (or European) friends.

I argue that schooling and education have provided the possibility of developing conceptions of friendship within pastoralists. Friendship categories are closer to the experience of the European colonizers (and African neo-colonizers) and their social systems rather than to those cultural parameters associated with Boorana kinship. Thus, letters as a vehicle of communication express a certain change in pastoralist society. Letters also express the possibility of a communal and universal way of communication, not used primarily between Boorana kin. National para-meters of sameness that have been built by using Western education and Western social parameters as cultural foundations have therefore complemented the kinship relations.

The Symbolic Construction of Friendship

Such social processes have also been bridged and re-ordered by another wider level of friendship within pastoralism, the membership of symbolically constructed and more globalized communities. Thus, churches or mosques have also provided another realm where pastoralists can perceive others as friends rather than as kin. Allegiance to a particular religious tradition has meant that pastoralists have interacted with non-pastoralists through a symbolic construction of community that requires a momentary suspension of their cultural ways of interacting and their own pastoralist construction of kin and friends. Ritual activities have therefore created other symbolic relations between pastoralists and others and at the same time have increased their sense of relatedness with others in non-kinship terms.

In the pastoralist world of the 1990s, associated with constant redefinition and appropriation of land, a process of religious diversification has taken place

(Aguilar 1995). Monolithic ritual traditions, constituted as cultural foundations of a single grouping of ethnic communities, have expanded into a polythetic cultural world, where myths of origin are contested and negotiated in the context of several traditions. While during the colonial encounters between pastoralists and European missionaries there were very few conversions, the situation changed with the post-colonial period of interaction between pastoralists and missionaries who did not necessarily represent the political interests of a European colonial power.

If in the past, and in the eyes of the pastoralists themselves, to have been a Christian or to have been a Muslim was to be somehow a different Maasai or a different Boorana, one can argue that today there are Maasai who are Christians, while there are other Boorana who are Muslims. As a result, Maasai and Boorana have other relations of friendship outside the realms of age-mates or village relations, outside their ethnic networks of social acceptance and co-operation. Such diversi-fication of religion (Aguilar 1995) has meant that if kin are certainly located within the home, the camp and the settlement, friends do exist within the parameters of the schools, the churches and the mosques. Moreover, and in the case of symbolic and ritual relations within the world religions, the level of friendship relations within a village only represents a micro-reflection of some other relations of friend-ship at the level of other villages, the locality, the town or the larger urban centres. As suggested by Abner Cohen in the case of West Africa, ritual realities at the local mosque have other social consequences aside from the proper ritual so that:

> Men come to the ritual some time before it begins and linger on in company long after it ends. Through the social interaction occasioned by the performance of the ritual, members of the ritual assembly develop small, intimate, primary groupings of various sorts, which are characterized by intense sentiments of loyalty, affection, co-operation, and mutual help (Cohen 1969:156).

During my fieldwork in the early 1990s, groups of Boorana Christians made trips to Nairobi in order to participate in youth retreats and assemblies. While in Nairobi they were hosted by families who were participating in the same activities. Therefore on their return to their homes, they spoke of the friendship they had experienced and the friends they had made while outside their pastoral areas. Some of them complained that friendship was not present within kin, and that it was easier to co-operate with friends rather than with kin. It was a new experience!

While those experiences of friendship can be considered universal, and indeed the idea that friends are easier to deal with than kin can be considered a human reality, such social experiences were in the past rare within arid areas inhabited by pastoral societies. At one point or another Muslim and Christian proselytizing had failed, due to the fact that semi-nomadic peoples rarely became attached to symbolically constructed sacred places such as churches or mosques, where non-kin gathered.[6]

Conclusion: The Pastoral Diversity of Friendship

I have described three levels of human interaction important for the cultural understanding of friendship within pastoralism: the localized, the extended educational and economic network, and the globalized, expressed by symbolic and ritual communal ties. In relation to categories of space and time, I have shown that those three areas of experiential friendship described in this chapter tend to coincide with the historical experience of pastoralism within a changing national and globalized society.

Pastoralists interact with each other within close kinship ties and by using cultural categories of exclusion/inclusion signified by similarities and differences in language, rites of initiation, and the practicalities of economic resources and ecological niches. Within such geographical isolation and cultural self-containment, pastoralist societies centre themselves around kinship ties, and the primary relationship between different groups is defined by inter-marriage on the one hand, and ethnic warfare on the other. Within such symbolic constructions, friendship arises out of cultural and social parameters of co-operation rather than out of any conscious search for other agreeable individuals outside kinship co-operation.

The second social manifestation of friendship takes place with the introduction of post-colonial systems of education and the subsequent manipulation of such models by independent African states in order to create new social roles. One of those roles, that of citizen, requires individuals to have many things in common and therefore to depart from the differentiation associated with ethnicity and the subsequent importance of localized languages and cultures. Thus, as a result of the politics of modernity, the children of pastoralism have been exposed to other places and other peoples within the unifying project of the state and its concerns for the cultural creation of Kenyans or citizens rather than Boorana or Kikuyu or Luo. The conditions of such imposition of modernity have nevertheless been negotiated so as to incorporate new cultural elements within the ideological contexts of pastoralism, rather than vice versa.

In a third sphere of friendship, religious traditions associated with even more globalized spheres of influence have provided new experiences and as a result new conceptions of friendship within pastoralism. Christianity and Islam in particular have symbolically constructed social relations not associated with kinship that have in reality made pastoralists from one area encounter pastoralists from other areas or other peoples from diverse ethnic and language groups.

Therefore, it is possible to suggest that there is a direct relationship between social and cultural constructions of nomadism and kinship, sedentarization and friendship. While pastoralist societies in East Africa have for the most part been semi-nomadic, there has been a tendency to pursue processes of sedentarization as a result of droughts and famine, wars and conflicts. There has been a constant increase of pastoral settlements geographically connected with centres of famine relief, schools and hospitals, and NGO-oriented projects. Such conditions have undermined strong kinship ties associated with processes of ritual and cultural initiation, and family ties of economic and pastoral co-operation that nevertheless require some kind of economic and cultural independence. It is a reality that economic and cultural dependence have created cultural changes, but any relationship with other non-pastoralists and relief agencies has required mutual negotiations of networks and friendship that were not culturally accentuated before colonial times.

Taking into account the cultural diversification of pastoralism and the actual diversification of social relations, it is plausible to argue that friendship will increase its social importance and cultural value within a world of pastoralism that will continue to expand into other areas of social life outside the arid lands of East Africa. Therefore, two larger spheres of influence have made conceptions of friendship possible in that pastoral world. One of them, religious modernity, understood as the presence of different religious traditions, has provided a basic change from the geographically isolated pastoral societies, formerly perceived as unified and distinct by the sole existence of their ritual and symbolic unification. Be it by the *gada* system in the case of the Boorana (Legesse 1973) or by a gerontocratic system of age, as among Maasai (Spencer 1993) age-systems were self-contained, and based on self-regulated social and political relations. The other sphere of influence, education, has created a pastoralist 'educated self', a Westernized neo-colonial product of the post-colonial African nations who is the subject and the agent of new cultural perceptions and the cultural creation of friends, as well as of globalized kin.

It is my suggestion that such manifestations, perceptions and social constructions of friendship will always remain closely related to changes and cultural perceptions of kinship relations and kinship co-operation within pastoral society. Thus, it will not be possible to understand kinship relations, that is the basis of pastoral societies, without understanding the growing social contingencies of friendship.

Notes

1 The term East Africa could certainly be deemed problematic. On the one hand, boundaries and perceptions have changed since colonial times, and places such as the contemporary Congo or Malawi have sometimes been included within East Africa. For the sake of clarity, I refer in this chapter to ethnographic materials and ethnocentric anthropological perceptions related to British colonial construc-

tions. Thus, when I talk about East Africa, I refer to the world of pastoralism within Kenya, Tanzania and Uganda, plus the studies of pastoralism conducted by E.E. Evans-Pritchard among the Nuer of the Sudan.

2 Such a 'Survey' was worked out by the International African Institute in 1944.

3 I came across letters such as those used in this chapter at the offices of the Wolfeda Program of the Catholic Mission in Garba Tulla, and during my conversations with Boorana women, who usually keep letters and indeed communal possessions in tin boxes.

4 Paul Baxter has remarked that 'Booran and Arsi take great care both in the selection of spouses and in the fostering and maintenance of good relations with their affines' *sodda*', so that 'the selection of useful and congenial affines is the main concern of the marriage arrangers' (Baxter 1996:182).

5 Young Boorana men and women refer to one another as brothers and sisters. After all, and in the case of the Boorana proper, all Boorana belong to one of the two moieties, Gona and Shabo. Those belonging to one moiety have to marry somebody from the other, and therefore brothers and sisters are numerous within the Boorana social and relational structure.

6 However, it must be said that such notions of symbolic and ritual isolation had played down the fact that pastoralist groups still make pilgrimages to sites that are problematic in relation to political boundaries but justified by their myths of origin (Schlee 1990:52).

References

Aguilar, M.I. (1995), 'African Conversion from a World Religion: Religious Diversification by the Waso Boorana of Kenya', *Africa* 65:525–44.

—— (1998a), *Being Oromo in Kenya*, Lawrenceville, N.J.: The Red Sea Press.

—— (1998b), 'Reinventing Gada: Generational Knowledge in Boorana', in M.I. Aguilar (ed.), *The Politics of Age and Gerontocracy in Africa: Ethnographies of the Past and Memories of the Present*, Lawrenceville, N.J.: Africa World Press.

—— (1999), 'Pastoral Memories, Memorials and Imaginations in the Postcoloniality of East Africa', *Anthropos* 94, (1–3).

Barnard, A. and Good, A. (1984), *Research Practices in the Study of Kinship*, London: Academic Press.

Baxter, P.T.W. (1996), 'Toward a Comparative Ethnography of the Oromo: The Importance of Affines', in P.T.W. Baxter, J. Hultin and A. Triulzi (eds), *Being and Becoming Oromo: Historical and Anthropological Enquiries*, Uppsala: Nordiska Afrikainstitutet and Lawrenceville, N.J.: The Red Sea Press.

Baxter and Almagor, U. (eds), (1978), *Age, Generation and Time: Some Features of East African Age Organisations*, London: C. Hurst

Cohen, A. (1969), *Custom and Politics in Urban Africa: A Study of Hausa Migrants in Yoruba Towns*, London: Routledge and Kegan Paul.

Evans-Pritchard, E.E. (1940), *The Nuer: A Description of the Modes of Livelihood and Political Institutions of a Nilotic People*, New York and Oxford: Oxford University Press.

—— (1956), *Nuer Religion*, New York and Oxford: Oxford University Press.

Fratkin, E. (1998), *Ariaal Pastoralists of Kenya: Surviving Drought and Development in Africa's Arid Lands*, Boston and London: Allyn and Bacon.

Fukui, K. and Turton, D. (eds) (1979), *Warfare among East African Herders*, Osaka: National Museum of Ethnology.

Gulliver, P.H. (1955), *The Family Herds: A Study of Two Pastoral Tribes in East Africa. The Jie and Turkana*, London: Routledge and Kegan Paul.

—— (1971), *Neighbours and Networks: The Idiom of Kinship in Social Action among the Ndendeuli of Tanzania,* Berkeley, Los Angeles, London: University of California Press.

Hogg, R.S. (1981), 'The Social and Economic Organisation of the Boran of Isiolo District, Kenya', Ph.D. dissertation, Faculty of Economics and Social Studies, University of Manchester.

Holy, L. (1996), *Anthropological Perspectives on Kinship*, London and Chicago: Pluto.

Legesse, A. (1973), *Gada: Three Approaches to the Study of African Society*, New York: The Free Press.

Leus, T. (1995), *Borana Dictionary*, Sebijadel: W.S.D. Grafisch Centrum.

Manger, L., Abd el Ati, H., Harir, S., Krzywinski, K. and Vetaas, O.R. (1996), *Survival on Meagre Resources: Hadendowa Pastoralism in the Red Sea Hills*, Uppsala: Nordiska Afrikainstitutet.

Schlee, G. (1990), 'Holy Grounds', in P.T.W. Baxter and R. Hogg (eds), *Property, Poverty and People: Changing Rights in Property and Problems of Pastoral Development*, Manchester: Department of Social Anthropology and International Development Centre, University of Manchester.

Spencer, P. (1988), *The Maasai of Matapato: A Study of Rituals of Rebellion*, Manchester: Manchester University Press.

—— (1993), 'Becoming Maasai, Being in Time', in T. Spear and R. Waller (eds), *Being Maasai: Ethnicity and Identity in East Africa*. London: James Currey.

—— (1998), *The Pastoral Continuum: The Marginalization of Tradition in East Africa*, Oxford: Clarendon Press.

Wilson, M. (1951), *Good Company: A Study of Nyakyusa Age-Villages*, London: Oxford University Press.

Index

Index

Index

Index